Goddess

Goddess

Be the woman you
want to be

Elisabeth Wilson

Acknowledgements

Infinite ideas would like to thank the following authors for their contributions to this book: Rob Bevan, Linda Bird, Sally Brown, Eve Cameron, Jem Cook, Kate Cook, Peter Cross, Sabina Dosani, Penny Ferguson, Helena Frith Powell, Lisa Helmanis, Mark Hillsdon, Andrew Holmes, Lynn Huggins-Cooper, Ken Langdon, Anna Marsden, Cherry Maslen, John Middleton, Lizzie O'Prey, Marcelle Perks, Tim Phillips, Steve Shipside, Alexander Gordon Smith, Karen Williamson, Elisabeth Wilson, Tim Wright.

First published in 2006 by
The Infinite Ideas Company Limited
36 St Giles
Oxford, OX1 3LD
United Kingdom
www.infideas.com

A CIP catalogue record for this book is available from the British Library

ISBN 10: 1-904902-77-4
ISBN 13: 978-1-904902-77-5

Designed and typeset by Baseline Arts Ltd, Oxford
Cover designed by Cylinder
Printed in China

Brilliant ideas

4   MAKE EVERYBODY LOVE YOU

Finding a partner if that's what you want

How to impress...your lover

How to impress...at work

The fast track to goddesshood

What is a goddess? She's a woman living a 100% sorted life – who knows what makes her happy and has a plan for getting it.

So the first question is: What do you want? To become the woman you want to be, you have to understand what motivates and inspires you, what forces are shaping your life, and which areas you are ignoring. These are the areas which you run the risk of leaving unfulfilled forever.

'Multi-tasking' is a very modern word for an ability of women that has been recognised for millennia. Women have the potential to fulfil many roles. The ancient Greeks understood this and immortalised this huge potential for choice in their pantheon of goddesses – all of them powerful female archetypes. We can choose any of these archetypes – indeed all of them in one lifetime. But somehow life gets in the way, and we get catapulted off in one direction. We're too busy or too scared to listen to all those other goddesses clamouring inside us to get out and play. We can flit between different goddess energies during our lifetime, but we have to recognise them first.

This isn't always easy. In the ancient Greek myths the goddesses were in constant conflict and that's no coincidence. It's hard to be an Athena and a Demeter at the same time, but it's possible to honour both goddesses within you at different times. With insight comes the ability to integrate the characteristics of the goddess archetypes who have most to teach you now. And at least if you don't fulfil all of them in this lifetime, it will be your choice – not just something that happened.

Take the following quiz to find out which goddess you identify most strongly with.

1. **You are at a party and a good-looking man makes a bee-line for you and spends most of the night chatting to you.**

    ☐ a. You give it all you've got. You may not do anything about it, but you want to make sure he won't forget you in a hurry.

    ☐ b. How long you talk to him depends on what he has to say – if he's interesting, he'll get more of your time.

    ☐ c. If he seems like a thoughtful, caring person, you'll prolong the conversation, but if he's superficial, he'll bore you.

    ☐ d. You're more likely to spend time with him if he's got a problem or needs some advice.

2. **Whether you have children or not, what is your truthful response to this statement: 'A life without children is a life half-lived.'**

    ☐ a. Kids are fine if that's what you want, but they can ruin relationships.

    ☐ b. Obviously not true. More people would probably be more fulfilled if they could rid themselves of the idea that reproduction is all there is.

    ☐ c. A life without caring about something more than yourself is probably a life half-lived, whether or not it's your biological children.

    ☐ d. Yes, I do think it's true, even if it's not politically correct.

3. **How often do you get the feeling, 'If I don't do it, it won't get done properly'?**

    ☐ a. Practically never.

    ☐ b. All the time but it doesn't mean I'll do it – I have only finite time and I save it for the big stuff.

    ☐ c. Hardly ever – and if I get to feel like that, I know it's time to start saying no.

    ☐ d. Frequently.

4. **Do you put as much effort into your clothes and make-up as you did when you were younger?**
   - ☐ a. Yes, I enjoy it.
   - ☐ b. No – but I spend a lot more money on looking smart even if I don't spend hours in front of a mirror.
   - ☐ c. No – but I do spend more on keeping fit and eating well than I ever thought I would.
   - ☐ d. No, who has the time for that juvenile primping?

5. **If you're honest, you learned to cook...**
   - ☐ a. Because it impresses other people.
   - ☐ b. Because it's an essential life skill and I might as well do it well.
   - ☐ c. Because it relaxes me, it's absorbing.
   - ☐ d. Because I like to sit down at a table with loved ones around me and cooking is the most reliable way of making that happen.

6. **It's Saturday afternoon and you're lying on the sofa relaxing, drifting off to sleep:**
   - ☐ a. It feels great.
   - ☐ b. It's fine if justified by a week of achievement.
   - ☐ c. It's fine – I have to recharge my batteries.
   - ☐ d. I always feel slightly guilty completely indulging me.

7. **How comfortable do you feel with someone else organising your holiday arrangements?**
   - ☐ a. Fine.
   - ☐ b. OK, if it's someone you can trust.
   - ☐ c. You like to have some input.
   - ☐ d. You'd be fine with it but you can't even imagine what that would be like.

8. **If you worked in an office with mostly men, would you feel**
- ☐ a. Great, you'd probably prefer it. Men are easier to work with.
- ☐ b. Fine if they were good at their jobs and didn't spend the time grandstanding.
- ☐ c. Fine, you don't get too involved with personalities so if they're reasonable it will be OK.
- ☐ d. A bit nervous. In all-male environments, work tends to take over and it's more difficult to have any life outside work.

9. **When a friend has been talking about her problems for about an hour, you are:**
- ☐ a. Sympathetic but don't know what else to say.
- ☐ b. Still brainstorming ways you can help her.
- ☐ c. Listening intently to her.
- ☐ d. Offering any help you can.

One way to make sure that we live our best lives is to integrate all the different aspects of our personality, giving them a chance to grow and shine. The quiz will help you identify the qualities personified by particular goddesses in yourself. Read those which correspond to the letters you tick most often. They are the archetypes with whom you align most closely. Then turn to the chart for some guidance on how moving towards some of the other archetypes can give your life more balance.

The number of As reveals how closely you align with Aphrodite, goddess of love and desire

You are adventurous, charismatic and passionate and your love relationships tend to dominate your life – you become obsessed with the drama of your relationships. You are a true romantic, and tend to get disappointed in relationships when the first flush has passed, and commitment can be a problem. Yours is a sensual nature and you have a tendency to become introverted; your inner life is vivid and it can seem more fascinating to you than other people.

What this looks like in real life:

✿ Modern-day movie goddess Angelina Jolie. When younger there was a definite Persephone energy – defensive of her mother against her absent father. As she grew to womanhood and success, her prevailing energy is Aphrodite – passionate, charismatic, irresistible. By adopting children and having them herself with Brad Pitt, she seems to be flirting with her inner Demeter – but despite her family commitments she is still very much in her Aphrodite energy.

✿ Nicole Kidman has maintained a dignified front and achieved her best work since her divorce and on the surface looks like an Artemis. But she was all Aphrodite during her intense marriage to Tom Cruise, and although her behaviour since is classic Artemis it could be that she is hiding behind an Artemis face for protection to disguise that underneath she is still an Aphrodite who has been hurt, waiting for her next big love.

The number of Bs reveals how closely you align with Athena, goddess of wisdom

You are clever, resourceful and perceptive and recognition is important to you. You are happy mentoring others and are a source of inspiration and good advice. Your career can take precedence over just about everything including personal life. You guard your private life and don't show your vulnerability. You risk regrets in later life if your intellectual and working life fails to keep moving forward, supplying challenges and garnering you the respect of others.

What this looks like in real life:

❀ Oprah Winfrey is a classic Athena – she has a personal life but she guards it jealously and it seems to be her career and its opportunities that give her life definition. She has decided that by resisting the urge to have a family of her own, she has the energy to help thousands (she has set up foundations to mentor young, poor women), and that, logically, seems more attractive to her.

❀ Kylie Minogue has spoken often about her desire for a family and a settled relationship, but behaves like an Athena. If she had followed the Demeter path, would she have made the jump from being a minor pop star to becoming respected for her avant garde music while achieving a sort of icon-hood as a survivor? She is an Athena and though drawn towards Demeter isn't convinced it gives a sure way to happiness.

The number of Cs reveals how closely you align with Artemis, goddess of hunting and wild places

You are independent, creative and hard-working and your passion is for reaching your full potential in life. Your space is very important to you and you are good at setting personal boundaries. You may choose to live alone unhampered by domesticity but that doesn't mean you don't expend a lot of love on other people. You only want love relationships on your own terms and this can mean you prefer to be on your own. You risk becoming overly self-reliant.

What this looks like in real life:

✿ As a young woman, Diana, Princess of Wales had a definite Persephone complex but by the end of her life she was Artemis, fearless, bold and provocative – and though willing to love, happy to live alone.

✿ Her history of broken, intense relationships hint at an Aphrodite, and her talk of wishing for a family point to a frustrated Demeter, but underneath it all, Jennifer Aniston could well find she's an Artemis. She wants life on her terms – and has a very definite idea of how she wants it to be.

The number of Ds reveals how closely you align with Demeter, goddess of harvest and motherhood

You are strong, wise and nurturing and the embodiment of all the traditional female virtues we associate with a 'good mother'. You may not have children but you almost certainly put the needs of others before your own. Being needed is really vital to your sense of your self and this self-sacrifice can slip into self-neglect.

What this looks like in real life:

✿ Julia Roberts was a classic Artemis – creative, independent, resistant to being tied down – but in recent years she has 'retired' from public life and put all her energy into bringing up her twins and being with her husband. She is moving into a Demeter role but will it last?

✿ Mia Farrow is a classic Demeter. They often trail a sense of betrayal behind them because sacrifices that Demeters make for their family are not always recognised or appreciated by those they lavish their love on. Mia's was the ultimate betrayal, her partner went off with her adopted daughter.

Aphrodite	Athena	Artemis	Demeter
You can learn from Artemis by building emotional distance and turning passion into compassion	You can learn from Aphrodite by coming out of your head and focusing on your body	You can learn from Demeter by living out what you know – that you need to love and be loved	You can learn from Athena by realising that fulfilling your ambitions is crucial to living a life without resentment.
Try: facing problems rationally rather than emotionally.	Try: appreciating the pleasure your body can give you.	Try: seeing the world differently.	Try: making time for yourself part of your everyday life.
See ideas 95–101	See ideas 33–45	See ideas 85–94	See ideas 1–6

Is Persephone part of your personality?

Do you feel that:
❀ you have overcome many difficulties?
❀ loss has defined your life?
❀ you experience more pain than other people?

Persephone was the daughter of Demeter. She was abducted by the god of the underworld and thus torn away from everything that gave her life meaning and security. Nearly all of us are cast down by loss at some points in our life – after disappointment, the break up of a relationship, the loss of a child or parent. We all know Persephones who have become stuck there. But it is meant to be a transitory phase. Eventually Persephone reached some level of acceptance of the hand fate had dealt, built up her strength, and moved on. Modern-day Persephones must do the same if they are to reach their full potential.

Now here's an Elite offer to get you started...

COUNTRY HOTELS OF DISTINCTION

Here's the first of many special offers you'll find throughout Goddess. Spoil yourself rotten with this special offer from **Elite Hotels**. You and a guest will receive a **free room upgrade** on any booking you make. Plus the first ten lucky readers to make a booking will also receive a complimentary champagne afternoon tea for two.

Elite Hotels presents a portfolio of outstanding country house hotels situated in prime locations throughout South East England. The hotels are some of the UK's most beautiful historic houses and have been restored to their original splendour. They include Ashdown Park Hotel in East Sussex, Tylney Hall in Hampshire and The Grand Hotel, Eastbourne. The unique charm and character of each make them the perfect retreat for girly weekends or romantic breaks. **Elite Hotels** have created havens away from the stresses of every day life, catering for every service required in a friendly and relaxed atmosphere.

For further information on individual hotels please visit www.elitehotels.co.uk

For details on how to take advantage of this fantastic offer please go to page 487, where you'll also find information on all the other great deals throughout *Goddess*.

Terms and conditions
This offer is valid between Sunday and Friday, excluding bank holidays, Christmas & New Year, Valentine's Day or Easter. Offer is good until 30 November 2007 and valid for new bookings only. Applicants must be aged 18 years or over. Holiday insurance is not included. The room upgrade and free cocktail prize is non-transferable – there is no cash alternative. Accommodation subject to allocation and availability at the time of booking.

Getting what you want – the easy way!

'Just don't give up trying to do what you really want to do. Where there is love and inspiration, I don't think you can go wrong.'

ELLA FITZGERALD

Whatever you want to achieve in life, it helps to know the shortcuts. What you'll find in this section are some tried and tested techniques for getting what you want — fast. First, decide what you want and then turn to some brilliant ideas for finding out how to get it.

You want more time

How do you relate to time?

We all have an innate way of organising our time. Experts estimate that you could be up to 20% more efficient if you understood how to manipulate these natural tendencies. Read through each of the following four profiles and then turn to the idea recommended as a starting point. (You may find you recognise yourself in more than one profile.)

1. ☐ My work space is pretty messy.
   ☐ I spend a lot of time looking for things I need.
   ☐ I work on several tasks in one morning.

2. ☐ Leaving things until the last possible minute feels very familiar to me.
   ☐ I spend a lot of time getting together the tools I need for a job and 'tidying' my space so that I'm 'ready' to work.
   ☐ I am easily distracted from a task.

3. ☐ I'm organised but I never seem to get everything done.
   ☐ I'm frustrated by having to depend on other people.
   ☐ I seem to get more anxious about deadlines than other people do.

4. ☐ I get distracted by other people's demands and agendas.
   ☐ I often find myself saying yes when I know I should say no.
   ☐ I feel like I get stuck with the jobs that no one else wants to do.

How can this help?

1.   You're a **chaotic**. Perhaps you subconsciously feel that you're bucking the system and being your own person but it leads to you being less productive. Try idea 5.

2.   You're a **procrastinator**. You don't have enough time because you find it hard to get started. Try idea 3.

3.   You're a **perfectionist**. You can't let things go but this leads you to being perceived as inefficient. Try idea 4.

4.   You're a **people pleaser**. You're simply too busy looking after other people's needs, which means you don't have time for your own. Try idea 2.

1. Find an hour a day to play

No, seriously, is that too much to ask?

Shut your eyes. Breathe deeply. Picture what you'd do today if you had a whole hour each day to yourself to spend doing exactly what you wanted.

'Yeah, right', I hear you say. Like there's any chance of that.

So here's a question worth asking

I think that the 'desirable' things we'd like to spend an hour doing fall into two categories:

✿ The stuff we yearn to do because it's relaxing and fun.

✿ The stuff that's usually prefixed with a sense of 'ought to' because we know the rewards are worth it

In the first category is lying in bed watching a movie, in the second going for a run or quality time with the kids. We need to find the time for both. But both categories tend to get shunted to the sidelines of our life because of general business.

Exercise especially is one of the things that goes by the wayside when life gets stressful. How many times have you said 'I'd love to go to the gym – but I don't have the time.' So here's the useful question to ask yourself: how will I feel in five years' time if I don't?

Here's an idea for you...

On the move and stressed? Running cold water over your wrists for a minute cools you down on a hot day and it works to bring down your stress levels, too.

More to the point – how will you look?

Nothing in your life will change unless you take action. If you don't take the time to exercise, if you consistently allow family and work demands to be more important than your continuing good health, then at best you'll be more vulnerable to illness; at worst you'll be fat (and still more vulnerable to illness).

This goes for 'life dreams' that fall into the first category, like writing a novel or learning Russian. These have been called 'depth activities' because they add meaning to our lives. If I had a fiver for every time someone said to me 'I'd love to write a book but I don't have the time', I wouldn't be writing this one. Wannabe authors miss the point that in just an hour a day, you can make a start. Here's the big question: how will you feel in five years' time if you haven't at least tried?

People who spend at least a bit of their time doing the stuff that they want to do tend to feel that they're in control, and that's majorly destressing.

First get the big picture...

Get out your diary and write down everything you're expected to make happen in the next month. This could take some time. Include everything from work projects, organising baby-sitters, buying birthday presents, decorating the bathroom, taxing the car, medical appointments.

OK, finished? Right, go through the list and mark the items that you can delegate to someone else. Be honest. What I said was the items you 'can' delegate, not the ones that no one else wants to do, or the ones that no one else will do as well as you. Don't worry. I'm not going to make you hand over all these tasks, just 10% of them.

In a spirit of solidarity, I've done this too. And guess what? On a list of thirteen things only two of them have to be done by me. Actually, only one – writing this book. (I could ask someone else to do it but the publishers might notice; or maybe they wouldn't, which is an even scarier thought.) The other one is to take my youngest for an injection and I could even delegate this if I wanted. But I don't. By actively thinking about it and deciding that it's something I want to do I've turned it into a positive – a choice rather than a chore. Big difference.

Now you've offloaded 10% of your work for the next month, think about dumping 10% of what you have to do every day. Jot down your 'tasks' for tomorrow. Quickly, without thinking too much, run through them marking each entry.

A Must do
B Should do
C Could do

Now knock two of the Bs off the list and three of the Cs off and put down in their place an activity that you know would destress you or add depth to your life. Mark it with a whacking great 'A'. Soon, giddy with success, you'll be prioritising yourself all of the time. Well, at least for an hour a day. Life really is too short to wallow in the C-list – feeling busy but achieving nothing that matters.

Defining idea...

'Life is what happens when we're busy doing something else.'
JOHN LENNON

2. Cure yourself of the 'disease to please'

Make 'just say no' your new mantra.

A huge amount of stress is caused by the inability to say 'no'. Result? We end up running to other people's agendas.

This is traditionally seen as a female problem. But I'm not so sure. On Saturday night I had dinner with a male friend who told me that for the first time in his ten-year marriage, he'd managed to get his wife to agree to going on holiday on their own without inviting at least two other families. Extreme? Yes. But I know many men whose entire domestic life is run to their partner's agenda and who feel that somehow they're being a bad dad or husband if they say no to the relentless socialising, child-centred activities and DIY set up for them by their driven other halves. I also know men who don't want to stay at work until 8.30 most nights, or go to the pub for an hour on the way home, but can't say no to the pervading culture of their workplace.

Now and then, all of us have to do things that don't benefit us much in order to feel that we're pulling our weight. But if it's a daily occurrence then we're going to get run down and ill. Worse, we're going to get seriously fed up.

Try this quiz. Answer True or False to each of these questions:

I can't relax until I finish all the things
I have to do
T/F

If I wasn't doing favours for other
people most days, I wouldn't think
much of myself
T/F

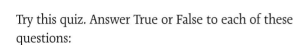

Here's an idea for you...

If you just can't say no, try an
intermediate stage. Next time
someone asks you to do
something, say: 'I'm not sure,
let me get back to you.' The
breather is often enough to
stiffen your resolve.

I seldom say no to a work colleague or family member who asks a favour of me   T/F

I often find myself changing my own plans or working day to fit in with
other people's wants   T/F

I rarely, if ever, feel comfortable with what I've accomplished   T/F

I often feel I'm so exhausted that I don't have time for my own interests   T/F

I feel guilty relaxing   T/F

I find myself saying 'yes' to others when inside a voice is saying 'no, no, no'   T/F

I honestly believe that if I stop doing things for others they'd think less of me   T/F

I find it hard to ask other people to do things for me   T/F

Add up the number of Ts you scored. If your score is between 7 and 10, you think it more important to please others than please yourself. If it's between 4 and 6, you should be careful. You're on the slippery slope to terminal niceness. If your score is 3 or less, you're good at saying no and keep your own needs in balance with others.

Aim for a score of under 3. Here are some ways to get there.

1. List your top 10 'no's', the things you want to eliminate from your life. Start each sentence 'I will no longer…'

2. Think of situations where you need to say no to improve your life. Imagine yourself in these situations saying no. Practise the exercise in front of a mirror if necessary. (This is brilliant. I tried it myself and the experience of actually saying no out loud, albeit in private, makes it much easier in real-life situations.)

3. Whenever you're asked to do anything, ask yourself: 'Do I really want to do this?' rather than 'Should I do this?' If the answer is no, then let someone else pick up the baton.

Defining idea…

'I cannot give you the formula for success, but I can give you the formula for failure, which is: Try to please everybody.'
HERBERT BAYARD SWAPE, journalist

3. Never procrastinate again

Procrastination is stress's best friend. It's not big, it's not clever but for most of us, it's a way of life.

But no longer. Here is the best method I've ever found for overcoming it, here's how to get going when you have absolutely no motivation.

It was taught to me by life coach Mark Forster. An interesting man, he achieves more in a day than most of us do in a week. But he used to be disorganised and chaotic (he says!). None of the advice on procrastination ever worked for him (we all know that feeling), so he invented his own techniques. (You can read more in his brilliant book *Get Everything Done*.)

Mark calls this the rotation method. You need pen, paper and a watch but a kitchen timer with a bell works best.

1. First make a list of your tasks. (Here is my list for this morning: write two ideas for this book, organise dinner party, do washing, make phone calls to pay some bills.)

2. Against each item write 10, 20, 30. These represent blocks of minutes that you are going to spend on each item in turn. So my list would look like
   Write book 10, 20, 30
   Organise party 10, 20, 30
   Laundry 10, 20, 30
   Phone calls 10, 20, 30

Here's an idea for you...

Scan your diary for big projects coming up. Tomorrow spend just 10 minutes working on each project. By giving a tiny amount of focused attention regularly to projects, well in advance, you accomplish them without even noticing.

3. Start with the task that puts you off least. Set the kitchen timer for 10 minutes. Do the task for 10 minutes. (I choose the laundry – a mindless chore that I quite enjoy. I have my load on comfortably within the 10 minutes.)

4. When the timer rings. *Stop*. Wherever you are in the task. *Stop*. Take a pencil and score through the 10 next to the task.

5. Set the timer for 10 minutes. Start the next task. (In my case, it's paying bills. It takes me the whole 10 minutes to get the paraphernalia together. Note: I'm no longer resentful about paying the bills, I'm irritated that I can't get on with it.)

6. Score through the 10 on the list and start the next task (Writing. The task that is most formidable, but buoyed on by the fact that I've made a start on the mundane tasks, I sit down, make some notes and start typing. The timer rings mid-sentence. Note: I'm disappointed that I have to leave my task and move on.)

7. Score off 10 and start the next task. (I look through recipe books for 10 minutes and make some notes on whom to invite.)

8. Score off 10 minutes. Now move on to the first task again but set the timer for 20 minutes. Repeat the entire process. (Laundry again. The first load isn't finished, so I sort the laundry so that it's ready to go in the machine. That takes 10 minutes but I score off the 20 next to laundry as there's nothing more I can do. I set the egg timer to 20 minutes for the bills. For most of that time I listen

Handel's *Water Music* played on a xylophone but I am halfway through paying the last bill when the timer goes. Score off 20. I move back to the writing with a sense of relief – that's the job that's most important but because of my 10-minute start I'm raring to go. When the timer goes after 20 minutes, I go back to the party, finalise the guest list and decide on the menu. Back to the laundry – 30 minutes. Unload and hang out the washing, set off the next load – well within the 30 minutes that they have now been allocated. Now I go back to my computer and complete another 30 minutes. After 30 minutes I pause and look at my list. All the chores have been completed. I don't need to do any more on the party – I've made a real start. And I'm where I want to be – sitting at my computer and enjoying writing, so I set my timer for 40 minutes and carry on, promising myself a cup of tea at the end. I'm so into it after 40 minutes that I bring the cup of tea back to my desk and carry on until lunch time.

Why this works for me when nothing else does

- ❀ It helps you overcome resistance. You can assign a task 5 minutes to begin with – although I started on 10 here. Anybody can do just about anything for 5 minutes.

- ❀ It has built in end-effect. This is the phenomenon well observed in employees in the two days before going on holiday – they get more done in two days than they usually achieve in a month. The rotation method keeps you focused because you build in artificial 'deadlines'. In other words, you'll get more done in 3 × 20 minute blocks than in an hour of unfocused grind.

> Defining idea...
>
> **'Procrastination is the art of keeping up with yesterday.'**
> DON MARQUIS, American humorist

- ❀ It has an innate momentum of its own. The easy tasks propel you into the difficult ones.

4. The perfection trap

Your need to 'get it perfect' isn't about perfection. It's about staying in control.

And staying in control is not a virtue if it's making you miserable.

I have a friend who ran her first marathon. And she did run the whole way, never once slowing down to a walk. She felt fabulous for about six hours afterwards – she deserved to. Then before she'd even had her evening meal, the self-doubt began – she should have run faster, pushed herself more, achieved a better time. All she'd wanted beforehand was to complete the race but now that she had, she couldn't stop beating herself up for not doing it 'better'.

When she told me this story, I sat dumbstruck by her perfectionism. She looks better than me, earns more than me, achieves more than me, but the price for her success is a small voice inside telling her endlessly that she's just not good enough. Does it have to be that way? I think perfectionists can achieve just as much if they let that voice go for good. They tend to think not. They know their perfectionism is neurotic but they cling to it because they think they are lazy and that without the voice they would just give up and slope around the house in old tracksuits not brushing their teeth.

This is unlikely. However, only you can learn to ignore the little voice. What I do know is that if you don't ignore it, you'll never be free of stress. Often that little voice belongs to someone we know, often someone who brought us up, who has no idea of the complexity of our world. In their world, with one role to fulfil it was easy to do it perfectly. In the world we live in, chocka with choice, where we can fulfil so many roles, there's no way we can do all of it perfectly. And even if you did, you still wouldn't be happy. Give it up!

✿ Ration your perfectionist behaviour. You probably won't ever lose it completely. However, you can limit it. One woman I know whose energy levels had plummeted finally made the connection between her habit of staying up late reading and answering emails and her inability to get to sleep (duh!). So now she allows herself two nights a week to check emails late. Go through your own life working out where you can cut down or cut out perfectionist habits.

✿ Lose your fear of the person who made you this way. Even if you were always the sort of kid who liked to colour code your books, no one becomes a perfectionist unaided. Someone somewhere had high expectations of you. Accept something pretty basic: if you haven't earned their unconditional approval by now, you probably never will. Let it go. And if you can't, get therapy.

✿ Walk barefoot in the park. Remember Jane Fonda begging Robert Redford to stop being such a stuffed shirt and to walk barefoot in Central Park. You could try the same – just to see if you like it. You probably won't – but it might teach you something valuable: that nobody cares but you. Whatever your version of mad devil-may-care spontaneity – asking friends to dinner and ordering a takeaway curry, or letting your roots show, or putting on a few kilos, or refusing

> *Here's an idea for you...*
> **Restrict your 'to-do' list to seven items only. Less a 'to-do' list than an 'I absolutely have to do' list. Chinese medics say that any more and you get stressed out by the sheer volume and fed up when you don't complete them.**

to take the kids swimming on Sunday morning because you simply can't be fagged – go on: *do it*. The kids will not implode with disappointment. The world will not fall apart. Slip up and nothing happens.

No one cares if you're perfect but you (and the person who made you this way, see above, but we've dealt with them already).

5. Stop acting on impulse

Focus, concentration, sticking to what you've started. That will cut your stress levels instantly.

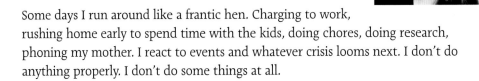

Yes, yes, yes, But how?

Some days I run around like a frantic hen. Charging to work, rushing home early to spend time with the kids, doing chores, doing research, phoning my mother. I react to events and whatever crisis looms next. I don't do anything properly. I don't do some things at all.

When I get to bed I remember the stuff that I didn't get round to and feel disappointed and frustrated with myself. When that happens it's time to go back to basics and use this idea. It helps you finish what you start and makes you feel on top of your life. Besides helping you become more focused, it also helps you curb your impulse to wander off and do other stuff rather than the one task that you have set yourself. It will show up the numerous times you have just got started on a project when it suddenly seems terribly important to water the plants, call your mum or make a nice cup of tea. But now you will be prepared and will observe your impulses as just that – impulses. And you will stay put with a wise 'Oh there I go, looking for ways to waste time again.'

Besides training you to focus and resist the impulse to waste time, this idea will achieve two further objectives: (1) It will build your self-esteem by fostering your sense of yourself as a person who follows through on their word. (2) It will clear your life of a ton of annoying little irritations that have been stopping you mentally from moving on.

> Here's an idea for you...
>
> **Making a promise to yourself every night and keeping it the next day is the route to mental toughness. Every time you keep a promise to yourself, stick some loose change in a jar. It's a good visual record of your growing focus and strength – and, of course, you get to spend the cash at the end of it.**

Step 1   Before you go to bed tonight, think of something you want to achieve tomorrow. Keep it really small and simple. It doesn't matter what it is, but you have to do it. Make it something restful – you're going to read a chapter of a favourite novel. Make it useful – you're going to clean the cutlery drawer. Make it worthy – you're going to take a multivitamin. Take this promise extremely seriously. Promise yourself you'll do it – and follow through. If you don't, no excuses. You've failed. But you're aiming too high. Make your next promise easier to achieve.

Step 2   Make a promise to yourself every evening for a week. And follow through.

Step 3   OK, now you're going to make a list of some tasks that you need to undertake but have been putting off. You will need seven, one for every day of the week. Some ideas: starting on your tax return; making a dental appointment; cancelling the gym membership you never use; sorting out your wardrobe; cleaning out the inside of the car; tackling just one pile from the many piles on your desk; grooming the dog; making a start on the garage.

Step 4   Write these down and keep them by your bed. Each night for the next week, pick one and promise yourself you'll do it tomorrow.

Step 5   Write another list. This time put on it things that are worrying you and driving you mad. Suggestions: discover if your pension plan will pay out enough for you to live on; write a letter to that friend you're upset with; paint the kitchen. Put on the list everything that is driving you nuts. Then pick one and break it down into manageable steps. Promise yourself to do the first of these steps tomorrow, and every day from now on, make a promise to take another step forward. Don't let impulse drive you off course.

This is an exercise in mental toughness. Making promises to yourself that you never keep brings you down and, over time, breaks your heart. But by breaking difficult tasks down into manageable chunks and building the strength of character to follow through and get them out the way, you take a huge step forward in reducing stress in your life.

Warning: don't make more than two or three promises a day. Keep it simple.

6. Leave the office on time

Reduce interruptions. Reclaim your evenings.

Take control. Don't let your working day be hijacked by others. The secret is to have your goals clear in your mind.

Think weekly, then daily

Don't be a slave to a daily 'to-do' list. See the big picture. On Monday morning lose the sinking 'I've got so much to do' sensation. Instead, think 'What are my goals for this week?' Decide what you want to have done by Friday and then break each goal into smaller tasks that have to be undertaken to achieve all you want by Friday. Slot these tasks in throughout your week. This helps you prioritise so that the tricky and difficult things, or tasks that depend on other people's input, don't sink to the back of your consciousness. It also means you are giving attention to all that you have to do and not spending too much time on one task at the beginning of the week.

Concentrate on three or four items on your 'to-do' list at once. You won't be overwhelmed.

Work with your energy cycles

Some of us operate better in the morning, some in the late afternoon. If your job demands creativity, block out your most creative periods so that you can concentrate on your projects. Don't allow them to be impinged upon by meetings and phone calls that could be done anytime.

Make the phone call you're dreading   Right now. That call that saps your energy all day. Just do it.

Have meetings in the morning   People are frisky. They want to whizz through stuff and get on with their day. Morning meetings go much faster than those scheduled in the afternoon.

Check emails three times a day   First thing in the morning, just after lunch and just before you leave are ideal times. Keeping to this discipline means that you don't use email as a distraction.

> *Here's an idea for you...*
>
> **Create a 'virtual you' if you're getting stressed out in the office by the demands of others. When you're an administrative lynchpin, set up a shared file where people can go to find the information or resources they'd usually get from you.**

Limit phone calls   Talk to other people when it suits you, not them. The most time-effective way of using the phone is to limit your calls as you do your emails – to three times a day. Make a list of calls you have to make that day. Call first thing. If someone isn't there, leave a message and unless you have to talk to them urgently, ask them to call you back at your next 'phone period'. Just before lunch or the end of work is good. That means neither of you will linger over the call. Of course, you can't limit phone calls completely to these times but most of us have some control over incoming calls. I don't have a secretary to screen calls, but I very politely say 'Sorry, I'm in the middle of something.' I tell the caller when I'll be free and most people offer to call me back then, saving me the hassle of calling them. The point of all of this is to keep phone calls shorter by putting them in the context of a busy working day. Social chat is important and nice but most of us spend too much time on it. And this goes for personal calls too: give yourself five minutes maximum. Or better still save personal calls as a treat for a hardworking morning.

You want more money

Where does it all go?

You earn enough, so why are you always skint? Read these three profiles, ticking all statements that apply, and pick the one that most closely applies to you. (You may find you recognise yourself in more than one profile.)

1.
☐ You have been known to file* bank statements unopened.
☐ You don't know how much is in your bank account to the nearest £50.
☐ You have no idea what percentage interest your credit card charges.

2.
☐ You see an overdraft not as debt but as a bonus.
☐ 'Save' – to you, it's a foreign concept.
☐ Life is for living. Something always turns up to help you pay the bills.

3.
☐ You have a 'challenging' mortgage but don't miss payments.
☐ You have debt but move it onto low interest or 0% interest deals.
☐ You have moments of freefall anxiety about your future because although you have a pension you don't put enough into it.

* 'File' may be a euphemism for stuffing in the bottom of a drawer or your handbag.

Your profile

Note the sections in which you ticked the most boxes:

1. You're an **ostrich**. Money is a dirty word. You'd rather not think about it. But ignoring money usually goes along with ignoring other things and your life probably feels stressed and overwhelming quite a lot of the time. See idea 12, Red is the new black.

2. You're a **philosopher**. For you money is an abstract concept – it doesn't really exist. You are probably right. It's just that the rest of us – specifically your bank manager – don't share your reality See idea 7, Love your money.

3. You're a **worry bunny**. In some senses the worst of all worlds because you don't feel secure but you don't get the fun either. See the ideas in the next section: 'You want a secure future'.

7. Love your money

And it will love you right back. When that happens life gets a lot less stressful.

Quickly, without thinking too much about it, write down three phrases that come into your head when you think about your finances.

(Hint: unless your three words are 'abundant, balanced, life-enhancing', then you need this idea.)

This idea is about respect. If you're disrespectful of your money, I'm prepared to bet that money is a stressor in your life. If you don't take care of your money, the chances are that, just like a neglected teenager, it's never going to amount to much. Worse, the relationship will probably deteriorate further. One day your money is going to do the equivalent of coming home pregnant with a crack cocaine habit.

Here's a quick test
Get out your wallet or purse. Check out how it looks. Is it neat with bills folded, receipts tucked away. Or is everything stuffed in higgledy-piggledy?

Here's a quicker one
How much money have you got in your wallet right now? If you're out by more than the price of a coffee, you need this idea badly. Your money is your friend. You should love it like a member of the family. You wouldn't go to the shops and forget to bring home one of the kids. Well, why the hell would you misplace your money?

Look for your latte factor

Make a list of everything you spend in a day. Keep a notebook with you and write down how often you take money out of the 'hole in the wall' and what you spend it on. Every cheque you write. Every card you swipe. Every time you spend a penny. Literally. Keep it up for a week, preferably for a month. Now multiply (by 52 or 12). That's what it costs to run your life. Go through and highlight the big essentials – the mortgage, the essential bills. Now get out a calculator and work out what you spend on lunches, clothes, magazines, newspapers.

You're looking for what has been called 'the latte factor', those items that are completely expendable and add very little to your life but cost a fortune. It will frighten the bejasus out of you. My latte factor was £472. I needed that money a whole lot more than Starbucks. You also realise how much it costs to run your life. The very first day I practised this exercise I spent £197.45. All I came home with was a pound of cherries. The rest was debt I couldn't remember accruing. Shocking.

We're not going to talk about debt here but if you've got personal debt, do this for a month and you are going to work out exactly why.

Writing down what you spend is a fantastically useful exercise whether you're overspending or not. It sure as hell won't destress you in the short term but it will in the long term. It allows you to see almost instantly who or what you're spending your money on and then decide if you're happy with that. It allows you to take control, and every way you can find to foster the illusion of control is helpful if you want to be less stressed. Spiritual teachers tell us that money is neither bad nor good, it's simply a way we register our presence on the world. If you fritter away money as a distraction, you'll never focus long enough to work out what's really important to you. If you spend what you don't have, your spirit as well as your bank balance is going to be overstretched. Your bank balance isn't important. Your spirit is. Respect it, protect it – and you're going to make someone very happy and that someone isn't your bank manager.

> Defining idea...
>
> **'The safest way to double your money is to fold it over and put it in your pocket.'**
> KIN HUBBARD, American humorist

8. I think therefore iPod

If you've ever bought something and then regretted it almost immediately, then this idea is for you. You'll learn how to save money by avoiding impulse purchases.

There's a Marx Brothers' film – I think it's 'A Night in Casablanca' – where Groucho is hired to run a hotel.

On arrival, he makes an announcement to staff, which goes something like this: 'There are going to have to be some changes around here. From now on, if guests ask for a three-minute egg, give them a two-minute egg; if they ask for a two-minute egg, give them a one-

> Defining idea...
>
> **'Immediate gratification just isn't soon enough.'**
> CARRIE FISHER,
> Postcards from the Edge

Here's an idea for you...

Part of the intention of having a 28-day list is to introduce a cooling-off period into the purchasing process. Another way to give yourself pause for thought is to try an experiment along these lines: work out how much you put on your cards last month and draw that sum out in cash. For the next month, try paying for everything with that money. Turning barely noticed credit card spend into extremely visible cash-burn can be quite a shocking way to discover just how much you get through. Alternatively, you may find that using real rather than virtual money inhibits your spending impulses.

minute egg; and if they ask for a one-minute egg, give them the chicken and tell them to work it out for themselves.'

Maybe Groucho's motives are questionable but he did manage to hint at today's retail world in which speed of delivery and instant gratification have become the norm. There's an episode of *The Simpsons* where a gigantic new deep fryer is being installed. Perhaps you remember the following exchange:

Shop owner: It can fry a whole buffalo in 40 seconds.
Homer: (wailing voice) Oh, I want it now!

As ever more demanding customers, we want better quality, we want cheaper prices and, above all, we want it more or less immediately. The bookshop owner who tells us that it will take two weeks to order the book we want is seeing increasing volumes of business going to internet booksellers. 'Now' is becoming the only acceptable delivery time.

There's physiological evidence to suggest that going on a spending spree gives us a short-term high. We actually enjoy buying stuff. Just as we're prone to comfort eat to cheer ourselves up and to allay anxiety, so comfort spending is a path to retail orgasm.

Let's be honest, it's probably something we've all experienced. There we are, wandering through a department store and we see *it*. It could be a TV, a cool top, a DVD... but it's a must-have. Chances are that until you saw it, you didn't even know that it existed. But now you've seen it and you want it – badly. You know you're a bit short this month really, but you reach for your plastic chum and it's yours.

Feels good, doesn't it? The weird thing is, of course, that a few weeks down the line, that must-have doesn't always seem quite so necessary to your life. If you've ever thought to yourself that you have a wardrobe full of clothes and nothing to wear, chances are that you've been a victim of premature retail ejaculation.

Defining idea...

'**When you look at the buying habits that have taken hold in our culture over the past 30 years or so, you can see that we made the decision somewhere along the line to work longer hours so we could acquire more things. We've exchanged our leisure time for stuff.'**
ELAINE ST JAMES,
50 Ways to Simplify your Life

Incidentally, don't imagine that you're only at risk when you're out shopping. It won't be long before most retail accidents happen at home. Shopping online is just as dangerous when gratification is only a mouse click away.

So here's an idea that will save you money and help reduce the clutter in your home. From now on, every time you come across an item that you would normally be tempted to splash out on and which costs a significant amount (you decide what counts as significant), hold back from buying it. Go home and put it on your 28-day list. Make a note of the item, the date you saw it and the cost. If after 28 days you revisit your list and still think it would be a good buy, then consider acquiring it. If you do buy it, the heightened anticipation of finally getting your hands on it after a wait of 28 days and more is quite something.

(A friend of mine calls this tantric shopping. The method works particularly well with singles and albums made by contestants in reality TV programmes. That amusing version of 'Jungle Rock' produced by early rejects from *I'm a Celebrity, Get Me Out of Here* seems less essential six months down the track.)

If after four weeks you're still unsure about the merits of buying a particular item, put it back on the list for another four weeks. Apart from keeping your home a bit freer from clutter, this will save you a fortune. Not a bad return for a *soupçon* of discipline.

9. Jump start your salary

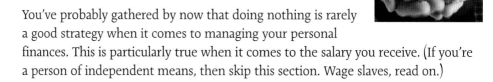

Do you deserve a higher salary? Well of course you do. Let's look at tactics and techniques for making a persuasive case to your boss.

You've probably gathered by now that doing nothing is rarely a good strategy when it comes to managing your personal finances. This is particularly true when it comes to the salary you receive. (If you're a person of independent means, then skip this section. Wage slaves, read on.)

Although we might fondly imagine that our natural talent and unstinting commitment and contribution will bring its own recognition and reward as surely as Day follows Doris, the more likely scenario is that you'll end up as some kind of overlooked organisational Gollum, driven to embitterment and quietly convinced that you've been diddled out of your rightful reward.

But if nobody knows how good you really are, why on earth would your company throw more money at you? The prerequisites for getting your salary increased are that (a) you are reasonably competent, and (b) you're well regarded by your employers. If these basic elements aren't in place right now, I'd point you towards another book in this series – *Cultivate a Cool Career.*

But taking these as read, here are some tips for negotiating your way to an optimal package. The first decision you'll have to make is, in the words of Joe Strummer, 'Should I stay or should I go?'

If you decide you want to stay where you are – for the time being at least – then you'll need to start gathering evidence that shows why you already deserve an increase. Perhaps you can make the case that some colleagues are getting more pay for doing the same work, or that others are getting more pay even though you do more work.

Before you fix a time to talk with you boss, make sure you know what you want out of your negotiation. This means having three figures in mind: your ideal salary (i.e. the most you dare ask for without alienating your boss), your bottom line (i.e. the lowest figure you'd settle for) and your realistic goal (i.e. the figure that you think you have a good chance of getting).

Here's an idea for you...

Be prepared to be flexible. If your boss accepts the validity of your case but pleads emptiness of the department piggybank, come back with something like 'Greg, I can see the problem so let's see what else we can do. Maybe I could have an extra week's holiday and a company car as an alternative.'

This particular response obviously works best if you have a boss called Greg. But it is worth bearing in mind that your salary is only one part of the total compensation package.

Defining idea...

'For they can conquer who believe they can.'
JOHN DRYDEN

Armed with this information, prepare your case and book a meeting with your boss. Make sure you time the meeting to your best advantage. If you've only been with the company a few months, or if you've just made the mother of all cock-ups, hold off for the time being.

More precisely, go for a time of day which gives you a fighting chance of finding your boss receptive and in good humour (e.g. not immediately after they've come back from the weekly knackers-in-a-mangle meeting with the MD).

When you go to the meeting, have all the facts and figures at your fingertips. Take along relevant reports, sales figures, performance stats and any other documents that support your case. It might even be worth putting together a supporting document to leave with your boss.

If there's nothing doing, don't despair. Career-wise, it might be an excellent time to position yourself for recognition when the money does become available again. You can ask for added responsibilities or a new job title. You're taking a risk, of course, that you might be working harder in the short term for the same pay, but you've bolstered your bargaining position down the line. If nothing comes through eventually, then, to be honest, I'd be looking for a new place to work.

Apropos of which, here are a few negotiating tip and wrinkles to deploy when you've been offered a position with a new company.

❀ Always aim to negotiate with the decision-maker rather than through intermediaries.

❀ It's always preferable to negotiate on the basis of having received a written offer. Not only will this help to prevent misunderstandings, but it also helps to depersonalise the situation if you are negotiating over a piece of paper. Remember that you are often dealing with somebody who could soon be your new boss. It pays not to antagonise them.

❀ Keep the tone of the negotiation positive by reaffirming your real interest in joining the company, by emphasising how pleased you were to receive the offer, and by looking forward to working with the new company – it's just a matter of clearing up a few contractual points to everybody's satisfaction.

❀ Try to give the company a few options to respond to rather than box yourself into a corner.

❀ Don't let the process drag on. Negotiate crisply and settle quickly.

By the way, if you decide to reject the job offer, keep it courteous and professional. Remember that the people you are dealing with are probably good networkers also. The last thing you want is to be bad-mouthed within your industry for buggering people about. For that reason, drop the company a line saying that you were pleased to have been offered the job, but that you regret that you can't accept the offer. Give your reasons why, thank them for taking the time to meet with you and wish them well with filling the post.

10. What's it worth?

Are you selling some sort of service? Here are some pointers about how you can get the best rate of pay for your services.

According to management guru Charles Handy, there's a marketplace for every skill. Whether you're an expert in your professional field, a damn fine cook, a great gardener or a dab hand at repairing brass instruments, somebody out there is looking for somebody just like you.

Whether it's as your main income stream or as a hopefully lucrative sideline, one of the key challenges for anybody who provides a service is setting a price for your offering.

It's a process fraught with pitfalls. Let's use the example of a business consultant to illustrate this point. It can be tempting when trying to establish a daily rate to set your prices based on the level of income you want to generate. At one level, it seems entirely logical. You want to generate £50,000 a year and reckon you'll be able to achieve 100 days of chargeable work. Ergo, your daily rate is £500.

Very rational, but very wrong

What's missing from this equation is any sense of the price range that your customers expect to pay. The question we need to ask ourselves is, 'What's the market rate for this type of work?' Think about it for a moment. Would you really rather work 100 days a year at £500 a day when you might be able to work 50 days at £1,000?

There's another question linked to this: how price sensitive are your customers? Or put it a different way, to what extent would you lose customers by raising your prices, or gain them by reducing your charges?

In my experience, consultancy is a relatively insensitive market. People bring consultants into their companies to help them address thorny issues: getting a solution is typically more important than saving a few bob. Can you imagine a project manager being held to account by their MD for a poor result and defending their choice of consultants by saying: 'Look I know that they cocked up big time, but at least they were cheap!' Show that man the door.

As a general guideline, consultants submitting proposals for work can afford to charge at the higher end of the price range. If the rate is genuinely problematic for a company, then the option is there for the consultants to drop their daily rate. Curiously, perhaps, undercharging is more problematic than overcharging. Once you allow yourself to be secured at a knock-down price, your customers assume that is the rate that they will pay in the future. The other irony of putting a low price on your services is that you fall through the floor of credibility. Particularly when it

---

Here's an idea for you...

One way to build your knowledge of the marketplace you're in is to find out what people who provide a similar service to yours are charging. If you're setting up a coffee shop, it would be relatively easy to find out what the Starbucks down the road expects customers to cough up for a cappuccino. Likewise, you can establish what the going rate for a piano lesson is in your parts through the judicious use of Yellow Pages and a couple of phone calls.

Armed with this research, you also need to decide how your service matches up against your competitors quality wise. If you're a conservatoire-trained pianist, you are well placed to go for the upper end of the range. If the service you offer has no obvious competitors, try a bit of market research to ascertain what people consider to be a reasonable amount to pay.

> *Defining idea...*
>
> **'If you are the seller, you must set a minimum price below which you will not sell. Anything above that is a bonus.'**
> RICHARD DOBBINS AND BARRIE O. PETTMAN, What Self-made Millionaires Really Think, Know and Do

comes to hiring consultants, most companies have a sense of the going rate for the work on offer. If you charge significantly less than your competitors, the working assumption is that you lack the experience or gravitas to carry off the work required.

That's all very well for consultants, you might be thinking, but what happens in a more price-sensitive market. If you're convinced that the main factor in buying is price, then of course it makes sense to take a less cavalier approach. The key is knowing your marketplace and your customers.

The biggest single danger you face is being seduced by the most popular price-setting model around. While it might make sense for the likes of Tesco to pile it high and sell it cheap, for most of us it's just a recipe for being overworked and underpaid. Which is bad. Obviously.

11. Become a top-notch bargain maker

Haggling is for life, not just for holidays. You'll save money if you adopt the six habits of highly effective hagglers.

As a recently resigned member of the Society of Life's Underpaid Overtippers (don't bother checking for an amusing acronym – there isn't one), I know all too well some of the curious habits and attitudes we develop around money.

Once, after a crap meal and contemptuous service in a place that ought to have known better, my response to a 'suggested gratuity of 15 per cent' on the bill was to signal my displeasure by leaving a tip of only 10 per cent. (Using coins rather than notes was the *coup de grâce* I felt – a social stiletto wielded with devastating precision.)

The moral of the story, of course, is that the £20 tip should by rights have stayed firmly in my trouser pocket. So why do we habitually pay over the odds? Why can't we pay what we need to, not what we feel we have to?

Social conditioning aside, I'm convinced that much of our reticence stems from a lack of tutoring in the art of haggling. So try the following on for size: they are my six habits of highly effective hagglers. Chances are that you're already adept in at least some of these areas, in which case pick 'n' mix to your wallet's content:

Here's an idea for you...

There's an old Chinese proverb which goes something like this: if you want to find out about water, don't ask a fish. Because we tend to approach bargain-hunting from a shopper's perspective, we don't always appreciate some of the tactics deployed by sellers. You'll improve your bargaining powers no end by reading a few books on sales techniques. And if you want to understand how retailers try to manipulate us, you won't find a better book than Why We Buy by Paco Underhill.

✿ **Cultivate a pained expression.** When the seller mentions a price, give them a clear facial signal that the price is not acceptable. If you're struggling with how this might look, imagine you've just been told by your lovable but overzealous secretary that he has just simultaneously shredded your appointments diary, passport and jackpot-winning lottery ticket. Now look in the mirror... that look will do nicely.

✿ As well as managing the visual signals you give, **keep an eye and ear out for the signals coming back at you.** A pause before a reply comes back to you often indicates that there's a negotiable stance being offered to you rather than the bottom line. Really pay attention to the words people use: when people tell you they can't reduce the price 'at the moment' or 'in these circumstances' or 'as things stand', they're actually letting you know that perhaps they could reduce the price at some point or under different circumstances. Press them to find out what these conditions are. For example, if there's going to be a '50 per cent off across the store' sale coming up, maybe you want to hold back and take the risk that you can elbow your way to the front of the sales queue.

✿ **Research the market.** Whatever the price quoted at you, if you can say 'I know I can get it cheaper elsewhere' and can back the assertion up with evidence, there's a good chance you'll get a reduction.

❁ Questions like 'Is this the very best price you can offer me?', 'Have you ever sold this for less?' and 'What does [insert name of company's chief rival] charge for this?'

❁ **Create possibilities.** Salespeople worth their salt should be doing this for you anyway, but it never does any harm to drop in hints and phrases that might move the negotiation along. You know the sort of thing: 'It's still a lot to pay all at once. Are there any credit deals going which might mean we could afford to buy now?' or 'Suppose we took half now and half later – would you still guarantee the price?' Questions like these can help to move a bargaining session out of stalemate, so go into your next negotiation armed with phrases like 'What if...?', 'Suppose we/you...' and 'How would it be if...?'

❁ If the item in question is something you really, really want, it might be worth delegating the bargaining to somebody who is emotionally detached. If the reality is that you are so desperate to lay your hands on something, your language and your non-verbal signals will give you away and you'll end up paying top price.

Now the trick with any of the above is to get practising them. Have a go and I'll be very surprised if by the end of the week you haven't saved yourself at least the cost of this already keenly priced book.

12. Red is the new black

Awash in credit card debt? Here are some strong pointers for how you can manage your way out of financial trouble.

Health experts are bemoaning the fact that we're fast becoming a nation of fatties. The thing about the population carrying a few extra kilos is that it's pretty obvious to the most untrained of eyes. Take a walk down your local high street and watch people waddle.

Our readiness to take on previously unheard of levels of debt is a different story. Barring a spectacular fall from monetary grace, our financial health is our secret. How could the couple two doors along afford to have that conservatory built? Who knows? How can the neighbours manage to put all three of their children through private education? How can the office administrator go on quite so many expensive holidays?

What we *do* know is that collectively we are carrying more on our credit cards and mortgages than any previous generation. The average household has debts of around £38,000, with many of us owing between *six and twelve times our household's annual income.*

Debt's the way to do it

We're debt junkies. Go to college and come out with a qualification and a pile of bills. You've chanced on a bargain in the sales but you're a bit short this month? No problem – stick it on the credit card. Whether it's buying a house or a car or just paying for Christmas, resistance to debt has never been lower.

Somewhere along the line, we've succumbed to the delusion that owing money is sophisticated. We look on that elderly uncle who'll only buy something when there's cash in the bank to pay for it as some kind of financial *ingénue* rather than as a model of financial prudence.

And, of course, it's getting ever easier to pile up the debt. Credit card companies seem to fall over themselves in their haste to bump up our credit limits, and then send us a letter telling us the 'good news' that our capacity for debt is now that much greater. Damn their eyes.

Even worse, they're now sending us blank cheques every few weeks. Aside from the fraud risks posed by these unsolicited letters falling into the wrong hands, these cheques usually have punitive conditions – no interest-free period, a transaction fee and often less than attractive interest rates.

Don't get me wrong. Used sensibly, credit cards can be a neat budgeting tool, which can provide a bit of financial flexibility. And borrowing money via your credit card can be extremely positive if you use it to buy smartly. If, for example, you had used your credit card to buy some tickets for a big theatrical or sporting event and then put them up for sale on eBay, you can make a tidy profit. Part of the trouble is that most of our credit card spend tends to go on buying liabilities rather than assets.

Here's an idea for you...

When Marlon Brando cries out 'The horror, the horror' towards the end of Apocalypse Now, he hadn't, to the best of my recollection, just opened his latest credit card statement. When the statements for your cards turn up over the next few weeks, make a note of the interest charged in each case, tot up the total interest you pay each month and multiply it by 12. That will give you a ballpark figure for the year. If that doesn't make you cry out in anguish, you may be beyond redemption.

Borrowing money to buy things that go down in value is a very bad habit to develop.

According to some estimates, most households in the UK have at least five active credit cards, including store cards, at any given time. Do you know what your total credit card debt is? Do you know what rates of interest you're paying on the cards you use? Chances are they vary quite widely.

Defining idea...

'I don't borrow on credit cards because it is too expensive. There's no question that a credit card is an expensive way to do borrowing. I would not recommend to anyone that they chronically borrow on a credit card.'
MATTHEW BARRETT, chief executive of Barclays Bank

Target your most expensive cards

Here's my advice. Find the card that's charging the highest rate of interest and focus on paying that off as soon as you can. Don't add to your woes by using it to buy anything else. All those other cards? Just send them the minimum payment until you've cleared public enemy number one. Once that's done, turn your financial firepower onto the card with the next highest rate of interest. And so on.

You might be thinking at this point that a suggestion to clear off your credit card debt is hardly ground-breaking advice. Maybe it isn't, but I do know that poorly managed credit cards are the source of many a mate's financial woes. Also, there's a world of difference between people that understand the concept of good credit card management and those of us who adopt an active strategy. As the wise old Chinese proverb says (although thinking about it, maybe it's a Klingon *bon mot*), *'Thought without action is sterile.'*

13. How to deal with severe debt

Hopefully, you'll never get so seriously into debt that you are dealing with credit management agencies. In case you ever do, though, you need to know how to manage the situation.

Most of us have been strapped for cash from time to time. Generally we are able to dig ourselves out of trouble with a bit of financial belt-tightening or some creative use of credit cards. It's not always that easy.

Remember the character played by Kevin Costner in the movie *Field of Dreams* who felt impelled to build a baseball stadium in the middle of nowhere on the basis of advice from a mystical friend that 'If you build it, they will come'? There's a variation on this that applies to many people who get deep into debt and are unable to extricate themselves: if you owe it, they will come. The 'they' in question are either the people who are owed money or their appointed debt collectors.

Know what you're signing up to

If you should fall into serious debt, here are a few tips on how to handle the situation:

* Don't panic or ignore the problem: unopened bills won't go away.
* Decide which debts take priority – like mortgage or rent – and which cost you the most through penalties or higher interest rates.
* Only agree to pay off debts at a rate you can keep up. Don't offer more than you can afford.

Here's an idea for you...

The days when lenders would send the boys around armed with baseball bats are largely the stuff of fiction and these days are confined to the extreme fringes of society. But watch out for the dodgy practices given above. They still happen from time to time.

❀ Contact those who you owe money to as soon as possible to let them know you're having problems.

❀ Remember that's it's better to make a small payment than send nothing at all.

❀ Keep copies of *all* correspondence. You will need them if you *want* to seek help and advice from a third party.

❀ Seek advice if organisations won't accept your repayment offers.

Lenders have responsibilities too

Lenders and debt management companies have to behave properly. Examples of their (illegal) deficiencies include:

❀ Failing to investigate or provide proper details/records when a debt is queried or disputed.

❀ Failing to deal with appointed third parties such as Citizens' Advice Bureaux or independent advice centres.

❀ Pursuing third parties for payment when they are not liable.

❀ Falsely implying or claiming authority – such as claiming to be working on court authority.

❀ Contacting debtors at unreasonable times and/or intervals.

❀ Claiming a right of entry when no court order has been obtained.

❀ Misleading debtors by the use of official-looking documents such as letters made to resemble court claims.

Lenders aren't allowed to ignore the dodgy practices of debt collectors acting on their behalf. If they do, their fitness to hold a credit licence can be called into question. Generally though, according to the Office of Fair Trading (OFT), complaints about debt management companies have dropped substantially in recent years.

> *Defining idea...*
>
> **'It is very iniquitous to make me pay my debts. You have no idea of the pain it gives one.'**
> LORD BYRON

So if you do get into debt, at least you shouldn't be unreasonably treated by the people you owe money to. Which leaves you free to concentrate on the task in hand, namely rebuilding your financial reputation.

14. Annualise your savings

I'm now going to outline a way in which you can save decent sums of money without too much pain. It's the financial equivalent of 'large oaks from little acorns grow'.

Imagine that you've just been given some bad news by your garage, or your builder, or your dentist. For example, your shower's causing a major damp problem in your master bedroom and it really needs attention soon (how your dentist knows this is another matter).

The upshot is that you're going to have to find £1,500 to sort out the problem.

Of course, you don't necessarily have to keep this going for a year. A 2004 survey suggested that abstaining from chocolate, alcohol, coffee, crisps and cigarettes during Lent could net savers around £660. The bank calculated that giving up a daily latte between Ash Wednesday and Easter can leave savers £86 better off, while foregoing a daily pint of lager could save £92. Smokers who buy a packet of cigarettes a day could save over £200.

How are you going to find this money? You could put it on the credit card but that's just shuffling the debt around. Or maybe you could dip into your emergency savings fund, but you were hoping to put that towards the cost of buying a new car. Or perhaps you could cancel the holiday you had planned for the summer, but that would be such a drag because you really could do with a break.

Or you could give up eating Snickers for a bit.

OK, so that's a bit of an exaggeration for dramatic effect, but the point is that our cash has a habit of dribbling away in lots of small amounts here and there, and that if we could harness a whole bunch of small (and probably relatively painless) savings, we can quickly build up a healthy financial stockpile.

Psychologically, pocketing 40 pence on the back of a Snickers unconsumed doesn't seem like a saving worth having. What can reinforce the impact of a bit of confectionery-related restraint is to try multiplying out the saving over a 12-month period. Imagine that Snicker is one of five you eat each week; that makes the saving £2 a week, or a starting-to-get-impressive £104 a year.

When I was faced with a unexpected £1,500 bill a little while back, this is how I raised the money over a 12-month period:

Item given up	Annualised saving
A bottle of wine a week	£260
Sunday newspaper	£73
A Mars Bar a week	£22
Packet of crisps a day	£75
Coffee on way into work	£480
Evening paper on way home	£100
A DVD a month	£195
A CD a month	£140
A paperback a month	£85
A bottle of lager a week	£75
Total saving	**£1,505**

These numbers get even more significant when you bear in mind that they come out of our take-home pay. Try working out what proportion of your annual salary is needed to fund these items. If you're on the average wage, for example, this little lot above are broadly equivalent to one month's pay.

I have a friend who describes this focus on realising a series of small savings as moving from 'penny profligate to pound proud'. Mind you, he works in marketing.

Defining idea...

'**If you want to appreciate the cumulative effect of saving, think of Nassau in the Bahamas: Note All Small Savings Adding Up.**'
JOHN VILLIS, writer and educator

You want a secure future

15. What's your plan B – take the insecurity out of life

It could be your best friend in stressed out times.

The life you're living is Plan A. Plan B is what happens if it all goes pear-shaped. Know how you'd get from A to B and you remove a huge chunk of the stress that is caused by worry about the future.

It was a former boss who taught me the value of having a Plan B. Magazine editors have one of the most glamorous jobs going – great pay, company car, free holidays, free clothes...

And they have one of the most insecure jobs you can imagine. The higher they climb, the faster they can fall. Their job is highly stressful and they routinely work their butts off for an employer only to be shunted to the side in a matter of hours if they don't deliver. 'How do you stand it?', I asked my former boss. 'Always, always have a Plan B,' she told me breezily.

Deciding on plan B

Every life has its fair shares of upsets and reversals of fortune. An essential of the Plan B is to be able to look at your life dispassionately and see potential stress lines – where your life is likely to come apart. For instance:

✿ If you work in a volatile industry, it's work. Your Plan B is what you'll do if your dismissal slip lands on your desk.

✿ If your relationship is struggling, your Plan B is what you'll do if you split up.

✿ If your health isn't good, your Plan B is to research methods of financing your life if bad stuff happens.

Now please, don't get cross. I'm not trying to rain on your parade or say that your happy world is about to fall around your head. I'm merely concerned with stress proofing your life, and Plan Bs are brilliant for this. No one says you'll ever need Plan B but having one is invaluable comfort when you wake in the middle of the night and can't get back to sleep because of catastrophic thoughts swirling around in your brain. You know those nights? Well, with a Plan B, you worry for about 30 seconds, go 'Oh, I remember, I've got a plan B', roll over and doze off again.

Here's an idea for you...

Tomorrow open a completely new bank account for your Plan B. Start a direct debit and pay in until you've built up your emergency fund total of three months' expenses. Knowing you've got enough money to finance your dream makes your present life a whole lot more fulfilling.

Defining idea...

'Reality is the leading cause of stress amongst those in touch with it.'

JANE WAGNER and LILY TOMLIN, comic writers

For Plan B to work it has to be a fantasy built on reality. By that I mean it's not just a vague 'Oh, I'll sell the house and move to France.' It's more concrete than that.

Building the dream

First, decide on your Plan B and start a file. Add cuttings, pictures, information to it. Suppose you were going to sell your house and move to France. Your file for this would include information on people who had done the same thing, and research on how much you'd need to live on per year in France if you were mortgage-free. You'd also put in notes on the school system if you have young children.

Your Plan B should be realistic, but it should be awesome. It shouldn't be a case of 'Oh well, I could always move back in with Mum.' It should be training to become a chef, starting your own business, backpacking around Mexico. It should make your heart sing. Plan realistically but dream big.

Building emergency funds

Think about the financial position you'd need to be in to make it work, and take steps to achieve it. The ideal sum for a 'just-in-case fund', whatever your Plan B, is eight months' worth of living expenses. Go through your bank statements, adding up your outgoings for a year – this is truly frightening – take the total, divide by 12 to get your average per month and then multiply by eight.

Still reeling? Yes, it does that have effect. OK, eight months is ideal but it's that – an ideal. However, I'd say that a priority for anyone who wants to stress proof their life is to build up at least three months' living expenses. That's the bare minimum that you should have easily accessible in a bank account according to the experts.

What happens when you spend more of your time thinking about Plan B than worrying about Plan A? Then it's time to move your life on.

16. Make the most of your property

For most of us, our home is the single biggest component of our wealth. How can you get the best price for your property when the time comes to sell?

Well, dress me as a fop and pass those paint charts. I am, I confess, a little out of my comfort zone on this one. I know the airwaves are awash with TV programmes about house moves and makeovers but watching them has never been a personal priority of mine.

However, I fully recognise that when it comes to our personal finances, our homes are highly significant. Households around the world have far more of their wealth tied up in property than in shares or any other form of investment. Housing accounts for as much as 30–40 per cent of total household wealth in Western Europe and almost 25 per cent in America.

Here's an idea for you...

Don't spend a fortune trying to turn your current property into your dream home. In strictly financial terms, it's generally better to avoid major renovation and instead to find another house with what you are looking for. Major improvements rarely recoup their full cost if the house is sold within two to three years.

...and another

If you want your property to sell for the maximum amount, it's essential that you spend time ensuring your property looks its best. This needn't cost a fortune – simply cleaning and sprucing up the most tired parts of a house can often make a big difference. If you're lucky, investing £500 could add £5,000 to the resale value of your home.

This being so, spending a few moments contemplating how we might enhance the value of our home is actually far more relevant to most of us than any discussion about the state of the stock market. The financial sections of the weekend papers might be full of informed thinking about whether to buy Consolidated and sell Conglomerated, but we would potentially get more financial benefit out of some analysis of the merits of converting a bedroom into a bathroom.

So what can really add value to your home when you come to sell it? Interestingly, advice about the property market is not unlike that proffered in other financial areas, i.e. somewhat contradictory in places. But taking into account the range of views expressed by building societies, estate agents and surveyors, there are some areas of broad consensus. Not surprisingly, location is a dominant factor but the type of property, overall size, number of bedrooms, garage and central heating also have an impact.

Improvements that generally add value or will at least recoup their cost

✿ Installing an energy-efficient condensing boiler pays for itself. Central heating is viewed positively by buyers and will generally recoup your outlay.

❀ Adding a garage is very beneficial, especially where parking in the area is difficult. You should get your money back.

❀ Creating more living space generally works well: new conservatories and loft conversions should pay for themselves. An extra bathroom should pay for itself as long as it isn't at the cost of a bedroom.
So should adding French doors and a patio to create an outside room.

Improvements that won't add value

❀ Turning a bedroom into a bathroom: the value added by the bathroom is more than offset by the loss stemming from a reduced number of bedrooms. And beware of chopping a bedroom in half to make two oddly-shaped rooms.

❀ Knocking through walls to create an open-plan look – losing rooms generally reduces the price you'll get.

❀ Digging up a garden to build a swimming pool – you'll do well to recoup 20 per cent of your outlay.

❀ Unnecessary enhancements. For most properties, there's no merit in creating a third bathroom.

❀ Improvements that are disproportionate to the overall value of the house. Adding a £30,000 kitchen to a million-pound property might make real financial sense; adding it to a £100,000 semi is a waste of money – you won't get it back.

✿ Smokers could be reducing the value of their homes by £16,000 according to a poll by ICM

A final warning: don't improve a house to a point where it needs to attract more than 20 per cent above the going rate for similar houses in the area. You're taking a real risk.

17. Conduct an annual stock take of your finances

This idea will prompt you to come up with an overall view of your financial position.

So, all things considered, how well off are you right now? Do your assets outstrip your liabilities, or are you in debt overall?

Here are 20 questions that are designed to give you a pretty good handle on the general state of your 'finances':

✿ What's the state of your mortgage? Are you paying a competitive interest rate? If you have an endowment mortgage, review the latest information and make an informed guess as to whether this will pay off your mortgage when the time comes.

✿ If you are in debt, how much of it can you clear over the next 12 months?

Here's an idea for you...

An important measure of your financial health is your net worth. Your net worth is the difference between your total assets and total liabilities.

You'll probably have three types of assets:

■ LIQUID ASSETS. Assets that can be turned into cash more or less immediately – current account balance, any savings accounts, cash in jam jars, etc.

■ PERSONAL ASSETS. The current estimated market value of your home, car, furniture, electronic equipment, jewellery, books, CDs and any other personal items that have monetary value.

■ INVESTMENT ASSETS. Stocks and bonds, pension plans and any other type of investment you may have.

And you'll (sadly) have two types of liabilities:

■ CURRENT LIABILITIES. Credit card debt, any outstanding loan balances, any money you've borrowed and need to pay back.

■ LONG-TERM LIABILITIES. Your mortgage, and any other debt that you are repaying over a long period of time.

To determine your net worth, deduct your liabilities from your assets. You now know your overall financial health. Determining your net worth is a key plank in getting your financial life in order.

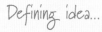

Defining idea...

'Never ask of money spent
Where the spender thinks it
went.
Nobody was ever meant
To remember or invent
What he did with every cent.'
ROBERT FROST, The Hardship of
Accounting

✿ Do you have your credit cards under control? Can you reduce the number you hold?

✿ Can you reduce your outgoings?

✿ How's your pension looking? Should you be investing more?

✿ Does your investment portfolio need rebalancing? Is it appropriate to adjust the level of risk you're exposed to?

✿ What are your spending priorities for the coming year? Do you need to update your spending budget?

✿ Do any of your major possessions need upgrading or replacing? How do you aim to pay for this?

✿ Have you scored any financial own-goals over the past year that you can avoid in future? For example, have you incurred any late payment charges on a credit card? If so, consider a direct debit arrangement.

✿ Have you made a will? Does it need updating to reflect changes in your life circumstances?

✿ Have there been any changes in your life over the past 12 months and are there any coming up? What's the impact on your finances?

✿ Are you on top of your tax commitments? If you're self-employed, do you have enough money set aside for your next tax bill?

✿ Have you claimed all the allowances – tax, state, etc. – that you're entitled to?

✿ Do you need to talk to your accountant or financial adviser?

✿ When you review your income stream(s), do you feel you are being fairly rewarded? Should you be booking a meeting with your boss to try to negotiate an increase? Is it time to move on?

✿ Are there other sources of income you might tap into?

✿ Do you have any longer-term savings challenges? Are you doing enough to meet them?

✿ What were your financial objectives this time last year? To what extent have they been met?

✿ What's your biggest financial fear for the next year? Is there anything you might usefully do to counter that fear?

✿ Can you take any pre-emptive action? For example, if you reckon that interest rates could go up later in the year, or if there's a risk that your income might suffer for whatever reason, trimming your outgoings now means that you might get away with a less draconian response down the line.

> Defining idea...
>
> **'Lack of money is the root of all evil.'**
> GEORGE BERNARD SHAW

There may well be other questions that you could usefully ask. At the heart of this process is the need to come up with an action plan. Don't be like the lemming who says 'yep, still marching to the edge of that cliff' and does nothing about it. Be like the lemming who dons a parachute and a life-jacket.

18. Stick or twist? – understanding the markets

Choose your level of investment risk. Are you a risk taker? Have you thought about risk versus financial return? I'm going to explain the idea of a hierarchy of investment risk that you can use to assess your personal finance comfort zone.

When I was at school, my old religious education teacher would invariably at some point of the lesson trot out his catchphrase: 'You know, boys, in life you pays your money and you takes your choice.' At around the same time, my horse-racing guru was telling me that I should 'only bet what you're prepared to say goodbye to'.

So when it comes to investing, what is an acceptable level of risk? (In the context of this book, let's define risk as the possibility of financial loss.)

Well, of course, it's up to each of us to determine the level of risk we're prepared to tolerate. You may be somebody who would happily contemplate descending a snow-capped mountain sat on a tea-tray. This outlook on life might translate into you feeling compelled to behave as the Indiana Jones of the investment circuit. Equally, if you wouldn't dream of getting on a bicycle without sporting at least two sets of cycle clips, your devil-may-care bypass might point you towards a less racy investment strategy.

When it comes to investing, it's vital to know what your personal level of risk tolerance is. For starters, let's be clear what some of the primary investment vehicles are:

Shares

When you buy shares, you are buying a small part of a company. As a part-owner, you are entitled to a portion of the profits that the company achieves. These are typically paid out in the form of an annual dividend. In a perfect world, as the value of a company increases over a period of time, the value of the shares you own also increase. However, you would do well to remember that time-honoured line about how the value of shares can go down as well as up. Also, a dividend payment is not guaranteed.

Bonds

Although the word might conjure up images of 007 and glamorous women wandering around nuclear plants in bikinis, a bond is really a very prosaic investment vehicle. When you buy a bond, what you get is in effect an IOU for the amount you invest from a company or a government which they promise to let you have back on a fixed date (called the maturity date). On top of that, the bond issuer also promises to pay you a fixed amount of interest at regular intervals. Bonds issued by governments are called gilts. As governments can always raise taxes if they're short of a bob or two, gilts are regarded as a pretty safe investment.

Here's an idea for you...

You may of course decide that you want to avoid any investment vehicle managed by a financial institution. You might prefer to put your spare cash into buying property, or buying and selling for profit in a field you know particularly well (e.g. stamps, CDs, red wine). This may not be a bad strategy but I would suggest that you sit down and make a clear-eyed judgement about your motives for doing so and where in the league table you might slot your alternative choice.

57

Unit trusts

Defining idea...

'**Risk comes from not knowing what you're doing.**'
WARREN BUFFETT, probably the world's most famous and influential investor

A unit trust is typically a managed portfolio of shares and bonds. The word 'managed' is significant – somebody else is making the day-to-day decisions about which shares and bonds are bought and sold. When you put money into a unit trust, you are buying a small portion of that overall portfolio. If the value of the portfolio increases (share prices rise, interest or dividend payments are made, etc.), then you share in the spoils. Equally a decline in the value of the portfolio reduces the value of your investment.

Derivatives

In essence, derivatives are high-risk financial instruments that can be traded on various markets. They are called derivatives because they are 'derived' from some real, underlying item of value (such as a stock, bond, currency or commodity). They are risky because they are time-fused and can expire worthless. The rapid growth in derivatives trading has played a major part in the growing volatility of the global financial system.

Building society savings account

You hand over your money and the building society periodically adds small amounts of interest. Dull but safe as houses.

19. Develop a penchant for a pension

I don't want to bang on about pensions too much, but many people still hold unrealistic expectations about the level of pension they'll receive. Here's how you can check whether your own arrangements are good enough.

Remember that classic 60s song by The Who called 'My Generation'? You know the one – it featured the line 'Hope I die before I get old'? Well, band member Pete Townshend, who penned that youthful expression of romantic fatalism, turned 60 in 2005.

Townshend's song may be an extreme form of the phenomenon but many of us have difficulty in imagining our old age. Yet, statistically, most of us will reach retirement, at which point we will be looking to our pension arrangements to fund our twilight years.

Given that, and the fact that governments are always banging on about how we all should be saving more for our retirement, you would have thought that we would be taking the idea of a pension very seriously. However, it seems that we are awash in unrealistic expectations. According to a report by Barclays Bank, UK workers expect to retire at 59 with an annual pension income of £20,730, and yet 40 per cent of workers are saving nothing at all towards their retirement. The bank says those who are making contributions are paying an average of just £45 a month. One estimate of the so-called 'savings gap' is that UK workers are saving £27bn less each year than they should.

It's bizarre really. We're acting as though tomorrow never comes when every indicator suggests that it almost certainly will. Another tempting argument advanced to justify pensions apathy goes, why bother, when falling returns and reduced tax breaks undermine the likely value of a pension?

Perhaps you remember how Robert Maxwell plundered the Mirror Group's pension fund. Or maybe the Equitable Life débâcle is fresh in your mind. Chances are, say the cynics, that company bosses will raid the pensions piggybank before we get to retirement age, and if they don't the government probably will.

Here's an idea for you...

At the heart of the whole pension issue is the need for us to ask ourselves what level of pension we are trying to achieve. Once we've got an idea of this, we can very readily identify what we need to be investing to achieve this.

OK, there may be some sound reasons for being a little sceptical about the pensions market, but scepticism is not a good enough reason for becoming some kind of conscientious objector to the very notion of saving for a pension. Doing next to nothing on the pension front and hoping that something will turn up is just plain irrational. State pensions are already meagre and are set to fall further.

Defining idea...

'Another good thing about being poor is that when you are seventy your children will not have declared you legally insane in order to gain control of your estate.'
WOODY ALLEN

The sooner you start saving seriously, the easier it is to accumulate the substantial capital sum needed to generate enough income for a comfortable retirement. Start saving £100 a month when you're 45 rather than 25 and the value of your retirement fund drops by around two-thirds.

You want more freedom

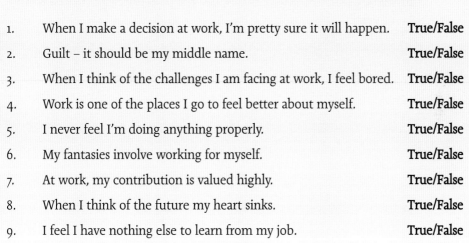

So why do you hate Mondays?
There are a whole lot of reasons for what's known as 'Sunday night syndrome' – headaches and nausea at the thought of the working week. If you suffer from it, these questions will lead you to some ideas that should help.

1. When I make a decision at work, I'm pretty sure it will happen.   True/False

2. Guilt – it should be my middle name.   True/False

3. When I think of the challenges I am facing at work, I feel bored.   True/False

4. Work is one of the places I go to feel better about myself.   True/False

5. I never feel I'm doing anything properly.   True/False

6. My fantasies involve working for myself.   True/False

7. At work, my contribution is valued highly.   True/False

8. When I think of the future my heart sinks.   True/False

9. I feel I have nothing else to learn from my job.   True/False

Which ideas can help me?

❀ If you answered FALSE to two out of three of the following questions – 1, 4, 7 – you feel undervalued and out of control at work. Turn to idea 21, Have a holiday at your desk, for a short term answer, and (you know this already) it might be time to look for a new job.

❀ If you answered TRUE to two out of three of the following questions – 2, 5, 8 – you may be struggling with the work-life balance. Try idea 23, Working by the pool, for a short term answer and what to do with it.

❀ If you answered TRUE to any of the questions 3, 6 or 9, you might need a new job, too – or possibly yearn to downsize. Try idea 24, Buy your way to freedom.

20. Perfect moments

The ability to create perfect moments is possibly the most valuable life skill you'll ever learn.

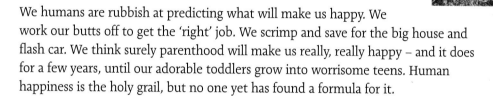

It's the only guarantee that tomorrow will be less stressed than today.

We humans are rubbish at predicting what will make us happy. We work our butts off to get the 'right' job. We scrimp and save for the big house and flash car. We think surely parenthood will make us really, really happy – and it does for a few years, until our adorable toddlers grow into worrisome teens. Human happiness is the holy grail, but no one yet has found a formula for it.

Or have they? In the last few years, neuroscientists have moved their attention from what's going wrong in the brains of depressed people, to exploring what's going right in the brains of happy people. And for the most part, it's quite simple.

Happy people don't get so busy stressing about building a 'perfect' tomorrow that they forget to enjoy this 'perfect' today.

It turns out that the surest, indeed, the *only* predictor of how happy you are going to be in the future is how good you are at being happy today. If you want to know if you are going to be stressed out tomorrow, ask yourself what are you doing to diminish your stress today? And if the answer's nothing, don't hold your breath. You won't be that calm and serene person you long to be any time soon.

We can plan the perfect wedding, perfect party, perfect marriage, perfect career. But we have absolutely no idea if when we get 'there', a perfect 'anything' is going to be delivered. The only thing we can do is guarantee that today at least we will have a perfect moment – a moment of no stress where we pursue pure joy.

> Here's an idea for you...
>
> **Invest in an old-fashioned teasmade. Waking up to a cup of tea in bed can get the day off to a good start for little effort on your part.**

What is a perfect moment for you? I can't tell. For me it is whatever helps trigger me to remember that unknown, unquantifiable, profoundly peaceful part of myself. Let's call it 'the spirit'. We could call it 'Joe' but it lacks that certain mystical something that I'm aiming for. Anyway. When I'm having a perfect moment, I'm absolutely happy, absolutely content. That doesn't mean everything is alright in my life, but it does mean that for this one moment, I've got enough to feel joyful.

Some people slip in to a perfect moment as easily as putting on an old coat. But me, I'm a pragmatist. I think if you want to have a perfect moment, you have to plan for it early before your day is hijacked. So I try to start each day with a perfect moment. All debris, mess and clutter is banished from my bedroom the night before. When I wake just about the first thing I see is a bunch of fresh cut flowers – big squashy pink peonies are a favourite. Before my eyes are quite open, I reach out and grab a book of poetry from my side table and I read for five minutes. I choose poetry because it reminds me that life is a lot bigger than me and infinitely more interesting.

But your perfect moment might be snatched late at night, listening to jazz by candlelight when the family are asleep. Or it could be a glass of chilled wine as the sun slips beyond the horizon. You might best be able to access a perfect moment by running round your park or through practising yoga. Listening to music while you exercise often heightens the sensations of being in tune with your body and tips you into joy.

Defining idea...

'**Happiness not in another place, but this place...not for another hour, but this hour.'**
WALT WHITMAN

Preparing, cooking, eating food can give perfect moments. Gardening is a good one. Sex is reliable. We all know the sensation of feeling 'bigger' than ourselves. All you have to do is give yourself the space to feel it more often – ideally, at least once a day.

But ultimately, only you know your own triggers. Write down a week's worth and plan for them. Schedule them in your diary. It obviously doesn't have to be the same activity every day and sometimes despite your best intentions, it all goes belly up. (I only get to read poetry when I'm not woken by the kids clamouring for cartoons and cereal.)

But planning for perfect moments means they are more likely to happen. Even if you don't believe now that striving for perfect moments will destress you, try it. At least you will be able to say 'Today, there were five minutes where I stopped and enjoyed life.' Enjoying life today is the only certainty you have of happiness and your best chance of being less stressed tomorrow.

21. Have a holiday at your desk

Imbue the old nine-to-five with a certain glamour and you'll be amazed at how much tension seeps out of your life.

Forty years has taught me that there are two ways to have a perfect day. One is in the grand tradition of the Lou Reed song. You hang out for a whole day with someone you really, really love who is loving you right back – or at least tolerating you. You don't have to do anything because just being with the beloved is so blissful it blocks out the boring little problems that usually stress you out. If you manage twenty days like this in your whole life time, you're doing pretty well.

And then there's the second way. You build a perfect day for yourself and by adding grace and glamour to your life, you remove stress. It takes a little thought. But it is more reliable than true love. You can have a holiday of the 'mind' on even the most mundane day.

Reboot your commute

Give your journey to work an overhaul. Set yourself targets. Instead of a drag, see it as a purposeful part of your day. If it involves walking, buy a pedometer. Learn a language. Use the time to repeat your mantras for the day. Be creative: write a page of free-hand prose on the journey in (not if you drive of course!). Start working up the characters for your novel. It's a terrific time to practice mindfulness, which can deliver the benefits of meditation. The list is endless.

Boost your environment

Your starter question: what five changes would make
your work environment more pleasant. Here's mine.
Getting rid of piles of papers and magazines that need
to be filed. Investing in a china cup and no more
sharing the office's grubby, chipped ones. Cheering up
my desk with a bunch of pink tulips. Cleaning my
keyboard – so filthy it's a health hazard. Turning down
the ringtone volume on my phone. Everyday find
some way to make your surroundings more pleasant.

> **Here's an idea for you...**
>
> **Clothes can play a huge part in
> improving the quality of our
> life. Every morning choose one
> thing that makes your heart
> sing – a colour you love, a fabric
> that embraces you, a piece of
> jewellery with sentimental
> attachment. Next time you're
> shopping buy clothes that help
> you radiate confidence.**

Beat the mid-afternoon slump

When you feel the slump kicking in, stop working and get away from your
workstation if you can. Go for a short walk in the sunshine, or take a nap. If you
can't, try this: palm your eyes in your hand for a few minutes and visualise a calm
and beautiful place. See this in as much detail as possible.

The journey home

This needs a different mood from the journey to work. If you listen to music, make
it different from the tunes you play in the morning – slower, deeper. Small stuff like
that really helps to emphasise that this is your transition period. Have a project that
you work on at this time (planning your holiday is good). And if you read, keep the
tone light. If in the morning you read French verbs or the novels of Dostoyevsky,
read P.G. Wodehouse on the way home.

Spread love

When you pass someone in distress send them 'serenity'
or 'calm' as a thought. Smile. Be gracious. Be kind,
compassionate, a force for good.

Not every day can be a high day or holiday, but changing
your mindset, looking for grace and sheer fun in previous
black holes of misery turns you into a force for light and
transforms your day-to-day grind – it's the art of living
lightly and it gets easier the more you look for
opportunities to practise your skill.

22. Walk don't run out of the day job

**Setting up your own business can be highly
lucrative... or a total financial disaster. Here we'll
focus on the key financial issues involved in
kissing goodbye to the corporate life in order to
do your own thing.**

It's said that sometimes you can be too busy earning money to be making money.

Except for an élite few, those of us in a salaried job are unlikely to see our pay increase by
25 per cent this year. It's not the way things happen. Pay scales, salary review processes
and the like are not the backdrop against which dramatic pay rises tend to happen.

This can make heading for the open road of self-employment – where there's no inherent cap on earning potential – seem like an attractive alternative. As organisations continue to downsize, outsource and generally give growing numbers of staff the boot, there are increasing opportunities for us to trade the company car for the mixed joys of working for ourselves.

Look, it's not my job to give you career advice in this book about whether this would be a good move for you personally, but you do need to be aware of the financial implications of going self-employed…and it's not all good news.

Oops, there go my pension and my life assurance

> *Here's an idea for you...*
>
> When you set up on your own, there will be nobody to insist that you put in place a new pension plan, increase your life assurance cover and so on. It becomes your call, and your call alone. Don't forget these, and check what insurance is compulsory. Some public liability insurance will probably be required if the people need to visit your premises. You may also need it if you visit the premises of your clients/customers, say to service equipment.

A move from salaried work to fee-earning work carries with it greater autonomy and the promise of increased income, but without the security provided by an employer's remuneration and benefits package.

When you stop working for a company, they stop paying you a salary. Alright, that may hardly qualify as a revelation, but have you thought about the whole raft of benefits that disappear along with your final pay cheque? The company pension goes, your death-in-service benefit goes, and you are no longer covered by group insurance schemes for public liability (the 'health and safety' insurance that protects you and visitors to your company in the event of accidents).

You'll also be saying goodbye to the world where the monthly salary cheque is for a predictable amount and hits your bank account on a predictable date. In its place will be…well, who knows what? Chances are that your income stream will flow in fits and starts, at least initially. Do you have a financial cushion in place to underwrite your living expenses until your business picks up momentum?

What are your chances?

According to a report by NatWest Bank, around 400,000 new businesses are launched each year in the UK. You've doubtless heard some of the horror stories about the number of new businesses that fold within a few years, sometimes just a few months. The stories are pretty much true. On average, *20 per cent of new businesses crumple within 12 months*, with over 50 per cent disappearing within three years.

Why you might fail

There are a number of finance-related reasons why your new business might go to the wall:

❖ Overestimating sales and underestimating how long it takes to achieve them

✿ Underestimating costs

✿ Failing to control costs ruthlessly

✿ Losing control over cash, i.e. carrying too much stock, allowing customers too long to pay, paying suppliers too promptly

✿ Underpricing

Cheer up, it might never happen

Look, there are financial upsides to being self-employed, not least of all because the tax regime is still a very favourable one. And if you make a roaring success of your business idea, you definitely have a big opportunity to put your corporate salary in the fiscal shade. The point I'm trying to get over is that the financial dice aren't entirely loaded in favour of self-employment. Please don't underestimate the benefits of salaried work in a rose-tinted rush to be your own boss. There may be gold in them thar hills but it will still need some digging out.

23. Working by the pool

OK, maybe not by the pool, but at least earn your salary from your kitchen. Other people work from home, so why not you?

For an ever-growing chunk of the population, working from home isn't a euphemism for skiving; it's a way of life. They've cut out that hour-long commute, the grumpy boss hovering over your shoulder, office dress policy, and sandwiches at the keyboard for lunch.

71

Here's an idea for you...

As part of the flexible working legislation you have the right to take a colleague with you when meeting the boss to discuss your proposal. So instead of reinventing the wheel seek out others in the company who have successfully applied for flexible working and get them on your side. A little flattery goes a long way and, after all, you are saying 'I want to be like you'. They in turn have already got good arguments for their (your) case: they can hardly sit there and admit that it doesn't work and all they do is slack off on company time.

For a start if you have kids under the age of six (or eighteen if they have a disability) and you have been working for a company for 26 weeks or more then you have the automatic right to apply to work flexibly. The idea is that you then have more time to spend taking care of your kids, but that could mean many things: for example, you could be applying to start work later so as to be able to take the kids to school, or to start earlier and finish earlier so as to be there to pick them up after school. It could also mean working at home a certain number of days a week.

Employers have a statutory duty to 'consider the applications seriously' and must follow a specific procedure when considering them, which means that they can't refuse you without giving precise reasons. So head them off at the pass by sitting down and putting together a killer application that can't be refused. What you will need to think about is the benefit to the company, not to you. Try to:

❀ Explain how you will make up exactly the same time so the company isn't losing anything.

❀ Point out that you will be more motivated and happy with your new timetable, and therefore more productive.

✿ Show that the company may stand to make savings in the office environment (perhaps they could do away with your desk or give your office workstation to someone else).

✿ Demonstrate that you have the appropriate technology and abilities to do your job from home (this may mean researching Voice over Internet Protocol (VoIP) telephony, for example, to handle phone diversions at no extra cost).

✿ Consider means of monitoring your performance that can be used to prove you are reaching agreed levels and so back up your claim to be more productive with the new timetable.

Your boss has 28 days from receiving the request to arrange a meeting with you and explore your proposal in depth. Fourteen days after that, the employer must write to you to either agree the new pattern and a start date or else provide clear business grounds as to why your proposal is unworkable. If that's the case, the letter also has to set out the appeal procedure for you to contest the decision. For more details take a look at the DTI website (www.dti.gov.uk).

When you're putting together your proposal you should consider how much experience your company already has of flexible working. Bear in mind that you may be seen as setting a precedent and so you are effectively establishing the benefits of flexible working in general to a company that may not yet be convinced about it. In that case, make doubly sure that you have the facts and figures at your fingertips and can explain how they would affect the company.

An interesting stat to bear in mind is that, according to the Equal Opportunities Commission, 80% of women return to work within 17 months of childbirth, but only 47% return to the same employer. By contrast, employers who offer flexible working patterns have return rates of 90%, saving the business replacement costs and retaining valuable skills and experience.

Finally, very few companies study their own productivity levels, and even fewer publish their findings. BT does both and found that home workers were actually 31% more efficient than their office counterparts. The happy worker, it seems, really is a more productive worker.

24. Buy your way to freedom

Controlling your money gives you control of your life. It buys your freedom. Money under control gives you a breather and can release you from a job you hate.

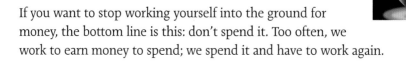

If you want to stop working yourself into the ground for money, the bottom line is this: don't spend it. Too often, we work to earn money to spend; we spend it and have to work again.

With a financial cushion, you can choose to work part time or take a risk and start a business. You tie yourself to a stressful, unsatisfying job by continually living beyond your means. You live from pay cheque to pay cheque, saving nothing.

What can you do?

Break down how much you spend each month. You could be in for a surprise. It certainly was for me when I carried out this exercise! I found I was buying myself little 'treats' to cheer myself up because I was so tired, and I was getting down about working so hard. What I couldn't see until then was that the 'treats' I was buying were getting more expensive as my income rose. That meant I was forced to work harder to afford the treats – so I worked harder. The upward spending spiral needed to be broken, and tracking my spending was one way to do that. Today, there are still many treats and rewards in my life. They might involve giving myself time to dig a new veggie bed (therapeutic, trust me), or they might involve a splurge on a meal out. I just make sure that I no longer live beyond my means.

> **Here's an idea for you...**
>
> Track your spending for a week. Be really anal and write down everything you spend, even including a cup of coffee. It's tedious and seems small minded, but it gives you an idea of where your money is going – and that could be a real wake up call.

It may be a nasty shock when you identify where you spend your money, but it's better than going on complaining that you don't know where your money goes. Do you spend a lot on takeaways because you come in late and tired? Do you spend a lot on ready meals because you have no time to cook? Are there things you are spending money on that you can do without? Don't get into the mind-set that it's about denying yourself – instead, think that it's about making choices to bring you towards a positive goal, such as working fewer hours.

Create a financial plan

Once you have a real picture of where your money goes, make a list of expenses such as your mortgage or rent, utilities, etc. Are there any ways to economise there? For instance, using energy saving bulbs and appliances can save money, as well as the environment. Then look at monthly bills such as satellite TV, club membership, etc. Is there anything you are willing to give up to move you towards being able to work fewer hours or to retire earlier?

Use any money you can gather from the savings and cut-backs you choose to make to pay off consumer debt. This is even more important than saving. Credit and store cards charge ridiculously high interest rates and should be paid off as soon as possible. Really think hard about whether it is worth buying anything on credit. That cute little piece of plastic does more than anything else to keep you on the work treadmill. Look at any debts you have closely. Prioritise them, paying off those with the highest rates of interest first. If you have credit card debt, shop around for a new card with a 0% offer on balance transfers. This can give you months of payments that hack lumps off the debt rather than merely pay off interest charges. Pay as much as you can every month. Once you are out of debt, think about saving. It is worth talking to a financial advisor at this point to find a savings plan that fits your needs.

These financial plans may mean that you can't buy everything you want. But, think carefully: what do you want more – consumer goods or the financial freedom to work less and enjoy life more?

25. Look before you leap: finding out more

If you are wondering how to get started with downshifting, becoming self-sufficient or productive gardening, you need to do your research.

There are many organisations, books, websites and courses out there designed to help you. Here's the pick of the bunch.

Books

I always start with books. Apart from being a writer, I'm a voracious reader. If you are like me, you'll like to pore over them, and dream your dreams – and never more so than with downshifting. Relevant books vary from extensive manuals to pamphlets, but they have all been really useful to me. You will find most of these books at the library, or you may prefer to buy them (many turn up in second-hand bookshops).

You won't get far on a book list about downshifting without bumping into John Seymour's *Complete Guide to Self-Sufficiency* (ISBN: 0-751-36442-8) in one imprint or another. This weighty tome covers everything from allotment gardening to scything and thatching. It has such a wealth of information that I would recommend it above most others.

Here's an idea for you...

Join a local allotment, community gardening or smallholding association. Apart from the material benefits, such as cheap seeds, tools, etc., there is a wealth of knowledge among members. You could even set up a 'lend and exchange' group, with seed swapping and larger tool loans, on a co-operative basis with fellow members.

Home Farm by Paul Heiney (ISBN: 0-751-30461-1) is another favourite of mine. It has lots of well-organised information and is easy to dip into at the level you want – be it garden farm, home farm or smallholding. The pictures – many of the author and his family – are great for fuelling dreams of what might be.

Henry Doubleday Research Association, *Encyclopaedia of Organic Gardening* (ISBN: 0-751-33381-6) is a 'must have' for me – and anyone who wants to garden organically. It is packed with useful, hands-on information and I return to it often. If organic gardening is of interest to you, you should join the HDRA or similar organisation. Apart from being a source of invaluable advice, you can also join the Heritage Seed Library and gain access to many heritage varieties of delicious vegetables that you just cannot buy. You can also very cheaply buy pamphlets that tell you everything you need to know to get started as an organic gardener.

Cottage Economy by William Corbett (ISBN: 0-953-83250-3) is a classic. The book was written in the 19th century with a view to improving the health of country labourers, but don't let that put you off. It has lots of useful – and cheap – ideas, and Corbett was a grumpy old bugger, so it makes for quite an amusing read!

Food For Free by Richard Mabey (ISBN: 0-00219060-5), together with its companion *Plants With a Purpose*, enriched the childhood of my sister and I as we gathered all manner of wild foods and lugged them home, much to my mother's horror. It's invaluable.

I could go on, as a book addict. But you get the idea. Read the books, dipping in and out to get an idea of what is – or can be – involved in becoming more self-sufficient at the level that suits you and your family.

Magazines

Without doubt, the number one 'must have' magazine for downshifting gardeners is *Kitchen Garden Magazine*. I've subscribed since I read the first issue and still wait eagerly for the magazine to arrive each month. It's full of 'readers' gardens' and allotments. As well as expert advice on growing, it has contributions from Sue Hammon, a chicken expert. Sue runs the Wernlas Collection, a supplier of rare breed chickens. Her columns have been invaluable to me as I have set up new trios of hens and bantams, etc.

A new magazine, *Grow Your Own*, published by Matthew Tudor, is also proving useful.

Country Smallholding is an interesting buy, with real life stories, and *Smallholder* magazine has some useful articles.

I have a set (bought second-hand) of a part-work I remember my parents collecting week by week in the 1970s. It's called *Grow Your Own* and it's well worth looking out for because it is full of practical, inexpensive ideas for growing food in the garden.

Websites and forums

Useful sites I know include rivercottage.net, countrysmallholding.com, smallholder.co.uk, and thekitchengarden.co.uk. They are all packed with great ideas. You could, of course, do worse than join my own forum ('Downshifting to the good life' on yahoo groups) and chat with others following the downshifting dream.

Courses

Many courses are available at agricultural colleges. Search for colleges near to you on the internet. You can also search for specific local courses in green woodworking, willow weaving, organic gardening and the like.

You want to jump start your love life

Burned out – or washed up?

Has the love gone for good, or are you just too exhausted by life?

1. You fight...
a. All the time.
b. You can't be bothered to fight anymore.

2. On your birthday...
a. It was just the usual token gesture, very little thought went into it.
b. He didn't make any effort whatsoever.

3. Your sex life is...
a. OK.
b. Non-existent.

4. When you think of your future together, you think:
a. 'We're just having a bad spell.'
b. 'I feel sick at the thought.'

5. If you had enough money, you'd...
a. Buy a really great holiday where you could spend time sorting things out.
b. Leave.

Which ideas will help?

Mostly 'a's. You may have just got so exhausted or lazy that your relationship is suffering. You may need small measures (ideas 28 and 29) or large ones (ideas 26 and 27)

Mostly 'b's. Your relationship may need remedial help. Try idea 27.

26. Search for the hero

We know the score. You fell in love with a hero and now your relationship isn't as wonderful as when you first met. We'll help you track down your partner's lost appeal.

Do you miss the good old days, when your lover listened spellbound to your stories, treated you like the sexiest creature on earth and made you feel warm and fuzzy?

Have you heard that after the initial glow of romance, you're left with something deeper, more mature, that's, well, a bit boring really? That, once you've settled with your mate, spontaneity, romance and heroics are just for high days and holidays? It's just not true.

Of course relationships change with time. As we get to know our partners better, we often love them more deeply and feel a closer bond. But this new companionship should be an add-on to the old intensity, not an instead-of. In the drudgery of our daily grind, it's often far easier to look for problems than solutions. At times it might feel as if the hero or heroine you fell in love with has sneaked off, leaving behind a dull git or crone. We believe the hero is still there, waiting in the wings to be rediscovered and nurtured back to health.

It takes a bit of effort to root out your partner's inner hero and you might have to look quite hard. We know that when you're in a rut of working, shopping, cooking, bringing up kids, cleaning, watching television, arguing and worrying, it can be hard to believe there's a hero inside your tired, sniping partner. If that sounds familiar, we suggest you ring-fence half an hour to yourself, grab a sheet of paper and answers the following questions:

❀ Why do I love my partner?
❀ What would I miss if we weren't together?

The tricky part is to then share your answers with your partner. Instead of attaching your list to the fridge, sneak your responses into conversations. For example, if you love your partner's sense of humour, instead of just guffawing at her jokes, try making a comment like, 'I like it when you make me laugh. Nobody makes me laugh like you do.' Or, if you appreciate hubby getting your kids to stick to bedtime, say something like, 'I love the way you're a really hands-on dad. I couldn't have got the kids to bed without your help.'

Peel off the label

Everyone, your partner included, lives up or down to others' expectations. Try to avoid labelling your partner. If you think 'he's not romantic' or 'she's always late', you're less likely to notice the times when he does buy roses or when she arrives ahead of you.

If your girlfriend usually leaves you to do the laundry but one day does the ironing on a whim, resist the temptation to make a sarcastic comment like 'Are we expecting the Queen round for tea?' and instead try 'I really like it when you iron the shirts' (and don't tell her she's missed a bit).

Nobody can be a knight in shining armour every day, so as well as noticing the big stuff, show appreciation for small acts of kindness. Say your partner has put off hanging a picture you were both given months ago. You come home one day and notice it up. Most of us would instinctively say something along the lines of 'I'm glad that picture is finally up'. The problem with that sort of comment is that it stresses the negative and sends your partner the message that he's a bit of a procrastinator. Hardly heroic. But if you breeze in and exclaim, 'Oh that looks fantastic. I really like the way you've hung that', he'll feel like a hero inside and be more likely to act like one. It's crucial to watch your tone as well as your turn of phrase, so that you sound more like an impressed temptress than a disappointed schoolmistress.

Defining idea...

'I remember a lovely New Yorker cartoon, so poignant I cried. The drawing was of an obviously poor, overweight and exhausted couple sitting at their kitchen table. The husband, in his t-shirt, had not shaved. The wife had curlers in her hair. Dirty dishes and nappies hung on a makeshift clothesline strung from a pipe to the fridge. They were drinking coffee out of chipped old mugs. The caption was the man smiling at his wife, saying, "I just love the way you wrinkle your nose when you laugh".'

LEIL LOWNDES, relationship expert and author

27. Take your love outside

Walking is wonderful. Need to clear your heads of clutter and put problems into proper perspective? Take a hike. Chances are you'll walk out with a problem and home with a solution.

Whether you saunter in companionable silence or amble in animated conversation, nothing quite matches a daily constitutional. It's an escape from domesticity and a chance to reconnect with the person who matters.

Let's be pedestrian

Unless you live in an offshore lighthouse, there is always somewhere to walk. The sort of journey we're talking about does not need to have a specific purpose or destination, though it might involve the collection of a newspaper or be broken up by a pint in a local pub; the real reason is to have a change of environment and a change of air. Open spaces have mind-expanding properties which help you to think more clearly; all of a sudden, difficulties become more doable and problems less problematic. Walking boosts your level of serotonin, the feel-good chemical in our brains. It also releases the body's natural opiates, endorphins, giving you a buzz. When we walk with our partners we associate feeling high with him or her.

> Defining idea...
>
> **'I have two doctors – my left leg and my right.'**
> ANONYMOUS

As we know all too well, small spaces can be constricting and close down creative processes. Try to walk every day, or at least a couple of times a week. Whether you live in the city or the country there will be something to explore, so try to take new routes every time rather than just going on the same journey every day. In the countryside, by the sea, in every village and town there is always something to see, hear, touch and feel. Life is different on foot, the pace is slower, there are fewer distractions and you don't have to worry about parking, drink driving or one-way streets.

Here's an idea for you...

Next time you find yourself getting into an argument, why not suggest you go for a walk together to take time out and regain your composure? You might agree not to discuss the contested subject, or do so only after an interval of, say, half an hour.

Marching orders

If one of you feels like walking out, go for a walk together. Walks give couples a chance to talk and think. And on warm summer evenings a chance to stop and drink. And it goes without saying that a walk will make any meal eaten afterwards all the more enjoyable.

Memory lane

Walking can perk up your relationship in different ways. Perhaps, like many couples, you went for more walks in your 'courting days'. Going for walks, years or even decades into a relationship, may take you not only down Pineview Avenue, but down memory lane as well. Indeed, if you make the same journey, retracing forgotten steps, those old passionate feelings will probably return.

> ## Defining idea...
>
> **'Where'er you walk, cool gales shall fan the glade. Trees where you tread, the blushing flow'rs shall rise. And all things flourish where you turn your eyes.'**
>
> ALEXANDER POPE

> ## Defining idea...
>
> **'I like long walks, especially when they are taken by people who annoy me.'**
>
> FRED A. ALLEN, American radio comic

Two's company, three or more is a rambling association

Many couples find that joining a walking club gives them a sharper focus and opportunities to meet like-minded saunterers or strollers. If there isn't a club within a short walking distance from your home, why not start one?

But if asked for a definitive reason for walks and why we continue to do so, one word comes to mind: serendipity – the faculty of making happy and unexpected accidental discoveries. Sometimes it is what we discover in the environment: a new building site to spy on, a skip to raid, an unexpectedly lovely garden, a mis-spelt ad in a shop window. More often, the happy discovery is something one of us says, triggered by something we have seen. A walk is a journey into your partner's head and heart.

28. Sorry seems to be the hardest word

Some of us would rather face a firing squad than admit we're wrong. If the 's' word sticks in your throat, it's time to bite the bullet.

Everyone screws up sometimes. We all make mistakes, forget important dates and break promises. But trying to blame your partner makes them feel bad and drags them down to the same level.

The trouble is, deep down you both know you've messed up, and it mangles trust. How do we know? Been there, done that and learnt the hard way that owning up and apologising helps rebuild damaged trust between lovers.

'I'm sorry.' Sounds simple doesn't it? But why do so many of us struggle to say it? Perhaps you are afraid of losing face or looking weak. After all, saying sorry means admitting you're wrong. Perhaps you feel resentful because you always end up apologising first. It could be that it's not your fault or you don't see eye to eye. It's hard to say sorry when you don't know why your partner is angry or upset. Maybe your partner made sarcastic comments when you tried to apologise last time or won't accept your apology, so you wonder what the point is.

Here's an idea for you...

Try saying sorry next time you catch yourself hurting your partner's feelings. In your mind, rate how difficult it was out of ten, where ten is 'will the ground please open and swallow me up'. Your first couple of apologies might feel off the scale, but once you've had a bit of practice, you'll get it down to an easier two or three.

When to say sorry

The best time to say sorry is as soon as you notice that you've hurt your partner. Now, we're not saints either, and know it's incredibly difficult to break mid-argument and offer an apology. Especially if you're winning. If you can express regret after, or even during, an argument, great. On the other hand, it's often preferable to calm down a bit so you don't sound sarcastic or insincere.

How to say sorry

Saying sorry is useless unless your partner knows why you're apologising. You need to acknowledge what you've done wrong. Be specific. It might make you squirm, but which of these apologies packs most punch?

'I'm sorry.'
'I'm sorry you're upset.'
'I'm sorry I upset you by calling you a lazy slag. I didn't mean it. I came home irritable and took it out on you. I know I shouldn't have said it.'

Sarcasm or a half-hearted apology, like 'You know I didn't mean it' or 'You know I'm not all bad', is worse than no apology at all because your partner will probably feel you are being disingenuous.

How to accept an apology

Apologies need to be accepted with grace and good will, rather than as ammunition for mud slinging and accusation. 'Ha! I knew it was all your fault, you horrid little worm, and now you've accepted it' is a great way not to accept an apology. There are millions of variations of it, but you usually know when you are not accepting an apology properly, as there's only really one right way: 'Thank you.' So if it's tempting to gloat, remember: you'll probably need to say sorry for something soon yourself.

More than words...

Words are sometimes enough, but actions usually speak louder. This doesn't mean proffering a potted cheese plant or box of peppermint creams every time you feel an apology coming on. Gifts can make your partner feel pressurised or even blackmailed into accepting your apology before he's ready. If you can't resist saying it with flowers, make sure this isn't the only time you buy your beloved blooms. Far better to follow your verbal apology with action related to your transgression. If your partner's cross because you never wash up, get the rubber gloves on or buy a dishwasher. If your girlfriend's upset after finding your stash of *Horny Housewife*, cancel the subscription. Whatever you've done, there's no greater crime than apologising only to commit the same sin again. If you've wounded with words rather than with deeds, action is still called for. When you've said sorry, hold out your hand. Invite your partner to come to you, not to lunge at you.

> ## Defining idea...
> **'You're either part of the problem or you're part of the solution.'**
> ELDRIDGE CLEAVER, founder of the Black Panthers

> ## Defining idea...
> **'Everyone makes mistakes. To forgive those mistakes is an action of love.'**
> JOHN GRAY, author of Men are from Mars, Women are from Venus

29. The biggest turn off

Looking for a quick fix for a dwindling relationship? This one's fast, free and fantastically simple. Unplug your telly and plug in to an amazing life together.

When did you last watch something on TV that transformed your relationship for the better? Time for some home truths: it's big, it's ugly and it rots relationships.

Not tonight, Joseph

Are you sick of your partner hogging the remote control? Do you continually fall asleep over soaps, reality shows or celebrity snowboarding? Most of us recognise the damaging effect that television has on our children, but what about our love lives? We think the hold television has on society is scary. Yet the role it plays in people's lives is rarely questioned. Decades ago, broadcasts only took place in the evenings and weekend afternoons. The service closed down at midnight and what telly there was, was watched on one machine in a communal area by whole families. Not any more. The telly is taking up more and more of lovers' free time and energy. Most couples watch around four hours of television a day. Television, like a baby cuckoo, insidiously pushes everything else out of the love nest. And at what cost? Is that manic machine in the corner interrupting your

> *Defining idea...*
>
> **'Television? The word is half Greek, half Latin. No good can come out of it.'**
> C.P. SCOTT, legendary editor of the Manchester Guardian

conversations, preventing candlelit dinners or maybe even stopping you trying out other ideas in this book? Whether you're channel hopping, station surfing or really engrossed in episode 307 of that sexy sitcom, you're missing four hours a day of prime time real life.

Unplug the box and plug into a wonderful life

When we tell people we haven't got a television, they think we're eccentric, mad or seriously weird. Usually they wink and ask us what we do in our evenings. We do a lot: mooch around markets, cruise on the river, see old movies on the big screen, snoop about in galleries, visit exhibitions, comedy clubs, musicals, quirky fringe plays and a lot of other fun stuff. We're not joined at the hip and use our bonus four hours to do lots of things on our own or with other friends.

Take up a sport, join a book club, learn a language or develop your artistic side. We're not saying you need to do all of these things, or any of them – you need to choose the activities that would suit you. How could you recharge your relationship in a few extra hours a day? Maybe you'd like to have time to go running together, make your partner a sculpture, become part-time puppeteers or join the local choir. Flick the off switch, get your life back and your relationship will prosper. Whatever you do, it's better than being passive voyeurs of other peoples' lives.

Here's an idea for you...

Getting rid of the telly seems too radical? Why not have a telly-free month? Put the box, or boxes, in the attic tonight and in four weeks time see how you've got on. Both keep a journal of your thoughts and feelings, and write down how you spent all that time.

Defining idea...

'Television displaces other romantic opportunities. Like brushing up against your wife's backside in the kitchen. The old fashioned challenge of having to entertain each other.'
JIM PETERSEN, author of Playboy's History of the Sexual Revolution

30. The least you need to do...

...to keep your relationship minty fresh.

Read, digest and ponder. Then get your diary, a big red pen and start prioritising your relationship.

This chapter contains the three golden rules of a healthy relationship – the *sine qua non* of sexual happiness. All the technique and creativity in the world isn't going to fix the sex in a relationship where the couple is together but not *together*. On the other hand, couples that spend time together, and anticipate and plan for those times, find it hard to lose interest in one another.

Rule 1: Daily...

How is your partner feeling right now? What's happening at work? How are their relationships with friends, colleagues, siblings, parents? Carve out fifteen minutes of every day to talk. If you find yourselves getting into a rut of busyness, when you pass like ships in the night for several days in a row without touching base, either go to bed before your usual time or get up earlier and have a coffee together so you can touch base.

Kiss each other every morning before you get out of bed. Take the time for a swift cuddle. Breathe deeply. Hold tight. Do the same at night. Never take your physical intimacy for granted. In this Vale of Tears we call life, you found each other. Pretty amazing. Worth acknowledging that with at least a daily hug, methinks.

Rule 2: Weekly...

Go out with each other once a week where humanly possible. Once a fortnight is the bare minimum. According to the experts, this is the most important thing you can do. Couples who keep dating, keep mating. Spending too long sloping around the same house does something to a couple's sexual interest in each other and what it does generally isn't good. So get out, preferably after making some small effort to tart yourself up so you're visually pleasing to your partner. Let them see why they bothered with you in the first place. (No, I never said this chapter was rocket science. I just said that it worked.)

Here's an idea for you...

Look for easy ways to cheer your partner up. Pick up a tub of her favourite ice-cream on the way home from work. Run him a bath and bring him a beer. Sappy gestures work – they build up a huge bank of goodwill that couples can draw on when life gets stressful.

Rule 3: Monthly...

Go for a mini-adventure – shared memories cement your relationship. Make your adventure as mad or staid as you like, but at the least make sure it's something that you haven't done since the beginning of your relationship. It really doesn't matter what it is, as long as it's not your usual 'date'.

What's the point? You see your partner coping with new environments and new skills and that keeps you interested in them. And them in you. Simple.

If you're shaking your head and tutting 'how banal', I'd get that smug look off your face, pronto. Research shows quite clearly that one of the defining differences between strong couples and 'drifting' couples is the amount of effort and time they spend on their shared pursuits. All of us have heard the advice, 'Spend more time with each other being as interesting as possible.' But how many couples do you know who actually do it? I'm prepared to bet that those who do seem happiest.

> *Defining idea...*
>
> **'Good sex begins when your clothes are still on.'**
> MASTERS and JOHNSON, sex research pioneers

31. The love's there, but the lust's gone AWOL

Hey sexual pioneer! Yes, we're talking to you.

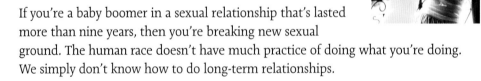

If you're a baby boomer in a sexual relationship that's lasted more than nine years, then you're breaking new sexual ground. The human race doesn't have much practice of doing what you're doing. We simply don't know how to do long-term relationships.

As Dr Alan Altman writes in *Making Love the Way We Used To, Or Better*, 'Many people are disappointed when they can't re-create those early thrilling feelings. [But] We don't really have many examples of how to keep a 25 plus year marriage alive sexually. At the turn of a century a 47-year-old male was considered old.'

Are we programmed to get bored with a long-term partner? There's a persuasive argument that we are. Psychologists believe that one reason we go off sex with long-term lovers is the powerful anti-incest taboos that are part of nearly every culture. Basically, in a 'functional' family, brothers and sisters who are brought up together don't fancy each other despite incredible proximity. However, brothers and sisters who are brought up apart often do. It may be that if we live too long with someone of the opposite sex, we stop reacting to their sexual charisma. This is why we must never get too cosy with each other or allow our boundaries to become too melded.

Here's an idea for you...

A long-term sexual relationship will go in cycles – sometimes strong, sometimes fading. Sexual desire is something you can rekindle, but make sure your partner is singing from the same hymn sheet. When the first flush of lust passes, it won't come back without will and compassion from each of you for the other.

We long for the thrills of the beginning of the relationship. We yearn for the time when our partners were mad for us. Sometimes we want it so much that we move onto another relationship to get the kicks. So there's the bad news. Your challenge is to decide what to do about it. Interview the sexual pioneers – women and men who have successfully lived with each other for many years – and they talk touchingly about the power that sexuality shared with one partner over many years can hold. One woman interviewed by writer Brigid McConville in her book *The Secret Life* says, 'We have been together for so long, when I look at him not just as my ageing bloke but as the man who made love to me on the beach in Greece, on the train across Europe, and tied to the bedposts in a hotel in Spain. No one else has those intimate memories, just us. No one else knows what he is capable of. It's a bond so strong it's a bit like having children together: nothing can change the history of our intimacy and what we have made and shared and I can conjure up images of us making love together any time I like.'

How do you get to the place where a lifetime's worth of loving experience informs your view of your lover? In a nutshell: don't get boring and don't get bored. Ask yourself some hard questions. If you love your partner but are no longer excited by them, reverse it. How exciting are you? How passionate are you? Would you fancy yourself? Do you feel alive?

Are you passionate about work or your interests? Do you have any interests?

Are you enthusiastic about your children, your friends and the things you talk about with them?

What projects do you have on the backburner for the future that excite you?

If you're drawing a blank here, it's time to get back your passion for life. There's absolutely no way you'll get it back for your partner without it. And be warned, moving onto another partner in the hope of regaining your passion for life will work in the short term, but never in the long term. This isn't always the complete answer to the 'love but no lust' dilemma, but it's the first crucial step.

32. Developing sexual mystique

Yes, it's possible. Even if you've shared a bathroom for years.

Last night I had a moment of despair.
I walked by a pub where I overheard a man saying to his (male) companion, 'So go on then, have a guess. How many clear shots did Portugal have at goal?'

Admittedly even his mate looked bored, but I thought, 'Here I am, working at building more understanding between the sexes in my own small way. And it's a total waste of time. Men and women? Different species. What's the point?'

Then my natural Pollyanna spirit kicked in, 'Differences – you know what? They're a Good Thing. In fact, if you want to keep your love life hot, they're an Essential Thing. To carry on fancying your partner and to have them carrying on fancying you, you need a little distance between you, a little mystery, a little wildness in your soul.'

And if that doesn't come naturally, you need to work at it.

'Male and female are different,' says relationship counsellor Paula Hall. 'And we've known since the sixties that if a couple want a stable relationship, it's worth working at maintaining that difference. It's what keeps the electric buzz between them.' She points out that studies by psychologists have already picked up on the dangers of becoming too alike. 'We call it "enmeshment" when couples become too similar,' says Hall. 'It's been known for a long time that it can have a detrimental impact on sexual desire.'

You probably think it's cosy that you share the same interests, friends, hopes, dreams, taste in soft furnishings. So it is. Congratulations. You're terrific mates. And carry on regardless if you want a great relationship without particularly exciting, or indeed plentiful, sex. However, if you want sex that makes your toes curl, you need a little separateness to keep desire alive.

You can be all things to a partner, but not to a lover. They cannot be all things to you.

There's an art to this. One woman I interviewed made a point of always being just a little bit cool with her husband every three or four months or so. 'Nothing serious,' she said, 'I'd just switch off from him a bit. Seem a little bit less easily pleased. A bit more interested in talking to my friends on the phone. Lock myself in the bathroom. Submerge myself in a book. Really trivial stuff. Worked like a charm. Within a week, he'd be suggesting weekends away in Paris and voluntarily arranging babysitting so we could go out to dinner.' (NB I can't resist the opportunity here to remind men of the huge aphrodisiac potential in occasionally arranging a babysitter. In most relationships, whether or not the woman works from home or not, she does the babysitting stuff – it's so goddamn nice when your partner sorts it out for once as it's such a clear signal that you want to spend some time with her. Try it.)

All this withdrawing interest sounds suspiciously like game-playing – and you know what, it is! You can fake it a little bit like my interviewee, but it doesn't always work. What does always work is if both partners do it for real – keep interested in

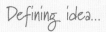

Defining idea...

*'An absence, the declining of
an invitation to dinner, an
unintentional, unconscious
harshness are of more service
than all the cosmetics and
fine clothes in the world.'*
MARCEL PROUST

life, stay full of vim and brio for other projects, remain
engaged with people outside of their relationship and
be passionate about the world. Then, and here is the
important bit, they bring that energy home and
translate it into passion for each other. They do that
by talking about their lives with such enthusiasm that
their partners can't help get a kick out of their
enthusiasm, charm, intelligence and all-round top-
quality personality.

The least you need to do...

Relationship psychologist Susan Quilliam points out that there are straightforward
ways of making sure your relationship doesn't sink into the mire of 'enmeshment'.

Rule 1. All couples fall into a pattern of doing the same thing and being scared to
suggest anything new because 'we don't do that'. But if you fancy doing something
different, suggest it anyway. Don't argue if they say 'no'. The point has been made.
You've reinforced in both your minds that you're different individuals.

Rule 2. Support your partner as much as possible when they're trying to be an
individual. Don't dismiss new ideas and interests without thinking them through
carefully.

Rule 3. Be yourself. Don't take on his or her interests and hobbies unless they
genuinely interest you, too. We're equal but we're not the same.

Any magazine subscription for £23.99*

Treat yourself or a friend to a subscription to any of these fantastic magazines for ONLY £23.99! With such a wide selection there's a magazine here for everyone – there couldn't be an easier way to get what you want.

COSMOPOLITAN
Save over £14

HARPER'S Bazaar
Save over £19

prima Baby & pregnancy
Save over £4

COUNTRY LIVING MAGAZINE
Save over £16

House Beautiful
Save over £11

RUNNER'S WORLD
Save over £21

Esquire
Save over £23

Men'sHealth
Save over £16

SHE
Save over £12

Good Housekeeping
Save over £14

prima
Save over £3

Zest
Save over £14

For details on how to take advantage of this fantastic offer please go to page 487, where you'll also find information on all the other great deals found throughout *Goddess*.

Look gorgeous every single day!

*'I don't want to make money.
I just want to be wonderful.'*

MARILYN MONROE (Aphrodite)

'Life is not about finding yourself, it's about creating yourself,' said George Bernard Shaw, and that's what this book is all about. Nowhere is this truer than when it comes to our appearance. It's relatively easy to transform the way we look — easier than changing our inner selves, for sure. And the great thing is that looking good does wonders for how we feel inside.

The beauty basics

Are you getting in your own way?

You feel less than gorgeous. Could it be you that's the problem?

1. Where is your latest gas bill?
☐ Paid and filed (score 0)
☐ In the bottom of your handbag (1)
☐ You're not sure (2)

2. You're meeting some friends at the weekend.
☐ You're meeting at 7.30 on Saturday (score 0)
☐ You know it's Saturday but you'll set a time by texting in the afternoon (1)
☐ You're not sure you're going to make Saturday – you've double booked (2)

3. A friend has blagged an entrance to a starry film premiere. She can take you with her – but it's this evening. Do you...
☐ Rush home to slip into your favourite outfit, pressed and ready to wear (score 0)
☐ Manage to rustle together something but don't have the right tights or handbag at short notice (1)
☐ Buy a new outfit because you have no idea if you have anything suitable (2)

How did you do?

Score 3 or more and there's every chance you're not organised enough to be gorgeous. It takes application, it takes time and you're too busy looking for your mobile phone to get gorgeous. Turn to the ideas on getting more time (ideas 1–6) before you start on this section.

4. The weekend, for you, is an opportunity to:
- ☐ Look gorgeous in cashmere and jeans (0)
- ☐ Get away with not wearing make-up (1)
- ☐ Get away with not washing (2)

5. You have been planning to lose 10lbs:
- ☐ And you will in time for summer/Christmas/John and Julie's wedding (0)
- ☐ It would be a lot easier if you could be bothered to exercise (1)
- ☐ And that's what it's likely to stay – a plan (2)

6. Your hair is cut
- ☐ Every six weeks (0)
- ☐ Every six months (1)
- ☐ When you can't see (2)

What does this mean?

Score 3 or more and you are too lazy to be gorgeous – we repeat, it takes application, it takes time. Your insouciance is admirable, just be careful it doesn't slip into total slobdom and if you'd like to be a little more appearance-orientated turn to idea 33, Boost your body image, to learn the basics of planning.

33. Boost your body image

Newsflash! You don't have to be beautiful to be perceived as such. The secret to looking good is feeling confident. Start with a few self-esteem tricks.

Take a minute to scroll through your list of female friends, colleagues and acquaintances. Not all lookers are they? Yet how many of those who aren't conventionally 'beautiful' exude a goddess-like aura nevertheless?

This is more than 'charm' and less obvious than raw sex appeal, although they may have that too. It's an intrinsic self-belief and *joie de vivre* that makes even 'homely' women somehow magnetic. Some people have bags of it. It may be something they were lucky enough to acquire in childhood. However, if *you* didn't acquire it, you don't need hours of therapy to get some too. Self-confidence (real or faked) is a beauty trick we can all learn.

Life coaches and shrinks suggest we tell ourselves at every opportunity how fantastic we are. In truth, most of us cringe at the thought, so I suggest listing your hottest qualities instead. Go on. Get a piece of paper and list them under a heading such as 'Things I Like About Myself' or 'My Best Bits'. See, I bet you feel better already. An alternative is to make a list of all the compliments you've received, from sweet nothings whispered by exes to ego-boosters that other women have bestowed upon you (which, bizarrely, often count for more). In moments of self-doubt, consult your list.

Here's an idea for you...

Fill a photo album with pictures in which you're looking your best and reach for it whenever low self-confidence is a problem.

Second, start focusing on and pampering the bits you love about yourself. So, if you've been told you have great legs, then capitalise on that. For example, indulge in some amazingly expensive body oil for them, buy yourself some unspeakably impractical shoes or add a few new leg-revealing mini skirts or floaty numbers to your wardrobe. And if your hair is your unique selling point, then get a haircut regularly and experiment with different looks or accessories.

The key to recognising and accepting that you're attractive is to do all you can to glory in your best assets and show them off to their best advantage.

Pampering yourself on a regular basis is a great way to boost your self-confidence. How much more attractive do you feel after a facial/manicure or even after a spritz of a new perfume? It's not about spending a fortune, it's about recognising that pampery girly treats can really boost your *amour propre* and help you to ooze gorgeousness, even if it's simply taking a luxurious, gorgeous-smelling bath, or wearing your sexiest, most expensive clothes just for the hell of it. Start taking pleasure in looking your best.

But what if you're overweight/out of shape/flabbier than you were two, five or ten years ago and your wardrobe is testament to the nubile beauty you once were and not the gallumping great oaf you now are and are evermore destined to be? Well, you have two options here. First, do all the above. Second, throw out all those thin clothes (they'll only depress you) and start building up a completely new wardrobe of clothes that fit and flatter you.

I'd suggest that you start doing some exercise as well. Nothing excessive, just something gentle but regular. Simply moving your body can help boost your mood, improve your complexion and give you confidence in your shape. And before you know it you'll have lost pounds! Aim for about twenty minutes of exercise three times a week. It's quite addictive so you'll probably want to do more, but if you start to see it as a chore remind yourself that you're doing something positive to make the best of your shape and regard it as a short cut to self-belief instead. And how much cheaper is that than a facelift?

> *Defining* idea...
>
> **'I'm tired of all this nonsense about beauty being only skin-deep. That's deep enough. What do you want – an adorable pancreas?'**
> JEAN KERR, writer

34. Water works

Water is a beauty tonic on tap. Eight glasses a day can boost your energy and make you slimmer, cleverer and more positive. Here's why.

GPs, nutritionists, dermatologists and beauty therapists all agree that drinking water is one surefire way to a longer, healthier life and plumper, firmer skin.

Water is involved in nearly every bodily function, from circulation to body temperature and from digestion to waste excretion. It helps your body to absorb the nutrients from food, too. When you get dehydrated, vitamins and minerals aren't absorbed optimally and toxins can't get excreted as efficiently. Food is like a sponge; if it's saturated with water it swells and allows the vitamins and minerals

109

Here's an idea for you...

You can eat your fluids, too. Fruit and vegetables are largely water – apricots, grapes, melons, peaches, strawberries, cucumbers, mangoes, oranges and peppers are all more than 75% water. Fish such as sardines, mackerel, salmon and tuna are also 50% water.

into your body, which can help heal you and boost your immune system. Water is also necessary for lubricating joints and providing a protective cushion for the body's many organs and tissues. And, when you're not getting enough water, your blood volume drops, which stops you from firing on all cylinders. All of this affects how you feel and how you look.

So, how much water do we really need? The Natural Mineral Water Information Service estimates that about 90% of us don't get enough fluids. This deficiency has been linked to headaches, lethargy, dry skin, digestive problems and even mood swings. Many medical bodies recommend that a 60 kg adult drinks 1.5 to 2 litres (between six and eight 250 ml glasses) of fluids a day, plenty of which should be water. Alternatively, aim for about 30 ml of water per kg of your body weight or 1 litre for every 1,000 calories of food you consume.

Your best gauge is the colour of your urine. You're after a pale watery colour with a tinge of lemon; yellow urine means you need to drink more.

If you're partying, match a glass of water for every alcoholic drink. And drink at least half a cup of water for each drink containing caffeine (such as tea, coffee or cola) to counteract their diuretic effect. Sipping is better than gulping huge glasses at a time. Experts say that the latter is just like pouring water on a dry leaf, so is certainly not the best way to absorb it.

Beauty booster: water can help you lose weight

How often do you confuse hunger with thirst and end up reaching for food instead of drinking? This is very common, but will cost you dearly in calories. Research shows that 75% of all hunger pangs are actually thirst, so if you get the munchies and fancy a Mars Bar, try a glass of water instead and save yourself some calories.

Defining idea...

'Beauty of style and harmony and grace and good rhythm depend on simplicity.'
PLATO

One study showed that you could increase your metabolic rate by about 30% by having a big 500 ml glass of cold water after each meal. This comes down to a process called thermogenesis, in other words the rate at which your body burns calories for digestion. Apparently, drinking cold water means you'll burn off your supper that much quicker! Another study found that drinking 2 litres of water daily can help your body to burn off an extra 150 calories a day. This can also flatten your tum because it can help you beat the water retention that causes bloated bellies.

Beauty booster: water can make you feel brighter and more energised

No one looks their best when they're exhausted. Drinking water has been found to refresh both physically and mentally so can enhance your performance. Studies show it helps concentration and assimilation of information, so if you swig regularly you'll feel brighter and radiate perkiness.

Beauty booster: water is great for your skin

Whenever you're dehydrated, your body effectively steals water from less important parts of your body and delivers it to the more important organs, so your skin is the first place it'll show if you're not drinking enough. Water can also help reduce puffy skin and eyes because it decreases the amount of salt in your body. Drink a glass before you go to bed and sleep on a thick pillow or with your head elevated to help prevent fluid from settling under your eyes.

35. Lose pounds without trying

Kiss goodbye to diets. There are easier, less painful ways to lose weight – and keep it off. A few simple lifestyle changes may be all you need to drop a dress size.

The year I gave up dieting I lost more weight than I'd ever managed before. Still, diets are a kind of rite of passage. Every woman's tried one – and has usually ended up obsessed with food and calories.

When I worked at Zest magazine, the editorial policy was never to cover diets that you 'go on' and 'come off' again. We knew from personal experience that they didn't work and dozens of experts had confirmed exactly that. Instead, we talked in terms of eating habits: healthier choices and food for lifestyle.

Diets don't work because they're offering short-term solutions that are impossible to sustain in the long term. You either feel so hungry, deprived or bored that you instantly crave that which you're not allowed or your nutrition is so unbalanced that your body steers you towards the calories it craves.

So, here are ten golden rules of healthy eating that really will help you to shed pounds without suffering:

Here's an idea for you...

Simplify your diet: experts say that if you're presented with a large variety of foods you tend to eat more.

1 Don't skip breakfast

Skipping breakfast won't help you to save calories and lose pounds. On the contrary, when you do eat breakfast you're more likely to make better, lower-calorie choices throughout the rest of the day because it'll kick-start your metabolism and give you the whole day to burn calories. Also, your body is more efficient at processing carbohydrates in the morning.

2 Eat lots of fibre

A high-fibre diet is one of the best ways to lose weight. One study showed that people who ate a low-fat diet that included 26 g of fibre per 1,000 calories lost more weight than those whose diet was higher in fat and lower in fibre (just 7 g per day). That may sound a lot, but you can up your fibre intake by eating bran cereals, wholemeal pasta, wholemeal bread and lots of fruit and vegetables.

3 Eat little and often

The aim of this one is to maintain your blood sugar level at a level where you don't get really hungry and end up reaching for the biscuit tin. It will also keep your metabolism working efficiently all day. So, divide your calorie intake into five or six smaller meals or choose regular healthy snacks such as crackers, yoghurt, fruit and nuts.

4 Watch your portions

As a rough guide, a portion of carbohydrate (e.g. pasta, rice or potatoes) should fit into the palm of your hand. The same goes for protein (fish, meat, cheese, etc.). As for fruit and vegetables, you can eat your fill.

5 Control the booze

Booze is full of empty calories that can't be stored so the body uses them first and then stores as fat anything else you've eaten surplus to your body's requirements. Booze can also weaken your resolve so that a curry, for example, is likely to become much more appealing after a few beers. Keep track of your tipples so that you don't exceed your daily alcohol allowance.

6 Eat more slowly

If you gobble your food you'll end up eating more. It takes about twenty minutes for your brain and stomach to compute that you're full up, so make mealtimes more leisurely. Always sit down to eat, put your fork down between bites and chew your food thoroughly before you swallow.

7 Be supermarket savvy

Never shop hungry and always make a list so that you're less likely to succumb to those tasty but high-fat 'two for one' offers or the crisps and chocolate at the checkout. And unless you're doing a big weekly shop, always use a basket rather than a trolley so that by the time you've bought your essentials, you can't carry anything else!

> Defining idea...
>
> **'The only way to lose fat is to take in fewer calories than your body needs. It's as simple as that.'**
> ANITA BEAN, nutritionist

8 Use smaller plates

Swap those whopping dinner plates for smaller ones about 20 cm in diameter (a dinner plate is usually about 25 to 30 cm in diameter), as people tend to clear their plates regardless of how many calories this means they eat.

9 Go easy on evening carbs

You're unlikely to use many carbs after dinner so they'll probably be stored as fat. Instead, eat protein, such as fish, and lots of vegetables.

10 Eat fruit or salad before meals

One study showed that women who ate a little apple or pear before each meal lost more weight than women who skipped the fruit but followed the same reduced-calorie diet. Fruit is full of fibre, so it can help fill you up. In another study, people who ate a low-fat 100-calorie salad before their meal ate about 12% less than those who didn't have the salad.

36. Luscious lips

Want plump, bee-stung, kissable lips? Before facing the needle try a few simple tips on how to fake them.

We can't all do pillar-box lips. Bold colours emphasise less than perfect lips but if you haven't the colouring or the requisite attitude, red lipstick can look more hooker than siren. Still, there's plenty you can do to enhance your pout.

Size up your lips

Assess their shape. You can minimise a large mouth and lips that are too full by choosing a neutral tone of lipstick. Use a lipliner to draw a line just inside the lips and choose a dark shade of lipstick to fill, which will help to make them look smaller. Stay clear of dark colours if your lips are thin, as they'll make them look even smaller. Instead, use a lipliner to draw a line just over your natural lip line to create the illusion of fuller lips and then go for a bright colour to plump them up even more. Glossy or pearl lipsticks can also make lips look fuller, as they reflect the light.

Select the right shade of lippy

Experts say that olive skins look their best next to berry shades. If your complexion and hair are fair, stick to reds with pinkish undertones. If you have pale skin and dark hair you'll find that strong, bright-red lipstick can look amazing. And if your skin is dark, then pick deep, rich reds.

Pay your lips due service

Take the time to care for your lips in the same way that you care for your skin. Gently buff them with a soft, baby's toothbrush to remove dry skin and boost the circulation, then regularly apply lip balm. This is also a great way to soften up dry, cracked lips.

Try the bee-stung look

There's an art to perfecting bee-stung lips, so even those of us with thin lips can pout with the best of them. Try this:

1. First, outline your lips using a lip pencil in the same shade as your lipstick or lighter (never darker, unless you're a lap dancer or would like to be mistaken for one).
2. Then, using a lip brush, 'fill in' your lips. Instead of using a block of matt colour, build up gradually using a sheer lipstick. That way you'll capture the light, which will make your lips look fuller and plumper. Using a highlighter pen, draw a fine line around your upper lip, just above your Cupid's bow. Alternatively, try blending little dots of reflective foundation on your upper lip, which will also help accentuate a natural pout.
3. Finish with a dab of lipgloss on the fullest part of your lips.

Here's an idea for you...

To get whiter-looking teeth go for berries, plums and blue-based red lipsticks. The contrast will help make your teeth appear whiter and brighter. Avoid any yellow- or orange-based shades, including corals and browny colours, as they can make your teeth look yellow.

Defining idea...

'Beauty, to me, is about being comfortable in your own skin. That, or a kick-ass red lipstick.'
GWYNETH PALTROW

37. Great gnashers

Confidence, good looks and success are the kind of qualities a brilliant smile can impart. Dig out that floss today.

I've always been a bit obsessed with teeth, as I had braces as a child. A full Hannibal Lecter number that tortured my poor wayward teeth into meek submission and earned me odd stares on the school bus.

As a result, I notice every detail about someone's smile – veneers, caps, chips, crowns, the works. I assess the teeth of everyone I meet with my own kind of Playtex barometer: 'has she or hasn't she?' When British starlets go off to Hollywood in search of stardom and come back with newly bleached, chiselled, perfected teeth it's as obvious to me as if they'd come back with a third breast.

Being a teeth person, I look at people with a naturally beautiful smile with awe. It's the first thing I notice about someone. Imperfect teeth can make the seemingly beautiful less so. And a gorgeous set of pearlies can transform the merely plain into a radiant beauty. Psychologists say this is quite a normal reaction. Apparently, we assign negative character traits to people with a bad dental appearance.

Having a pleasant smile makes you appear not just more attractive, but also more honest and trustworthy. And when you smile a beautiful smile, you make the person you're smiling at feel better and generate warmth, happiness and confidence.

Your teeth can even make you look younger. Anthropologists say that this is because white and even teeth, healthy pink gums and a convex smile are characteristics of youth. However, as the years go by, our teeth lose their luminosity and become dull, stained and chipped. A mouthful of fillings can also make your smile look dull and grinding your teeth can wear them down. So, taking care of them and investing in the odd procedure (whitening, straightening, etc.) can actually take years off you.

Here's an idea for you...

Stained teeth? Try this the old wives' tale: add a drop of clove oil to your toothpaste before brushing your teeth to help brighten your smile.

Considering all these plus points, it's little wonder that we're spending a fortune on our teeth these days and that there's a cosmetic dentist on every high street. To keep your teeth looking their best try the following:

- ✿ Dentists say it's vital to use a meticulous cleaning routine and to use the best tooth products you can. Brush your teeth at least twice a day and ideally after each meal.
- ✿ Make sure you visit your dentist regularly – at least every 12 months – and never miss a check up.
- ✿ If needs be, invest in cosmetic procedures or braces. Amazing techniques are available these days and full-on braces are a thing of the past.
- ✿ Floss at least once a day.
- ✿ Cut down on sugary snacks and try fruit, vegetables and calcium-rich low-fat yoghurt instead. If you must eat something sweet stick to chocolate, as with chewy sweets the sugar gets sloshed around in your mouth for longer.
- ✿ Finish meals with cheese, which helps neutralise the acid in your mouth and therefore helps prevent tooth decay. Cheese is rich in calcium and phosphorous and this helps replace some of the minerals in tooth enamel, thereby strengthening teeth.

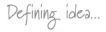

❀ Chew gum. Look for brands that contain xylitol because it's been found to help protect against – even reverse – tooth decay. Xylitol is found naturally in berries, mushrooms, lettuce and corn on the cob, too.

❀ Avoid stain-causing culprits such as coffee, tea, cigarettes and red wine. Try a whitening toothpaste to brighten your smile and have your teeth cleaned by a hygienist every six months.

Are you brushing correctly? And for long enough? In order to clean all your tooth surfaces thoroughly you need to spend at least two minutes at it each time. The brushing motion itself helps remove stains, so don't cheat!

❀ First, focus on the inner and outer surfaces of your teeth. Place your toothbrush at a 45-degree angle and use gentle, short, tooth-wide strokes following your gum line. To clean the inside surfaces of front teeth, tilt your brush vertically and use gentle up-and-down strokes with the toe of your brush.

❀ Then move on to your chewing surfaces, holding your brush flat and brushing back and forth.

❀ Next, brush your tongue. Use a back-to-front sweeping method to remove food particles, which will also help freshen your mouth.

❀ Finally, gently brush the roof of the mouth.

38. Beat the bloat

Bloating is the bane of many women's lives. It can add pounds overnight, immediately limit your fashion choices and force you to resort to your 'fat' wardrobe. Fortunately, you can beat it.

You know how it is. When your stomach is firm and flat the world seems a kinder, brighter place. You can slip effortlessly into jeans, flattering black dresses do actually flatter you and bikinis become less frightening.

Bloating is caused by trapped wind in your digestive system. The chief culprits range from food intolerances, constipation, too much alcohol, too much salt, eating too quickly or munching on too many gas-causing foods such as baked beans. Many women suffer premenstrual bloating too. And even stress can be to blame. Here are some ways to deflate that protruding tummy:

- ❀ Cut down on top bloaters such as wheat and replace them with rice or oats, which are usually better tolerated. Swap bran cereals for corn cereals, or breakfast on fresh fruit and yoghurt instead.
- ❀ Avoid constipation by eating plenty of fresh fruit and vegetables and drinking plenty of fluids. Also, go to the loo when you get the urge; resisting can muck up your digestive system further.
- ❀ Try a course of probiotics (acidophilus), which can help rebalance the good and bad bacteria in your digestive system. If the balance gets out of kilter your system will slow down, which can cause lots of gas in your gut. You can buy supplements from the chemist or eat a bio yoghurt or yoghurt-based drink everyday.

Here's an idea for you...

Stress can play havoc with your digestive system so aim to set aside plenty of time for quality rest and relaxation and develop some great strategies for nipping stress in the bud.

❀ Fill your fruit bowl. Apples, pears and rhubarb are a great source of potassium, which helps rebalance your body's fluid levels. They're also a good source of pectin, a soluble fibre that keeps you regular. Other good non-bloaters are cherries and citrus fruit. Pineapples are great for beating bloat, too, as they contain the wonder-enzyme bromelain that helps digestion, alleviates wind and can soothe your stomach. Fresh pineapple is better than tinned, which tends to lose much of its bromelain. Try papaya, too, which contains enzymes such as papain that can be good for your digestion, particularly if you've been eating lots of rich meaty foods.

❀ Cut down on alcohol and salty foods, which can cause fluid retention and inflate that bloated tummy further. That's because your body holds on to fluid to dilute the extra salt. Avoid adding salt to your meals, but also cut back on ready meals and processed foods, which often contain tons of salt. Try cooking from scratch more often so you can keep your eye on your salt intake.

❀ Eat plenty of natural diuretics to help beat water retention, including celery, onion, parsley, coffee, tea, aubergine (eggplant), garlic and peppermint.

❀ Check you're eating enough protein like fish, lean meat or tofu, as nutrition experts say protein can also reduce fluid retention. But, don't overdo the beans or pulses as they can make matters worse.

❀ Address those PMS symptoms and if you're plagued with bloating each month, try a supplement. There's evidence that taking 1,000 mg of calcium a day (the recommended daily allowance is 700 mg) may improve problems concerning water retention. Try evening primrose oil and vitamin B6 supplements too to help minimise those grim PMS symptoms.

- ✿ Drink at least eight glasses of water a day. Regular, small amounts are best.
- ✿ Slow down at mealtimes, stop eating on the run and aim to savour your food and chew everything thoroughly. When you gulp your meals down you can swallow air, which can bloat you.
- ✿ Try some tummy-toning moves. Pilates is a great way to work your stomach muscles. It gave me abs

of steel in just a few weeks when I first discovered it. It really helps pull your stomach up and in and is a great way to get your waist back after having a baby.

Defining idea...

'Like anyone else, there are days I feel beautiful and days I don't, and when I don't, I do something about it.'
CHERYL TIEGS, model

39. Fabulous foundations

Beautiful skin can be a sign of youth, good health, meticulous grooming, great genes or a combination of these. If you fall short in each department, you'll want to know how to get it out of a bottle.

A beauty counter is like an Aladdin's cave or a knicker draw: full of pretty things, yet you're really only interested in finding an item that works miracles.

Everyone knows that good skin stems from drinking lots of water, getting plenty of sleep and eating a healthy diet high in fruit and vegetables. If you're short on time, however, and haven't been all that saintly, you'll want results and you'll want them now. The key, as we all know, is to look natural, but not too natural.

123

Here's an idea for you...

If you've got open pores or spots, in the daytime avoid using bronzers containing shimmery particles that will draw attention to them. Save these bronzers for evenings, when the light will be on your side and you'll look sexy and sultry. For daytime pick matt bronzing powders.

Fortunately, these days foundations contain all sorts of silicone powders and light-diffusing pigments to disguise flaws and make skin glow. They've also been imbued with great sunscreens and vitamins to protect skin from the sun. And there are mattifying formulations to help even out skin tone.

How to apply the no make-up look

Gone are the days of Barbara Cartland-style make-up – trowelled on and proud of it. In fact, these days experts advise using foundation only where you need it, i.e. the often oily T-zone (forehead, nose and chin) and under the eyes. You may not need to apply foundation everywhere, but make sure you blend carefully, nay obsessively, into the skin, especially around nostrils, the sides of the nose and corners of the eyes. Beauticians recommend oil-free or matt formulas for oily skin, rich moisturising foundations for dry skin and stick or compacts for combination skin.

If you're trying to disguise broken veins on your skin, use a concealer that is one shade lighter than your skin tone, then dust with powder. Be sure to add concealer after foundation and not before else you'll wipe it away. If you have wrinkles or spots I suggest you steer away from heavy matt foundations, as sheer coverage is actually more flattering. And if you're prone to acne, avoid the compact foundations that are applied with a sponge, which attract bacteria that can make spots worse. Remember, you don't always need to splash out on concealer, just use the drier bit of foundation in the cap to cover blemishes.

Make-up by numbers

1. Start by moisturising your skin well, then leave it for a few minutes to let the moisture sink into your skin. If you're using an eye cream, now's the time to apply it. Foundation can often crease under eyes, which can be ageing.

> ### Defining idea...
> **'The best thing is to look natural, but it takes make-up to look natural.'**
> CALVIN KLEIN

2. Pour a penny-sized amount of foundation into your palm then dot it over your forehead, nose, cheeks and chin. Using your fingers or a sponge, blend it gently outwards using small strokes. Don't forget to sweep foundation over eyelids too; it can make a great base for eyeshadow. You're aiming to make the foundation disappear into the hairline and jawline. If you've been too heavy handed, dab the surplus away with a clean damp sponge. Always put your foundation on in good light and think blend, blend, blend.

3. Next focus on concealing blemishes such as spots and under-eye lines. Dot concealer over the areas you want to cover using a fingertip or tiny brush and blend well.

4. Now 'set' the foundation by dusting powder lightly over your T-zone (if you're using a light-diffusing foundation you won't need this as you're aiming for a dewy rather than matt look). Blot your face after applying powder so it doesn't lie on your face – never put powder under your eyes as it can accentuate fine lines. Always avoid thick bases as they're ageing too.

5. Then add blusher onto the apples of the cheeks. To find the apples suck your cheeks in and smile.

6. If you're going for the nude look, make sure you add plenty of mascara otherwise your eyes may 'disappear'. Use brown or black mascara and eyeliner to define your eyes.

40. Feed your face

When it comes to your complexion, diet can be far more valuable than make-up. Here's your guide to what to eat today for glowing, less troublesome skin tomorrow.

Experts tell us that diet can help fight certain skin conditions. For instance, oily fish alleviates the symptoms of psoriasis, and scientists have found a link between refined carbohydrates and acne. Brightly coloured fruit and vegetables can also reduce sun damage.

You know yourself that eating nothing but junk will take its toll on your face. Think about your most recent wild evening on the town. Perhaps it involved a couple of cocktails and a bottle of wine, followed by something greasy, salty and bursting with additives? How did your skin look the morning after? Pasty, dull and grey? The good news is that you can dramatically change your complexion in days simply by cutting out the rubbish and filling up on some skin-friendly foods.

So, what to eat? Well, omega-3 fatty acids, found in fish, for example, have good anti-inflammatory action and are great for improving the elasticity and texture of skin. And fruit and vegetables are rich in antioxidants that help fight the free radicals caused by pollution, sun and cigarette smoke that can lead to wrinkles. Free radicals not only cause cancer and heart disease, they can also wreak havoc on skin by damaging your cell membranes and the connective tissues that support it. Certain foods can help boost circulation too, including onions, garlic, nuts, pumpkin seeds and fish. When your blood is circulating at optimum levels, it means that your cells – including your skin cells – are getting a regular supply of life-giving nutrients and oxygen.

Here's an idea for you...

Patchouli is an essential oil thought to be good for skin as it can encourage the production of new skin cells. Add a few drops to your bath or mix three drops with 10 ml of a carrier oil such as sweet almond and give yourself a gentle massage.

Get a skinful

- ✿ **Fish** Oily fish such as sardines, mackerel and salmon are rich in fatty acids.
- ✿ **Turkey** A great source of lean protein, essential for making collagen. It also contains an amino acid known as carnosine, which can help prevent wrinkles.
- ✿ **Nuts** Packed with omega-3 fatty acids, which help control the lipids and fats in your body that can help skin stay soft and smooth. They're also rich in skin-friendly vitamin E. Brazil nuts contain the antioxidant selenium, which helps fight free radicals.
- ✿ **Spinach** Particularly rich in vitamin K, which is good for blood circulation, making sure nutrients and oxygen reach every cell. It's also rich in antioxidants.
- ✿ **Berries** Bursting with antioxidants.
- ✿ **Citrus fruit** Rich in vitamin C, which can help maintain the structure of collagen and help repair cuts and grazes.
- ✿ **Avocados** Rich in vitamin E and healthy monounsaturated fats.
- ✿ **Sweet potatoes** Rich in vitamins C and E, which help fight free radicals and may help prevent sun damage.
- ✿ **Pumpkin seeds** Packed with omega-3 fatty acids. They're also a good source of vitamin E, which is good for skin firmness.

✿ **Cruciferous vegetables** Broccoli, cauliflower, cabbage, etc., are rich in antioxidants and fibre, good for keeping your digestive system working properly and for stimulating the liver, which helps removes waste and toxins from the body. When you reduce your toxic load, your skin looks better.

✿ **Kiwi fruit** Rich in vitamin C, which helps build collagen and strengthens capillaries. They're also full of beta-carotene, which helps fight cell-damaging free radicals.

✿ **Water** At least eight glasses a day. Helps metabolise fat, reduces puffiness and helps your body flush waste from its cells.

The bad guys

✿ **Cakes, biscuits, white bread, etc.** Studies show a link between high intakes of refined starchy carbohydrates and acne. These foods also make your skin puffy, dehydrated and prone to allergic reactions.

✿ **Sugary foods** Can raise your blood sugar, which interferes with the way the hormone insulin behaves, making it flood your body with excess glucose. This causes collagen fibres to bunch up and results in loss of firmness and deep wrinkles.

✿ **Salty foods** Salt can cause fluid retention, which can make you look puffy and bloated and cause eye bags.

✿ **Coffee** Can dehydrate your body, leading to dark circles and puffiness.

✿ **Alcohol** Can increase the number of free radicals in your body and dehydrate your skin.

41. Quick fixes

Puffy eyes? Dark circles? Frizzy hair? Try these instant beautifiers for those hot date emergencies.

You know how it is. A huge bouquet of plump pink roses lands on your desk at work with a note saying, 'Darling, meet me at Claridges at eight. Wear something irresistible.'

In my dreams! Nevertheless, there *are* moments when we need to look super-gorgeous fast, like for a last-minute party, date or business lunch, for example. And since they'll undoubtedly arise on a bad nail, spot or hair day, here are some troubleshooting tips to catch the beauty demons off guard.

Cover up those spots

First, clean the spot area using cotton wool and a medicated lotion. Next, apply a mattifying product or gel to the area to remove any excess oil and prevent your concealer from sliding off. Pick a concealer that's the same colour as your face, ideally dry in texture rather than creamy, and apply it right in the middle of the spot. Using a brush or your middle finger, wipe away any excess. Remember, you're trying to camouflage the spot, not the area around it.

Instantly boost your complexion

Exfoliating to remove the layer of dead skin cells that dulls your complexion is the easiest way to brighten your skin and make you feel perkier. Splashing

Here's an idea for you...

For posh nails cut corners with press-on falsies. Pick the pre-glued ones and simply press them on over your natural nails. They should last up to three days.

your face with cold water is a great pick-me-up, too. Beauty doyenne Eve Lom (www.evelom.co.uk) has her own method. Start by massaging in a rich oil-based cleanser and then remove it using a muslin cloth. Next, massage cleanser over your face and neck gently, applying deep pressure with the pads of your fingertips. Start behind the ears to stimulate the lymphatic system, relieve congestion and reduce fluid. Repeat this three times, then rinse the cloth, rub off the cleanser and splash your face with cold water.

Fix puffy eyes

Give yourself a mini lymphatic drainage massage to help beat the fluid retention. Tap your middle finger around each eye in circular movements, then lie down and place cotton wool pads soaked in witch hazel or rosewater over your eyes. Alternatively, try damp camomile teabags that have been cooled in the fridge. Drink plenty of water too as dehydration can make puffy eyes worse. If you've time a quick workout can help boost circulation and lymph drainage. As a long-term solution, sleep with your head raised higher than your body.

Brighten dark circles

These nasties occur when your blood vessels become visible through your skin. Some people have naturally thin skin, but you do lose fat in this area as you age, so they tend to get worse. Start in the corner of your eye and apply concealer a shade lighter than your skin tone. Ideally, choose cream concealer as it's easier to apply and goes on more evenly. Some experts say that eye creams containing vitamin K, which helps boost blood flow, can help with dark circles.

Tame frizziness

You may have been born with frizzy hair. Or too much sun, too many colourants, blow-drying at too high a temperature and the need for a jolly good trim have left it crispy or wayward. Aim to condition your hair regularly and book that haircut if it's overdue. If you're on the point of going out use a leave-in conditioner before you blow-dry or add a few drops of smoothing serum that contains panthenol or silicone-based products to coat the cuticle and help it lie flat. Don't be afraid to spritz your hair with hairspray either as it will help prevent moisture in humid air (which causes your hair to frizz) from penetrating your hair.

Glam up your hair

Try this super speedy blow-dry. Lightly spray your hair with water then add a root-lifting product to give you instant body and volume. Start by blow-drying your roots, lifting the hair upwards as you go. Then smooth your hair into style using a natural bristle brush to give you extra shine. Finally, use your fingers to tousle your hair into a dishevelled but glam style, spray some perfume in the air and 'walk' into it. Instant gorgeousness.

42. Clever hair care

Simple tricks to turn a bad hair day good, plus hairdos to knock years off you.

Genetics, weather, hormones, diet and hair products (too many, not enough or the wrong type) can all take their toll. If you're frizzy, flat or frumpy, you need some professional help.

We've done the legwork for you, so try these invaluable solutions to everyday hair headaches.

Book that trim

A regular trim – every six to eight weeks – really is the best way to keep your hair in tip-top condition. Each hair on your head grows at its own pace, so within weeks they can look uneven and scraggly. Split ends happen when the individual layers of hair shafts separate due to chemicals, weather or too much heat from styling. You can help to seal split ends by using a leave-in conditioner, but the effect will only be temporary. Your hair grows between a third and half an inch per month, so you'll recover the length again in no time. A trim will make your hair look thicker, healthier and glossier.

The best blow-dry

✿ Blot wet hair first with a towel. If your hair is fine, only condition the ends because if you put it on the roots you'll make it lank. Spray some gel onto the roots and spread it evenly by rubbing with your fingers. To control frizz, use a small dollop of smoothing balm rather than gel, which can make hair drier.

✿ For added volume, use a handful of mousse about the size of a golf ball. Also, try wrapping the top layers of your hair around two large Velcro rollers when your hair is 95% dry and then finish blow-drying.

✿ Wait until your hair is quite dry before you blow-dry it and you'll do less damage; hair can lose up to 30% of its moisture when blow-dried.

✿ Clip your hair up into sections. Start with the hair at the back of your head first, then the side sections. Pull each section taut with a large round brush and dry from the root to the tip. Use the nozzle to tuck the ends under or to lift hair from the roots for volume.

✿ After drying each section, give it a blast of cold air to help 'set' the hair.

✿ When you hair is totally dry, part it. Now's the time to add a bit of serum to coarse, long or curly hair. Otherwise, wait until the hair is cool then spritz your hands with hairspray and rub it over your hair.

Here's an idea for you...

Put your hair in a high ponytail and you'll look years younger. It will help lift your face. A fringe can knock years off you too, plus it can emphasise your cheekbones. And highlights around your face are anti-ageing as they lighten and brighten your complexion.

Defining idea...

'I'm not offended by all the dumb-blonde jokes because I know that I'm not dumb. I also know I'm not blonde.'
DOLLY PARTON

Tips for curly or frizzy hair

Frizz is the result of too much heat, sun or chemicals used to bleach, colour, straighten or curl your hair.

❀ Choose conditioners with panthenol and silicone, which make the cuticle lie flat and make hair look smoother and sleeker.

❀ If you have naturally wiry or wispy hair, always use conditioner after shampooing and also invest in a deep-conditioning product. Also, wash your hair thoroughly to get rid of traces of shampoo and conditioner; otherwise it'll look lank. You'll know when you've washed away the last of the residue because when you run your hand through your hair, it should feel squeaky-clean.

❀ Never use too much conditioner even if your hair is thick. The right size for shoulder length hair is that of an almond, less if it's shorter.

❀ Blot hair with a towel to absorb excess moisture. A wide-toothed comb can detangle curly hair without tearing it and help to eliminate frizz. Anything else can break or tear your hair, leaving it with split ends.

❀ Apply a protective product before you blow-dry to prevent hair from dehydrating and then use a diffuser and your fingers to gently blow-dry. Avoid brushes or combs, as they'll just make your hair frizz. After drying, rub a few drops of serum into the palms of your hands then smooth it over your hair to calm wayward strands and seal in moisture.

43. The power of vitality

Discover the secret of that special joie de vivre that will make your eyes sparkle and your entire body radiate gorgeousness.

You can be dolled up to the nines, having just stepped out of the salon, but if you're feeling lacklustre you're simply not going to look your best.

One dictionary definition of vitality is 'the power of remaining alive, vigorous; liveliness, energy, durability'. Personally I think it's a combination of energy, liveliness and a passion for living that comes with seeing the best in everything and seeking out life's greatest sensations. It's about sensual pleasures – things that look, sound, taste, smell and feel great yet aren't too calorie-laden or illegal.

Here are a few vitality secrets to try today.

Initiate sex more
One study showed that people who had sex three times a week looked considerably younger than people who had it less often. Sex is great for your circulation, can release feel-good endorphins to keep you feeling happy and can help strengthen your bond with your partner.

Eat delicious foods
Choose healthy and decadent goodies such as artichokes, plump strawberries, huge asparagus tips and the finest organic chocolate. Research shows that men prefer normal-sized women with big, hearty appetites so combine this with the previous tip.

Here's an idea for you...

Make your own pick-me-up CD or tape. Pick your favourite energising and uplifting pieces of music and play them in the car, as you walk in the park or before that scary meeting. Instant joy!

Exercise regularly

Dance, run or swim three times a week – anything that involves moving your body is great for you. After twenty minutes of exercise, your body produces endorphins. Exercise is also great for your self-confidence and body image.

Go out to play

Indulge in regular girly rituals; take long soaks in delicious-smelling candlelit baths, splurge on a pedicure, wear flimsy strappy summer dresses, teeter around in an expensive pair of heels or have a pampering party night in with your friends.

Get out more

Get outdoors – it's a surefire mood booster. Surround yourself with greenery; make a window box and fill your home with flowers. Studies show fresh cut flowers in the office can boost productivity, too.

Perk up your extremities

Sore, aching feet squeezed into impractical shoes can radiate up your legs and make you generally sore and miserable. Treat yourself to a reflexology treatment or a darn good pedicure. Or try an Indian head massage; it's relaxing, energising and you can do it in your lunch hour.

Surround yourself with beautiful things

Splurge on a beautiful picture, spend a day at a gallery or museum or buy tickets to the opera or ballet. Think of it as a spiritual facial.

Cut down on chemicals

Chemicals can put your body under stress and rob you of energy. Hoover regularly, use a water filter, hang your washing to dry outside, eat organic when you can afford it and use chemical-free household products where you can.

Clean up your house

Decluttering has an amazingly positive impact on energy levels. Start small and devote just twenty minutes a day on a shelf, drawer or cupboard. And be brutal; if you haven't worn or used something for six months, get rid of it.

Inhale mind-sharpening scents

Pine, peppermint, eucalyptus and jasmine are known to stimulate the part of your brain that makes you alert.

Defining idea...

'There is a vitality, a life force, an energy, a quickening, that is translated through you into action, and because there is only one of you in all time, this expression is unique.'
MARTHA GRAHAM

Defining idea...

'Energy is eternal delight.'
WILLIAM BLAKE

44. Enhance your eyes

They're said to be the windows to the soul, the first thing people notice and capable of disarming a man at 100 paces. But what if your eyes are more Mole Man than Bette Davis?

According to anthropologists, the most attractive women's faces are 'child-like', with smooth skin, a peaches-and-cream complexion, a small nose and big eyes with long Bambi lashes.

These are all good reasons to take care of your eyes. Easy-peasy eye care includes taking off your eye make-up every night, keeping dirty hankies or fingers away from them and patting instead of rubbing the skin surrounding them. Make sure you get lots of sleep, drink gallons of water, apply a regular dab of eye cream and treat yourself to the odd cucumber or teabag session.

As for making them bigger and veiled in long, thick, fluttery eyelashes, you'll need a few good tools and clever make-up techniques.

Try these:
- ✿ Start with your eyebrows and pluck any stray hairs with a pair of tweezers.
- ✿ Apply a pale or neutral colour over the upper eyelid, blending over the outer edges, to give a good matt base on which you can blend and build darker and stronger colours. Even a dab of foundation can create a great base for colour and cover any redness or blotchiness.

- Apply a brown or grey eyeshadow, from the middle to the outer edge of the eye. Start with a tiny bit of colour and add more layers, blending as you go.
- Brush a thin line of a darker shade along the upper lid. Add a little shading under the eye, too, at the outer edge.
- Using white pencil along the lower inner socket of your eyes can make them more striking. Or dot a tiny spot of white shadow in the inner corners of your eyes to make them look wider apart.
- If your eyes are small, remember that you'll make them look even smaller by using eyeshadow or eyeliner around the entire eye as this will effectively close them up.
- False eyelashes can really open up the eyes so don't be afraid of them. Try a few individual lashes on the outer corner of the eye, then add a few shorter ones, and alternate between the two as you work towards the middle of the eye.
- Invest in eyelash curlers, which really help to open your eyes. They're easier to use than they look, too. Just hold them so that your upper lashes lie between the two rims, then squeeze and roll upwards.
- Eyeshadow spillage? Before you start, pop a layer of translucent loose powder underneath each eye to catch any of the eyeshadow that falls on your cheeks. You can then simply brush it away and you don't have to reapply foundation.
- Stick to black mascara for drama, brown if you're very blonde, or try the 'no make-up' look, which is also more flattering against older skins.
- Some make-up artists recommend you put mascara on the top lashes only and leave the bottom ones bare – it makes you look brighter and less tired.
- Don't dismiss coloured mascara. Try navy blue (not electric blue) to make the whites of your eyes look whiter, or plum, which can look great on blondes.

Here's an idea for you...

Bring out the colour of your eyes using contrasts. Pinks, mauves and greys look great on blue eyes. Or use really dark colours for stunning contrasts. Avoid pinks if your eyes are red and tired; stick to neutrals or ivories instead. Remember: blend, blend, blend.

✿ Avoid putting powder underneath your eyes, as when it 'cakes' it shows up every crease and fine line and can be very ageing.

✿ How many layers of mascara? Ideally two for maximum drama, but don't let it dry between layers or it may cake and flake.

✿ Invest in eyedrops, a great way to put a sparkle in your eye.

45. Photogenic fakes: looking great in photos

You know who they are – the plain Janes and Johns who somehow look like film stars when they're captured on camera. You can join them.

Models and celebrities know all the tricks of the trade – if you watch them carefully at red carpet events you'll catch them strike a carefully calculated pose as the paparazzi gather. So, next time you have to face your public, try some of these tricks picked up from celebrities and photographers.

✿ To look your slimmest try standing with one foot slightly in front of the other, and gently pivot on your feet so that your body including your shoulders are at a slight angle. Putting your hands on your hips can make your waist look smaller, so overall it'll take inches off your body.

✿ If you're sitting down, just lean forward and rest your elbows on your knees – you'll disguise any wobbly thighs and look slimmer.

✿ Look lively. Greta Garbo *froideur* isn't always the most flattering attitude to adopt in snaps. In fact, some professional portrait photographers insist the best pictures are always taken when the subject is looking animated and chipper – that way the subject's personality is captured. You can still engineer your 'best side' in front of the camera.

> Here's an idea for you...
>
> **Maximise your lips. To pout beautifully, try turning to the camera and say 'Wogan'. Sounds bizarre, granted, but try it. It somehow produces the perfect pout – glamour models swear by it.**

✿ Practise in the mirror. If you find a pose you're happy with, it's worth perfecting it, so you can strike it the moment the camera comes out.

✿ Brighten up. Dark colours can be slimming, but black can be draining against the face, so choose brighter colours on your top half to enhance your skin tone.

✿ Beware brightly patterned clothes; they can swamp you and detract from your face.

✿ Dark circles or bags under your eyes? Try lifting your chin – you'll avoid shadows falling on your face.

✿ Do smile. Forget looking moody – everyone actually looks more attractive when they're looking happy. Plus a lovely smile really does take the focus away from the bits you're less happy with.

✿ Poker straight hair can pull your face down. Putting your hair up can soften your features and draw attention to your smile.

Defining idea...

'With charm you've got to get up close to see it; style slaps you in the face.'
JOHN COOPER CLARKE, poet and comedian.

✿ Get them to take more than one! The more photos you have taken, the more likely it is you'll be captured from a flattering angle. Remember, safety in numbers.

Make-up tricks

You'd be forgiven for thinking that slapping gallons of foundation and concealer over spots and blemishes would create alabaster skin and produce wonderful photographs you'd display with pride. Forget it: overdo the slap and you'll look like a waxwork – or, worse, a cross-dresser. Instead, be subtle.

✿ Apply a light foundation only where necessary – sides of nose, over spots, that kind of thing.

✿ To avoid shiny-face, stick to matte formula make-up on your blemishes and only use creamy, reflective concealers on the eye.

✿ Flatter your best features – apply blush over to the apple part of your cheeks, sneak a couple of extra false lashes on your eyelids, slick on some glossy lipstick. Don't forget the golden rule of make-up, though: never overplay the eyes *and* the lips – choose between them before you open that make-up bag.

✿ Ask for a minute or two before the camera clicks so you can touch up and dab a bit of powder over shiny bits. Who cares if you seem vain – there are few things as insidious as unflattering photos of yourself *in someone else's hands...*

I want to be thin!

Are you an emotional eater?

When is food not food? When we start to get it mixed up with our best friend, looking to it for support and to make us feel better. Is your relationship with comfort food getting a bit too close for comfort? Respond to the following statements:

I eat when I'm not hungry:
Rarely/Sometimes/Often

If I have a bad morning ahead of me, I promise myself food as a reward:
Rarely/Sometimes/Often

Stressed out – and my first reaction is to turn to food:
Rarely/Sometimes/Often

I often think about my next meal when I've just eaten:
Rarely/Sometimes/Often

When I'm feeling low, foods 'call' to me and I can't think of anything else:
Rarely/Sometimes/Often

I'm always starting healthy eating habits or another diet, but even as I promise myself I'll change, I know I won't:
Rarely/Sometimes/Often

Which ideas do I need?

If you answered SOMETIMES 3 or more times, your attitude to food is ambivalent. Take the emotion out of food and see it for what it is – nourishing fuel. Understanding your energy needs will help, turn to idea 49, Top gear.

If you answered OFTEN 3 or more times, your attitude to food is as your best mate who will cheer you up when you're down. Food can't lift your mood in the long term. Turn to idea 53, Are you an emotional eater?, for more on curbing your cravings.

If you answered RARELY most of the time, your attitude is fine. If you're struggling on a diet, you might want to see idea 52, It's never too late to change your mind, on sticking to diets.

46. Bottom's up

Celebrate your curves. Having cellulite – as nearly nine out of ten women do – doesn't mean you can't feel gorgeous. Try some bottom pampering today.

The word cellulite was first coined back in the 70s, but it's no modern affliction. Just think of those Rubenesque lovelies, writhing about in the altogether. They'd never make the cover of today's Vogue, yet in their era they were considered the epitome of voluptuous sexiness.

Fashion has changed, and back in the days of yore, fatness (for that's essentially what cellulite is – body fat) would have been synonymous with wealth. Nowadays the smaller your thighs, the bigger your wallet. Women dread surplus pounds, aspiring instead to a neat peachy behind and racehorse legs. And cellulite, which becomes worse as you get older, is viewed as a sort of degenerative disease.

The truth is cellulite is just part of being a woman – 85–95% of us fall prey to it, including the world's most glamorous models and actresses.

There's nothing disease-like about it either: it's surplus fat held together by skin cells that have lost their elasticity. And it lurks about the areas of a woman's body that are designed to lay down fat – backs of thighs, bottoms, tummies, even your upper arms. The result? Fat cells squishing upwards against your skin and causing a cottage cheese effect – like stuffing bursting out of an old cushion.

That's not to say you have to embrace cellulite as part of your femaleness (that's why we've written this book, after all). But before you get stressed, depressed and obsessed about the cellulitey bits, take a moment here to get a perspective, and to celebrate your curves.

A friend's husband once took a mould of her behind, which was, refreshingly, generously proportioned. He gave it to her as an anniversary present – a wonderful pumpkin of a bottom cast in bronze.

So the first lesson is 'remember, men love curves'. In fact men particularly love fleshy bottoms when they're paired with a small waist; studies show a waist/hip ratio of 0.7 is the magic formula most likely to get a man's pulse racing.

Don't forget too that your curves are there for a reason: making babies, having babies, feeding babies, filling out bikinis/ridiculously expensive undies, that sort of thing.

Your curves also give *you* pleasure. Legs, bottoms, thighs, tummies – they're all part of your healthy, functioning, living, breathing body. So think of a slightly dimply bottom as a sign of a rich, happy and fulfilling life.

Oh, and a spongy bottom is also handy at weddings and on bikes; pews and saddles can be so uncomfortable.

So let's start by nipping that self-criticism in the bud. Time, instead, to celebrate that ass. Try some of these today:

> *Defining* idea...
>
> **'Everything has its beauty, but not everyone sees it.'**
> CONFUCIUS

✿ Savour the good things about your bum and thighs – that satisfying pain/exhilaration when you cycle up a hill, the sensation of rubbing lovely cream into your legs, someone else fondling your behind...

✿ Every day, promise yourself you'll do something that makes you feel good about your body – have something really delicious to eat, treat yourself to a day at a spa, go for a swim, book a fantastic holiday. Doing something pleasurable can make you feel happy.

✿ Stop buying clothes that don't fit but which you're aiming to 'diet into'. They make you feel worse about your body. Instead, buy yourself something big but gorgeous that you can wear now.

✿ Make a mental list of your best bits – hair, feet, long, beautifully shaped fingernails, trim calves, firm boobs. Stop focusing on your shortcomings and acknowledge your glories.

✿ Splash out on body treats: indulging really does boost your self-confidence – book a facial/manicure, buy new perfume, wallow in a luxurious, gorgeous smelling bath. Take pleasure in looking your best.

✿ Start taking some exercise. It can boost your mood, improve your complexion, help you focus and give you confidence in your body.

47. Brown girl in the ring

Cellulite looks less obvious on bronzed legs. If you can't beat it...hide it with a fake tan!

Faking it is so much safer than baking in the sun. And many of us would agree that we would be less tempted to soak up the rays if we arrived on holiday with a bit of colour.

It's also brilliant at helping disguise cellulite – fake tan somehow seems to even out those lumps and bumps. Plus the prep work you do before you apply it – exfoliating, moisturising and so on – helps hydrate the area, remove dead skin cells and even out skin-texture. So cellulitey skin can look better already.

Applying fake tan used to be a messy, smelly old business. And the shades were questionable. Mercifully, gone are the days of George Hamilton-style tans in a shade of tangerine that smelt of something you'd keep under the sink.

These days fake tans are sophisticated, easy to use, quick-drying and incredibly effective. They're a great way to prepare your body for your two weeks in the sun, or cover up pasty white bits when you're wearing that sundress/mini-skirt/strappy number. The magic ingredient is DHA (dihydroxyacetene), which turns the skin brown by oxidizing amino acids in the skin. And manufacturers usually add lots of other lovely softening, toning, hydrating ingredients too.

Fake tans come in mousses, creams, gels and lotions. Self-applied tans tend to last up to four or five days, or you can go the professional route and visit a specialist, who might put you in a booth and spray you with the stuff. Salon tans tend to last longer – some claim theirs last between a week and a fortnight. A salon is the best route if you want an all-over tan without the hassle of doing it yourself. Best salon choices include St Tropez, Guinot and Clarins.

Here's what to expect if you're a salon tan virgin. You disrobe (and usually pop on a pair of charming paper pants), after which the therapist exfoliates you, and slaps on handfuls of goo, covering you thoroughly. She'll then leave you there for up to an hour while the tanner works its magic, and she then removes the excess. When you shower the next day (if you can leave it that long) you look fantastic. Make sure you wear dark clothes to avoid staining on your clothes. Many fake tans take a few days to look beautifully natural, so if you're preparing for a special do, book your treatment a few days prior to the event.

If you're using a self-tanner at home, make sure you patch test the area beforehand to avoid an allergic reaction. Don't be tempted to go too dark; always choose one that matches your natural skin tone. The best tried-and-tested self-tanners include those by Decleor, Ambre Solaire, St-Tropez and Lancaster.

Follow the three golden rules: *exfoliate*, *moisturise* and *layer*.

✿ Start by exfoliating the area with a body scrub, loofah or flannel. Apply exfoliator with circular movements (it helps boost circulation). paying particular attention to heels, knees and elbows where the skin is rougher. A cheaper option is Epsom

> *Here's an idea for you...*
>
> **Fake tanning doesn't have to be a messy, painstaking business. You can buy packets of nifty little self-tan wipes, which you just rub over your skin, and a golden tan appears in a few hours. Keep a packet in your handbag, just in case you need to undress and impress pronto.**

salts – which will help to deep-cleanse your skin. Just fill a cup with salts and add enough water to make a paste. Massage over your skin, then rinse off.

✿ Always moisturise after exfoliating. Leave the moisturiser on for about fifteen minutes before you apply your fake tan so it doesn't interfere with the active ingredient in fake tanning products.

✿ Remove excess moisturiser with a damp flannel before you apply the tanning product – especially on bony areas such as knees, elbows and ankles – it'll prevent any uneven tanning.

✿ Apply the fake tan, smothering it on as you would a moisturiser. Don't forget backs of knees and hands, and your inner thighs.

✿ Then build up gradually. You don't need as much where your skin is thinner as the colour will stay longer here.

✿ Tan usually appears about three or four hours later – if you find you have streaks, try exfoliating the area.

✿ Avoid swimming or having a shower for about twelve hours after a treatment.

✿ Moisturise your body well over the next few days to prolong your fake tan.

✿ And always remember that a fake tan won't protect you from the sun so you still need sunscreen.

48. On the shelf

Cellulite creams abound. But what works, what doesn't and what's really worth the money?

There's no denying the placebo effect of using cellulite creams – there's nothing like rubbing on pricey, sweet-smelling, beautifully packaged unguents to make you feel you're spoiling yourself.

But, do they work? You might be seduced into thinking so. These days many products are impressively endorsed by various scientific studies, many of which claim that testers lost inches and pounds after using said unguent for a period of time.

But if you're hoping for a miracle in a bottle, you still have a long wait. Cellulite creams alone, however impressive, aren't likely to transform fleshy, saggy buttocks into a nectarine-firm bottom.

But they may certainly help. Cellulite creams can hydrate your skin, so if your thighs and bottom have been neglected, rubbing on a cream will moisturise the area and help plump up the skin. Big difference already.

Many cellulite creams also contain temporary toning ingredients, which help improve skin texture; the effects can be pretty immediate but are temporary – good for a hot date, beach day, black dress occasion, that sort of thing.

But the longer-lasting effects come down to a pot-pourri of active ingredients, which do anything from boost metabolism, facilitate cell turnover, help shed water, even break down fat.

Here's an idea for you...

Short on pennies? Try natural olive or grapeseed oil; you can buy them over the counter at chemists for next to nothing. Gentle enough for newborn babies, they're unlikely to cause reactions and are great for massage or for all over moisturising.

Defining idea...

'I will buy any cream, cosmetic, or elixir from a woman with a European accent.'
ERMA BOMBECK, humorist

Take *caffeine*, a common and effective ingredient in many anti-cellulite formulations. It's thought to encourage the metabolism of fats, and help drain accumulated fluids in your fat cells, and boost your circulation. It's also toning.

Another key ingredient used in the more effective anti-cellulite creams is *retinol*. It's a derivative of vitamin A that has been found to increase skin renewal and boost the production of collagen. Often found in face cream, it can improve the elasticity of the skin on your nether regions too. RoC's retinol-based product has many devotees, who claim to have lost inches and firmed up significantly using the formulation twice daily.

Another cellulite-busting ingredient is *aminophylline*, which is thought by some experts to enter the bloodstream and actually break down fat in the cells. One study found women using aminophylline cream lost as much as 8 mm from their thighs. Another study showed impressive results with aminophylline, although it was used alongside a calorie-reduced diet and daily exercise too.

Exfoliating ingredients such as *alpha-hydroxy acids* (AHAs) are often used in the latest cellulite-busting products. AHAs are found in plants (citrus fruits and apples) and are used in skin products to help remove dead skin cells, thereby promoting the turnover of new cells. Thus far research has found that the effects on cellulitey areas tend to be temporary, rather than permanent, but watch this space.

Natural ingredients

Most treatment creams are a combination of cutting-edge technology alongside tried and trusted natural or herbal ingredients. Here are a few to look out for:

✿ Gingko biloba can stimulate your circulation and boost blood flow. It's a strong antioxidant, so it may help slow down the ageing process and help fight the free radicals that can cause your skin to age.

✿ Gotu kola. This herb is thought to enhance the production of collagen. It's good for circulation and also has diuretic qualities. It's been found to help heal wounds and burns, so has positive effects on skin tissue.

✿ Guarana is a natural stimulant with a strong diuretic action. This seed is thought to help boost metabolism, and also has antioxidant qualities.

✿ Horse chestnut can help reduce water retention, boost circulation and increase blood flow to the skin.

✿ Butcher's broom is a plant extract with a diuretic action and may help boost circulation.

✿ Ivy has been found to help boost the circulation. It also has astringent properties, which may have a temporary toning effect on cellulite.

✿ Marine extracts such as carrageenan and alginic acid can help draw water into the skin, which may help make cellulite look less obvious by filling in the dimples.

✿ Co-enzyme Q10 is a powerful antioxidant thought to help beat cellulite by helping build collagen, thereby countering skin sagginess.

49. Top gear

As you age, your metabolism slows down, which means more body fat, and a saggier bottom and thighs as the years go by. Try some strategies to rev up your body chemistry.

Were you at the back of the queue when they were handing out metabolic rates? 'It's not me, it's my metabolism' is an oft-given excuse for erring on the lardy side.

To a certain extent, your metabolic rate is genetic. Experts say that the rate at which a person burns up calories can vary as much as 25% – that's between people of the same weight.

Your age also affects the rate at which you burn calories. Between the ages of 30 and 80, muscle mass decreases by 40–50%, which reduces your strength and slows down your metabolism.

So, if you've drawn the short straw, and you're gaining weight – and cellulite – as a result, it's time to get tough on your metabolism.

Start by working out how many calories you actually need, based on your metabolic rate. Remember, you gain weight when you take in more calories than you expend.

First, calculate your basal metabolic rate (BMR) – this is the rate at which your body burns energy even when you're not doing anything.

Your BMR = weight in kilos × 2 × 11 (if you prefer to work in pounds that will be your weight in pounds × 11)

So, if you're 65 kilos, your BMR = 65 × 2 × 11 = 1,430

Now work out how many extra calories you expend according to your lifestyle:

✿ Inactive or sedentary: BMR × 20%.

✿ Fairly active, i.e. you walk and take exercise once or twice a week: BMR × 30%.

✿ Moderately active, i.e. you exercise two or three times a week: BMR × 40%.

✿ Active (you exercise hard more than three times a week): BMR × 50%.

✿ Very active (you exercise hard every day): BMR × 70%.

So if you're a fairly active 65 kg woman, your additional calorie requirement is 1,430 × 30% = 429.

Add this to your BMR to find out how many calories you need a day: 1,430 + 429 = 1,859. So if you eat more than 1,900 calories and don't increase your activity levels, you'll gain weight.

Here's an idea for you...

Drinking 2 litres of still water a day can help your body burn off an extra 150 calories according to one study. It's thought to stimulate the sympathetic nervous system and increase the metabolic rate.

What's the best way to boost your metabolic rate?

Exercise

Move more: incorporate regular aerobic and weight-bearing exercise into your week (running, hill walking or weight training will do). When you increase the amount of lean tissue in your body, you use up more calories even when you're just sitting there; muscle uses more calories than fat does. Aim for 30–40 minute sessions, four or five times a week.

Eat regularly, and don't fast

When you eat less, your metabolism drops because your body tries to conserve energy in case its food supply is about to run out. Small, regular meals are better than scoffing a big meal then eating nothing for hours.

Eat protein

Eating protein uses more calories than other foodstuffs. If you're doing an aerobic workout three to five times a week you need more protein – about 1.1 g of protein for every kilo of body weight. If you're sedentary you need about 0.8 g per kilo of body weight. (As a guide, you get about 44 g of protein in an average lean steak, and about 25 g in a portion of lean chicken.)

Have a steak occasionally
Red meat and dairy produce contain conjugated linoleic acid (CLA). Research has shown this may increase the amount of lean tissue in your body, which boosts metabolic rate.

Go exotic
Add some chillies to your dishes – apparently they can raise your metabolic rate by about 50% for up to two or three hours after a meal.

Have a pre- and post-exercise nibble
One recent study found that people who performed gentle resistance exercise within two hours of eating a light, carb-based meal boosted their metabolic rate, and burned the food off quicker than those who didn't exercise afterwards. Plus, if you aim to eat something within half an hour of finishing a workout you'll increase your metabolic rate further. After exercising, your body will be low in energy. Replace it quickly and you'll keep your metabolism higher.

Have a coffee break
Caffeine can boost your metabolic rate – partly because it increases your heart rate and also because it makes you fidgety! Don't drink more than two or three cups a day though. Alternatively, try green tea. Studies show that drinking a cup of the green stuff twice daily could help you burn about 70 calories more each day – that's about 3.5 kg in a year! Researchers believe it's the catechins (antioxidants) and other flavonoids in green tea that help boost your metabolism.

50. Short cuts to supermodel looks

Yes, yes, we know – the key to looking great is lots and lots of sleep, eating well, working out daily, good skin care etc. Surely there must be an easier way.

The problem is that you haven't quite found the time for all that healthy living stuff but what you do have is a date/party/wedding and just a few hours to get ready. To heap up the pressure, you just *have* to shine. It's an emergency. Like your ex is going to be there and you have to make him jealous, even though he's going to be with the current squeeze – who happens to be Angelina Jolie. What to do?

As they said in *Reservoir Dogs*, it's time to go to work. First things first: first impressions do count, so make sure that you have all your necessary maintenance done for your special night out – hair and nails looking great. It's not just the look itself, it's the fact that the psychological boost will leave you with a glow that shows. For a small investment that goes a long way, a manicure is a must.

A full afternoon in the beautician's is the best way to go but if time and money don't permit and you simply have to polish up your crowning glory then the cheat's way to a shiny head of hair is Aveda's Purefume Brilliant Spray On For Hair (www.aveda.com). This adds instant gloss and shine to even the dullest locks.

The best way to great skin is a healthy diet and a couple of weeks in fresh air, sea and sun (not forgetting your SPF, natch). However, we're presuming that for you this is just wishful thinking so wipe the McDo remains from your mouth and resort to a facial for short-term cheating. If you can afford the time and the money for a salon-based treat then do so – the more you spend, the better you'll feel. However, if you can't, there's plenty you can do at home. Forget cucumber slices on the eyes – it'll make you feel too much like a distressed divorcee and not enough like a sex kitten. Instead go for the likes of Origins Clear Improvement (www.origins.com), which is a black charcoal mask to draw out pore-clogging impurities, followed by an Elemis Fruit Active Rejuvenating Mask (www.elemis.com).

Remember girls to have a hot bath before you go out to plump out your complexion with all that steam and to get the circulation going so that you appear rosy and, therefore, healthy.

Here's an idea for you...

Ignore Bridget Jones's nightmare, the gruesome fact is that granny gripper knickers (or 'pants of steel' as India Knight puts it) are the short-term solution to waistline emergencies. On this one, it's only right to go with the advice of India Knight herself (nothing nasty meant by that, India) and get yourself the ultimate pair – Nancy Gantz BodySlimmers High Waist Belly Buster. They are simply the best and the only trick they miss is that they should come complete with a suicide pill on the basis that obviously it is better to die than to let anyone know that they're what you're wearing.

Nutrition is a long-term thing but there are certain short-cutting cheats that will give you an instant hit of feel-good factor. Try taking a slug of supergreens, for instance. Supergreens are ground up superfoods – extremely health promoting vegetables, algae and sprouted grasses – which give a shot of optimum nutrition in one glass. Upside: you'll swear you can actually notice the difference in energy levels and well-being. Downside: they tend to taste disgusting. So, mix these life-giving powders with a little juice and down the hatch. Two that taste just about OK

Defining idea...

**'Grace in women has more
effect than beauty.'**
WILLIAM HAZLITT

and give you a spring in your step are Kiki's Nature's
Living Superfood (www.kiki-health.co.uk) and Perfect
Food by Garden of Life (www.gardenoflifeusa.com).

Depending on how fit you are, some people also
recommend performing a couple of press ups (yes that's
for girls as well as boys) to flush the blood through your
system and bring a healthy glow to your skin. Remember, though, healthy glow should
not be confused with out of breath and beetroot faced. Before you make your
entrance, try spritzing your face with a water spray, which helps cool you down and
also freshens up your make up – so carry your own supply with you at all times.

51. Dressing yourself slim

**If thinking of a hideously strict diet before that
date/interview/holiday drives you to the cake tin,
take heart. You can look thinner and more
elegant through your choice of clothes.**

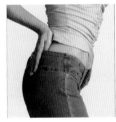

One of my friends used to be rarely seen out unless in black.
Neither did her magazine colleagues. 'It's the media uniform,' she explains, 'the one-
colour-suits-all for every event in your working life. And beyond, actually. I'd wear it to
every function too – weddings, christenings, bah mitzvahs, garden parties. Even at the
kind of outings that begged for the most feminine florals and pastel chiffon, I'd be
there head to toe in some billowy – or worse, silhouette-enhancing – black number,
believing it made me look barely there thin.'

Black can indeed look supremely elegant – the longer the streak you create, the better. But individual it rarely is. Dark colours certainly can minimise the bulges, but it's not the only sartorial route to a more slender you. Besides it can also be dreary, draining and make you look like 'the help'. Get it ever so slightly wrong at functions and you'll have half a dozen coats flung at you, or be asked for another vol-au-vent, both of which, when you're aiming for willowy Eva Herzigova-esque grandeur, will extinguish the joys of appearing to have a slightly smaller arse.

Instead of black, be inventive. Follow these guidelines:

✿ You can minimise bulges by sticking to one colour – and pretty much any colour. Obviously dark colours are the most flattering, but in summer you can still create the illusion of being longer and leaner if you're dressed head to foot in the same shade, even white.

✿ When you're shopping, make it a rule to ignore size tags. Don't buy the snug size ten just because that's your usual size. You look can lose pounds by wearing slightly looser clothes which skim over bumps and hang flatteringly.

✿ Where possible, choose lined clothes. They won't hug you so unforgivingly. Lined trousers are a godsend, particularly in summer because they drop crisply, however hot and sweaty you are beneath.

Here's an idea for you...

Colour experts say white, silver and mother of pearl are 'eternally feminine' because they're associated with the moon, stars and sea. Remember that luminous uber-gown that Nicole Kidman wore to the Oscars ceremony a couple of years ago? If the red carpets invites are thin on the ground for you, invest in striking silver or pearl jewellery instead; it's the easiest way to wear these colours. Alternatively tap into your inner goddess with a soft shell-pink wrap and mother-of-pearl make up – great against a tan. Light colours close to your face can reflect light, and take years off you too.

❀ Invest in an A line skirt. It flatters almost everyone because it doesn't cling to your curves, and it minimises your bottom. The best length is on, or just below the knee – and if you team it with knee length boots you can disguise thick legs and hefty unfeminine thighs. In the summer a light coloured skirt can look great with suede or denim boots.

❀ Don't be afraid of hipster jeans. They may seem the preserve of nubile girly band members but they can be really flattering whatever your age as they create the illusion of having smaller hips. Just keep a close eye on the flesh overhang because it can ruin the effect. Stick if possible to the boot leg cut – it's even more flattering since it makes your legs look longer and slimmer.

❀ Always wear a heel, however slight. Even tall women can get away with tiny tapering heels. The extra inch or two will add length and can make you more aware of your posture.

❀ Stick to textured fabrics. They can help to 'break up' flesh. Think linen, wool or even crinkled man-made fabrics.

❀ Disguise a big bust with V-necks and low scoop necks. Avoid slash necks and halter necks altogether as they just make you look bulky.

❀ Always choose trousers with hems long enough to skim the tip of a boot or shoe. They may feel too long, but they'll immediately draw the eye down, giving the impression of a longer, leaner leg. And avoid tapered trousers or clam diggers or pedal pushers for the same reason – they make almost everyone's legs look shorter and squatter, and thighs look bigger than they are.

✿ Investing in good lingerie can knock pounds off you; go for well fitting bras with uplift and knickers that flatten in the right places. With bras, aim to banish seams, puckering and surplus flesh bursting out of cups (unless it's what you're aiming for).

52. It's never too late to change your mind – sticking to a diet

Have you been on diets before, lost weight, then regained it and lost motivation? Change your attitude to dieting and use your mind to get ahead.

I have a friend who's been on every kind of diet going: cabbage soup, high protein, eating for your blood type, meal replacements and all the rest. The trouble is, she hasn't changed her poor mental attitude to dieting.

She uses diets like buses, jumping on and off. If she's just missed one, well, there will be another along in a minute, won't there? Has she lost weight? Yes, she has and then she's gained it, until the next period of dieting when the cycle repeats itself.

Why is it that most diets only seem to work temporarily? In my opinion the main reason is that they don't teach you much about healthy eating or help you learn a

Drink fruit juice not cola. According to new research from the American Diabetes Association, just one regular can of a fizzy drink a day is enough to increase your risk of diabetes by 85%. A can a day could also lead to a weight gain of around a stone in four years.

healthy attitude to food. All too often, entire food groups are banned, which, depending on the group, can be unhealthy or even dangerous if you follow it for a long time. Meal replacements, although designed nowadays to be nutritionally safe, don't really give the average dieter any idea of what a healthy meal looks like. If a diet promises you rapid weight loss, you can bet it will be due to consuming significantly less calories. It won't be because of some magical fat-burning enzyme found in the bongo-bongo fruit or whatever the angle is! Besides, you'll just lose water and lean muscle mass anyway, so it won't necessarily be sustainable.

Diets can be as dull as ditchwater, particularly if they are very strict about what you can and can't eat. Not only do you feel bored and start fantasising about bathing in jelly and custard (mmm, with some chocolate sprinkles too), but they can make eating out difficult, especially when you visit friends' houses. You have to be very good company indeed to make up for your inconvenient food requests. Let's face it, a diet can simply be hard to fit into your life, particularly when you also have a family to feed or if you work long or unusual hours. And then there's the hunger, the growling stomach and the faintness-inducing pangs that all too often lead to a binge. Then you feel guilty – and move on to another diet in the hope that it will be better.

Many people who sincerely want to lose weight are failing to stick to their diet regimes. So what does work? There isn't one single way to lose weight successfully. You need to develop a combination of tricks that work for you, and an acceptance of certain key points. The first is that you will probably need to change your idea of what a diet and losing weight is all about. The kinds of diets mentioned above are not going to help you. To lose weight and keep it off, you have to change your eating habits and lifestyle permanently. Before you shriek that this sounds even scarier than a wasp-chewing diet, remember that losing weight is about the long haul, not dieting in short four-week bursts. There are no quick fixes, but if you make small changes over a period of time, they will add up to big results.

Defining idea...

'I never worry about diets. The only carrots that interest me are the number you get in a diamond.'
MAE WEST

Next, you have to realistic about your weight-loss goals. Aim to be in the best shape you can be, which is to be healthy, not to look like a stick insect. Eat a balanced selection of foods with plenty of fruit and vegetables, protein and carbohydrate and a little fat. A balanced diet is essential for good health, keeps things interesting for you and ensures you won't suffer endless cravings because you're denying yourself certain foods. Remember that you do need to keep a check on the portion sizes. You'll also be doing yourself a big favour if you become more physically active. Exercise makes you feel and look good, helps to control your appetite and, in conjunction with sensible eating, helps you lose weight faster. Using these guidelines, weight should come off slowly but surely, without you feeling as though you've put your entire life on hold to accommodate a short-term diet. You might just enjoy yourself too!

53. Are you an emotional eater?

If you find that you often eat without being truly hungry, perhaps it's time to work out what's eating you instead.

On a physical level food is simply fuel for the body, yet our relationship with it is complex. It is a story filled with love and hate.

We read books about food, watch TV programmes about it and pay lots of money to go and eat what someone else cooks for us at restaurants. Over the years we learn habits and behaviours around food that can become inappropriate. These are often rooted in well-meaning parenting. How many of us polish off every last morsel from our plates because mum told us that the poor kids in Africa are starving or that in her generation all they got was bread, potatoes and water? How many of us will have a sweet treat in response to physical or emotional pain, recalling being soothed with confectionery after a childhood fall? We even give foods a moral value – some are bad or sinful, while others are good and virtuous.

It's a rollercoaster of a relationship, which is fine if you don't have any issues with weight. If you do, and food seems to be controlling you, remember you are not alone. Thousands of us are stuck in this kind of one-way relationship. You need to work out why you are feeding your emotions and what you will do about it.

The desire to eat is masterminded in the brain and involves more than twenty different chemical messengers in your body. Eating anything will stave off hunger, but not overwhelming cravings for a particular type of food. If you are hungry you have to eat, but when you want to eat for any other reason, you need to develop coping strategies that don't involve food. It is usually the negative emotions that drive us to munch more – unhappiness, stress and boredom, for instance. Different approaches work for different people; coping tactics could include talking to a friend, doing some physical exercise, confronting a situation at work that is troubling you or scheduling in some 'me time', such as a fun shopping trip, a facial or a game of golf. The point is to identify the where, when and how of your emotionally reactive eating and deal with that rather than continuing the behaviour that's holding your diet to ransom.

> Here's an idea for you...
>
> **Eat more slowly. It takes 20 minutes for 'I'm full' signals to reach the brain. Work with your body by giving it the time it needs to respond.**

Another trigger can be tiredness. Again, you need to get to the root cause. Are you exhausted because of work pressure or certain relationships? Or is it because night after night you go to bed too late? Tiredness lowers your mood, which makes you want to eat and perk yourself up, and it also makes your body send hunger signals because it is looking for more energy to get you through the day.

My downfall is boredom and procrastination. I often look for the answers to life in the fridge. I can also spend a long time seeking inspiration in a slice of cheesecake, especially the lovely crunchy bit at the bottom. The cure is to do something more interesting than the thing you're putting off. Alternatively, set yourself mini goals; for example, if you finish a task in one hour you will then reward yourself (not with food) before tackling the next task.

Defining idea...

'Stressed spelled backwards is desserts. Coincidence? I don't think so.'
ANONYMOUS

You don't have to finish up everything on your plate. You could try ordering or cooking a smaller portion to begin with. If you need to assuage guilty feelings, pledge some money to charity for every kilo of weight you lose.

54. Walk yourself thinner

If you're new to exercise or just don't fancy the gym, here's a simple way to drop some weight. It's easy to start, and requires no special clothing or equipment.

Most of us view walking as a way to get from A to B, and most of the time we'll choose to use the car or bus to get us to where we want to go.

There is a good reason to put one foot in front of the other more often: it's a great way to lose weight and stay slim. It is not expensive, it is not complicated and you can do it anywhere.

Half an hour's walking will burn up an average of about two hundred calories and help to tone up your legs and bottom. There's a catch; you won't see results with a gentle stroll to work or the shops once or twice a week. To make a difference, you'll need to walk at least three times a week, building up to five times a week, for half an hour. You'll need to do it at a reasonable pace, one that warms you up, makes you feel ever so slightly sweaty and leaves you feeling slightly breathless, but not so breathless that you could not hold a conversation. If you walk up some hills or on an incline on the treadmill in the gym, you'll increase the challenge and burn up more calories. It is simple. Here are a few other pointers to bear in mind:

Here's an idea for you...

Make your dairy product intake low-fat. In research, obese volunteers lost 11% of their body weight over six months on a calorie-controlled diet that included three low-fat dairy portions a day.

❀ You don't really need specialist gear for walking, but a decent pair of trainers will support you better than ordinary shoes. If you're planning to take up hill walking or hiking, you will need shoes or boots designed for the purpose, both for comfort and safety.

❀ You'll work harder outdoors than inside on a treadmill as you'll have to cope with changing terrain and wind resistance. This is a good thing as you'll burn calories faster and get extra toning benefits. Regularly spending time outside has been shown to keep you emotionally fit too, boosting feelings of well-being and staving off depression.

❀ Wear something comfortable! It might sound obvious, but if you get wet or too hot, you'll want to give up and go back home. High-tech sports fabrics are designed to draw away sweat and protect you from wind and rain without weighing you down.

❀ When walking, keep your tummy muscles pulled in to work your abdominal muscles and protect your back. Walk tall, avoid slumping and use your natural stride.

❀ If you swing your arms while you walk, you'll increase your heart rate and get more of a workout.

❀ For the best technique, hit the ground with your heel first, roll through your foot and then push off with your toes.

Rather than just randomly walking when you feel like it, try to schedule a daily walk, or at least every other day. That way, you are more likely to stick with it and see results in conjunction with your healthier eating habits, plus you'll be able to monitor your progress.

To reap the greatest benefits, set yourself a plan, say over six weeks, gradually increasing the length of time you walk and its frequency and the speed. For example, in week one you could walk for half an hour three times a week, slowly for 15 minutes and briskly for 15 minutes. Over the next few weeks, you would aim to add another walking session and making each one 5 or 10 minutes longer, and you would walk briskly for 20 or 25 minutes and at a slower pace for the rest of the time. By the end of six weeks, you could be walking for 45 minutes to an hour four or five times a week, and mostly at the faster pace. You'll be seeing a slimmer you in the mirror.

55. Stuck on those last 7lb?

That stubborn half a stone is hard to shift whether you are near the end of your weight loss programme or when 7 lb is all you want to lose to begin with.

It's such a small amount, you'd think it would pack its bags and leave without a whimper. But no, that half a stone always seems to be trickiest to shift.

I don't know why, but what I do know is that to make it go away you have to re-double your efforts and have more tricks up your sleeve than a magician. Make a start with my ten-point checklist.

1. Be honest with yourself about what you're eating. Keep a food diary for a week and note down everything that you consume. You might think you're eating sensibly, but a diary could help you spot the source of those extra kilos.

2. Do you suffer from portion distortion? Even healthy diet-friendly foods such as fruits have calories. If you eat vast amounts of anything and it exceeds your calorie output, you'll put on weight. Match it and you'll maintain that extra half stone.

3. How consistent are you? There are some experts who say as long as you eat sensibly for 80% of the time, you can relax a little for the other 20%. This could translate as making the healthiest choices all week and then eating whatever you like at the weekend. However, there's a big difference between relaxing a little and having a total blow-out every weekend. If you opt for the blow-outs, your week's calorie intake will stack up and your healthful efforts will be for nothing. That dull word 'moderation' springs to mind, but it really is a good concept to live by.

Here's an idea for you...

Limit your food options: too many choices can make you eat more. Research has shown that volunteers ate 44% more than a control group when offered a variety of dishes rather than the same amount of one dish.

4. Be more active, whatever your current levels of activity, to rev up your rate of weight loss. If you are sedentary start walking or swimming, ideally for at least half an hour five times a week. They are both safe effective exercises that, if done regularly, will pay dividends. If you are reasonably active, or even if you think you work out a lot, try to incorporate some new activities into your week to challenge your mind and body. Try working out for longer, more frequently or harder – or all of these together!

5. A simple way to cut a few calories is to cut out carbohydrates with your evening meal. You could try it every night for a couple of weeks, or every other night if that's more convenient. As long as your other meals and snacks are nutrionally balanced with some carbohydrate, you won't be missing out and you'll definitely see a difference of the scales.

6. Have healthy snacks. If you eat regular well-balanced meals and have a few in-between snacks that are also healthy – not a packet of crisps or bar of chocolate – your blood sugar levels will remain stable and you won't ever feel ravenously hungry, so you're less likely to binge or overeat.

7. Spice up your life with a few hot peppers in your lunch or dinner. Pepper eaters have less of an appetite and feel full quicker according to Canadian research. The compound capsaicin that is found in peppers temporarily speeds your metabolism.

8. Include calcium in your diet, as, along with other substances in dairy foods, it seems to help your body burn excess fat faster. In a study, women who ate low fat yoghurt and cheese and drank low fat milk three or four times in a day lost 70% more body fat than women who didn't eat dairy at all.

> *Defining idea...*
>
> **'It's OK to let yourself go, just as long as you let yourself back.'**
> MICK JAGGER

9. Get your rest. Sleep deprivation and a stressed out lifestyle can boost levels of cortisol in your body, which is associated with higher levels of insulin and fat storage. We can interpret the body's cues for sleep as hunger and end up snacking or drinking gallons of coffee to stay awake...and then not be able to sleep.

10. Don't eat when you're not hungry. It seems obvious, but think about it next time you put your food in your mouth. Ask yourself "Am I really hungry?" before that second mouthful.

56. Is stress making you fat?

Any sort of stress can lead to weight gain.

Stress causes your body to release cortisol and this stimulates the fat-storing hormone, insulin. Insulin causes your body to hold on to its fat stores.

And that's if you're eating what you always ate. The trouble is that you might be sabotaging yourself without realising it. When we're stressed there's a tendency to overeat, especially carbohydrates. (It's not called comfort food for nothing.) That's because carbohydrates cause the brain to release serotonin and this

173

is one of the feel-good hormones that raise mood. In a way, it's a form of self-medication.

As is booze. Terrific at relaxing you. Fabulous for adding layers of fat around your waistline.

Stay svelte even when stressed

It's not what you eat it's when you eat it

Researchers discovered that when women ate 'off piste' – whenever they wanted – they ate 120 calories a day more than those women who ate three meals and three snacks a day at set times. Decide on your meal times and stick to them. No grazing.

Make a conscious effort to cut out salt

We can feel more drawn to salty foods when we're stressed. There could be a physiological reason for this. Salt raises blood pressure and that in turn actually raises cortisol levels – which might have been an advantage when we only got stressed once a month but is redundant for the most part now. Wean yourself from adding salt to food and aim to eat no more than 6 g of salt a day in processed food. If the levels are given in sodium then multiply by 2.5 to get the grams of salt.

Get into green tea

Caffeine raises levels of stress hormones and makes you even more stressed. Try green tea. It has about half the caffeine of coffee and a little less than black tea. And

---

Here's an idea for you...

When you're stressed and feel the temptation to reach for comfort food, try sucking on half a teaspoon of honey instead (manuka honey from New Zealand is especially beneficial). Honey causes the brain to release the feel-good hormone serotonin almost immediately. You might find that just that tiny amount will satisfy you and prevent you pigging out on a bar of chocolate or a packet of biscuits which also cause serotonin release but pack a lot more calories.

it's good for your brain and your circulation as well as your waistline. There's another advantage. A recent Japanese study found that people drinking green tea lost 2.4 kg (5.3 lb) after 3 months, while those who drank black tea lost only 1.3 kg (2.9 lb). It's also thought that chemicals called catechins found in green tea trigger weight loss.

> *Defining idea...*
>
> **'My doctor told me to stop having intimate dinners for four, unless there are three other people.'**
> ORSON WELLES

Savour food
Apparently, it takes 20 minutes for our stomach to register that we've started to eat and switch off the feeling of hunger. It's certainly borne out by a small US study of women who were instructed to eat slowly, chewing each mouthful carefully, savouring their food. These women were told to stop eating when their most recent bite didn't taste as good as the first. They lost 3.6 kg (8 lb). In the same period of time, the control group gained 1.3 kg (3 lb). Our bodies know when we've had enough if we slow down long enough to listen.

Relax
One study showed that women who made a conscious effort to relax lost an average of 4.5 kg (10 lb) in 18 months without consciously dieting. The truth is you need actively to relax in order to switch off the stress hormones which could be contributing to weight gain.

Compete with yourself
The best possible antidote to stress *and* weight gain is to exercise. Buy a pedometer from a sports shop. Measure how many steps you take in an average day (most people average around 4,000), and then do a few more steps each day until you reach 10,000.

Special Champneys discounted offer on any stay

CHAMPNEYS
HEALTH RESORTS

Now you can put some of the tips and techniques from this section into practice. Pamper yourself at **Champneys** and enjoy a **15% discount** on any standard booking. You'll soon be on the way to looking and feeling like a true goddess.

Champneys offers a range of premier health resorts across the United Kingdom, all providing exceptional standards in beauty, fitness, nutrition and holistic health. Every resort is designed to be a haven from the stresses of everyday life. They are perfect to visit on your own, with friends or as a couple. Choose from the original **Champneys** Tring in Hertfordshire, the modern Springs in Leicestershire, the enchanting Forest Mere in Hampshire or the cosy Henlow in Bedfordshire. For more information visit www.champneys.com.

For details on how to take advantage of this fantastic offer please go to page 487, where you'll also find information on all the other great deals found throughout Goddess.

Terms and conditions
This offer is valid until 31 December 2007 and is subject to availability. This offer cannot be used in conjunction with any other offer or promotion and applies to new reservations only. The offer can not be applied on or during bank holidays.

Have mind-bending sex and be brilliant in bed
(partner optional)

'There are two kinds of women: those who want power in the world, and those who want power in bed.'

JAQUELINE KENNEDY ONASSIS (Artemis)

We ignore our sexuality at our peril. It's linked to our creativity, drive, self-esteem and personal happiness. When we neglect our sex drive, we close down to a lot more than just sex. You don't need a partner to be a sex goddess, as you'll find out if you read on. And if you might as well be single for all the good being hitched is to nurturing your inner sex goddess, well, there are some ideas here that will help with that, too.

Are you in touch with your inner sex goddess?

How many of the following have you done in the last two weeks?

- [ ] Massaged your skin with scented lotion or oils.
- [ ] Walked into a room thinking, 'God, I look hot'.
- [ ] Slipped on a pair of heels just to admire how they make your legs and feet look.
- [ ] Bathed by candlelight.
- [ ] Flirted with a stranger.
- [ ] Got totally caught up listening to a song that makes you feel 10 years younger.
- [ ] Made the first move.
- [ ] Exposed your body to a fabric that feels sensuous.
- [ ] Danced in the rain.
- [ ] Danced anywhere.
- [ ] Watched a sunset or sunrise.
- [ ] Eaten too much 'bad' food, drunk too much good wine.
- [ ] Got into bed naked.
- [ ] Contemplated buying a sex toy.
- [ ] Laughed so hard, you probably didn't look pretty.
- [ ] Bought a beauty product that you didn't really need.
- [ ] Read or written erotic fiction.
- [ ] Said 'I love you' and really meant it.
- [ ] Said 'I want you' and really meant it.
- [ ] Had a thundering orgasm.

If your score is five or less, reading through idea 65, *Lust – it's all in your mind*, will be a good start.

57. Solo player

One of the best ways to maintain your sex drive is to set regular pleasure sessions – with yourself.

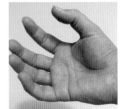

If you know how to turn yourself on, you can point somebody else in the right direction. Some feel a little dirty when they indulge, others frig themselves frantically in front of their partners, but sex researchers estimate that around 80% of women of all ages masturbate, and that means most of us are doing it.

Often in a stable relationship, the frequency of masturbation sessions drops off, but it's crucial to be able to make yourself come satisfactorily – you can separate desire from the whole range of complex feelings you may have about your partner.

Self-pleasure is often rushed or abrupt. This may be a legacy of sneaky sessions under bedcovers from the time when you lived with your parents. In The Illustrated Guide to Extended Massive Orgasm Steve and Vera Bodansky say that most people fail to take the best possible pleasure from masturbation because they 'do it to relieve themselves' rather than for pleasure. I suggest practising alone first so that you can experiment and work without expectations. Of course, you can add this to your lovemaking routine later.

How you prepare to masturbate is important. Some prefer to take advantage of the heat of the moment, or you might want to take a bath first, and perhaps dip into an erotic novel to get some saucy ideas. Don't dive straight in. By the time you undress you should feel pleasantly warm and stimulated.

Experiment with what feels good, tease your nipples, run your hands over the whole pubic region.

Open your legs wide; the sensation of air should feel pleasant. It's best to wriggle your hips now and wait until your labia lips are swollen: this way they will swell, increasing sensitivity and moisture. Dip an exploratory finger just inside your vaginal lips; if you are wet, now is a good time to find out what turns you on. (If you are dry, then use a little lubricant like KY Jelly to get things running smoothly.) Use the dribble of moisture on your finger to run your finger around your vaginal lips. Feel for the outline of the labia majora (outer lips) and contrast this with your inner vagina (labia minora). You might want to experiment with the perineum – the skin between the vagina and the anus. Try circles, figures of eight, and even tapping motions with your hand. What feels good? You should be nice and moist. Perhaps your clitoris is already retracting from its little hood of skin.

Now is a good time to explore your clitoris. Some women prefer to have one finger in the vagina while the other searches for the right spot. Feel for the clitoris and see which way and what type of strokes feel good. The clitoris is bigger than previously thought and has 'arms' which are buried underneath the skin – experiment with the whole area to find your soft spot.

If it doesn't feel sensitive, try using your other hand to pull your skin away from the clitoris. At the same time, look for a second erogenous zone to maximise your pleasure.

Here's an idea for you...

Before masturbating, try pressing your knees together and clenching your bum upwards in rocking movements. This helps to stimulate the flow of blood to the general area – after a few minutes you should notice a difference in your vaginal sensations.

This could be a finger or two in the vagina, massaging your outer lips, or some form of anal stimulation. You might want to use a vibrator, anal butt plug or some other toy to help you along. Continue experimenting until you feel a peak, a point where it no longer feels intense. Rest and repeat.

Don't worry if you feel that the earth hasn't moved – we still haven't worked out how to describe the female orgasm. The urologist J G Bohlen found there was little difference between the perception of orgasm by women and physiological signs of it as measured in the laboratory.

58. Toys R no fuss

Better orgasms mean more effort, and a buzzing vibrator and a drawer full of sex toys help you go at it longer. Will you go on till the end?

Using vibrators is the same as using your hands, except that they're faster and never get tired. You can use them all over your body or dive in and cut to the chase.

Sex toys are great tools for experimenting with, and are ideal for lazy days when you need a helping hand. There's a mind-boggling range: vibrators, dildos, specific toys for the anus and G-spot, clitoral and vulva massagers, as well as novelty and waterproof versions. And a lot of us have them stuffed in our sock drawer, as according to Durex's 2005 Global Sex Survey, more than half of couples use some form of sex aid to spice up their sex life. Don't worry about introducing them into sex games, you can do a lot more with them than just masturbation! Often men enjoy the tickle of a vibrator against their penis or testicles and you can use massagers and vibrators to stimulate each other's erogenous zones into action.

In countries like the UK, vibrators/dildos tend to be cheaper, more traditional models that look like a fake penis, but internationally, the trend is to use better quality materials like silicone and Pyrex glass and to incorporate new technology into the designs. The best thing about this, according to Cathy Winks, author of The G-spot, is that 'Manufacturers are now producing insertable vibrators and dildos that are curved to match the natural shape of the vagina and rectum'. Some men might feel intimidated by a huge dong-shaped dildo, but they're less likely to be threatened by products which don't even look like a sex aid. The Fresh Vibes range from www.funfactory.de have an animal design incorporated into their length. In an interview, spokesperson Jill-Evelyn Hellwig explained this: 'Many of our customers are women with children and they need something that's not going to be problematic if their children come across it.'

Here's an idea for you...

Masturbate with more than one sex toy. You can use a dildo/vibrator in your vagina and combine this with a vibrator tickling your clitoris (or Vielle's finger gloves). If you really want to push the boat out, you can use an anal plug as well. You stand more chance of having better orgasms if you have more than one area being stimulated.

You do need to experiment to find out what materials and shapes appeal to you.

If you don't feel comfortable about self-insertion, try a clitoral massager like the Fun Factory Layaspot which simply sits over your pubic bone and hums away, it has different speeds and programmes to vary the tempo. You can also keep it in place whilst you have sex with your partner (he'll share a bit of the thrill too).

The first time you insert a sex toy, don't feel a pressure to put it all in. You're more sensitive on the outer third of your vagina, so some women like to just nudge and stimulate this area. If your partner is using a toy on you, he can start by performing cunnilingus and then inserting a finger or two until you're ready, but always go slow and insert just a little. The time for shoving it in is when you're screaming with pleasure!

Specially curved toys also make it easier to find your G-spot. It's easier to turn off your vibrator, or use a dildo to find it first (generally the other end will be designed to tickle your clitoris to give you double stimulation). G-toys are the most problematic to fit as the length of women's vaginas varies. There are a lot of toys out there and you need to experiment to find out what works for you. Really every woman should have lots of different sex toys for different reasons, so start adding these to your Christmas list and build your own personal collection!

59. Giving it some

It feels good to give pleasure to your partner. You want to hear those moans. Here's how to drive your man wild.

Knowing you are a good lover gives you confidence, and making him see stars is an incentive for him to make an extra special effort getting you off!

Men find it easier to have an orgasm than women, but because their goal is ejaculation they often miss out on getting their full quota of sensual pleasure. In their Illustrated Guide to Extended Massive Orgasm Steve and Vera Bodansky reckon that 'They miss probably 80% of each stroke', so encourage him to slow down. Take a more active role so that he can take a back seat and enjoy himself more.

Just kissing him is sexier if you play with his lower lip. Suck it into your mouth and run your tongue down to his chin, it should send a shock wave he'll feel in his penis. The neck is also a known erogenous zone, particularly the area under the Adam's apple. Men also respond well to massage but before you get down to it search for other hot spots. Does he like having his nipples touched? Use your hands, tongue and a hot mouth to give him the once-over.

Don't forget to talk dirty to him, and let him see as much of your body as possible. Men are much more receptive to sight and smell, so if you want to give him a handjob, do it so he can see your excited vagina. It's less work if you use lubricant on your hands – his penis will automatically bump up and down, so use pressure that

Here's an idea for you...

Don't just mount him, do a reverse girl on top position so he can get a good look at you. Just before he climaxes, reach for his ankles and feel for his pressure points just below his ankle bones and press them as he comes. It'll feel electric!

feels good for him. The most sensitive part of the penis is the frenulum (where the head meets the shaft) so stimulate this extra well. One technique is to keep one hand on the penis at all times stroking its head (preferably slick with lube) while your other hand gives long strokes to the rest of his penis. You can add twists, move both hands differently or use one hand to nudge his perineum. Men like to have their testicles played with, and any time you stimulate multiple areas it boosts his arousal.

Men love oral sex. To increase his pleasure tie your hair back so he can see you doing it; even better, do it on your knees so that he can cop an eyeful of your breasts and extended neck. Brush your lips against his head, tickle him with your tongue and vary the sucking strokes. Some men like to masturbate the penis with their hand while you suck the top; encourage him to do whatever feels good. If you're confident with fellatio, you could try to deep throat him. To do this you need to be able to control your gag reflex which is easier to do with your neck straight. If you're not sure what to do, get him to move your head in the right rhythm.

During sex, just as he should be looking to stimulate your clitoris, look for his hot spots. Kneading the testicles works well, particularly the seam of it which contains lots of nerve endings. Some men can orgasm just from prostate stimulation, the male G-spot, which is just inside the anus. You could probe this with a finger or insert a well-greased butt-plug, but check first if he's game. Prostate orgasms feel different and are more of a full body experience, so stimulating this can give him a completely new feeling.
The ultimate in female power is to use a strap-on on him. In Brief Encounters Emily Dubberley reckons: 'About 30% of strap-ons sold by sex shops go to straight couples', so

it's not uncommon.

Use lots of lubricant and go slowly.

It could be that he only wants to take part of it, or even just experience the psychological thrill of your 'penis' tickling his nether regions.

Experiment with what works for both of you. Relax and slow down; his orgasm is better if it is delayed, so tease him and take him to the brink a few times, he'll appreciate the difference!

> Defining idea...
>
> **'Remember that in the beginning: An erection is like a dog with a concussion; it's just as likely to roll over and play dead as it is to come when you call.'**
> SHARYN WOLF, couples therapist

60. Be contrary

Put your love life in reverse gear. If you avoid sex, chase it. If there's a position you love, don't do it. Courting frustration could be just the trip you need to drive you over the edge.

Being intimate is a double-edged sword. Sometimes it brings you too close and you need to be a bit more sexually ruthless to enjoy getting off. Over time it's almost inevitable for a couple's sex life to decrease in frequency. Often we're simply unrealistic about our sexual expectations because our culture is saturated with images of sex and romantic longing. We feel like we should want more, and this unfocused yearning can lead to people seeking out affairs. It's possible to be in an endless cycle of falling in love, getting disillusioned, meeting someone else and repeating the whole cycle; Elizabeth Taylor once described herself as 'addicted to love'.

In reality the thing we have to deal with most when we grapple with sexual problems is our own psyche. During sex we have to open ourselves up to our vulnerabilities. Psychotherapist Dr Michael Bader says in Arousal: The Secret Logic of Sexual Fantasies: 'We go to bed naked in more ways than one.' We all carry insecurities with us that have been with us from childhood, and at first a new sexual liaison gives us a chance to work against this. If a woman has grown up feeling physically inferior to her beautiful mother, she might initially take refuge in a relationship with an especially attractive man. However, over time, her old insecurities will emerge and return to plague her, and this is why so many couples start to experience sexual problems after the 'honeymoon period' which were not at first apparent.

Some couples say they have less sex but it's more intimate; however, this has its own problems. The more intimate you become, the more you're aware of your partner's frailties. Dr Bader also says: 'As couples get to know each other, their deeper awareness of each other's vulnerabilities can become their undoing. The other's inhibitions and the shame upon which they rest begin to wear down spontaneity and passion. We are just too close, too identified with our inhibited partner, to escape the experience.' It's important for you to have a certain degree of sexual ruthlessness and sometimes we all need some kind of emotional distance (via fantasy or physical space) in order to be able to switch off and concentrate on our own sexual needs.

If your sex life is nothing to write home about, try deliberately avoiding it for a while. If something's on tap you take it for granted. See how long you can go without having sex together. It's a good idea not to stop all physical activity: you could try masturbating separately and telling each other all about it when you do get together. The idea is to get you hot, but you can still agree whether to postpone sex or not – and maybe tomorrow when you eventually succumb to passion it'll be even better. Sometimes being frustrated, that feeling of suppressed longing, leads to the best sex of all so it's worth waiting until you just can't hold back.

To objectify your partner a little, you could also try playing around with sexual fantasy. Get him to dress up a little differently or speak to you in bed in a different voice. You're trying to think of him erotically as a means to give you great sex, rather than your soulmate with lots of problems he wants to talk over.

Over time we can desexualise our partners, so now's the time to inject some throbbing desire into the proceedings. It could be that he's treating you gently when you really want to be ravaged, so try talking dirty and see if this makes it easier for you to get excited. Force yourself to expose your throbbing desires. That's it – get low and dirty and sex up your relationship.

Here's an idea for you...

Ask your partner to describe your contribution to your lovemaking; make a careful note of what he says, then for a limited time reverse this behaviour. If he normally initiates sex, you do it for a change. You'll have sex sessions using completely different methods and techniques to the ones you're used to, and perhaps you'll be pleasantly surprised!

61. The power of lovely lingerie

Underwear. It's crucial. Get it right and you feel great. It's an essential part of being incredibly sexy.

It boosts your confidence and helps you look marvellous in and out of your clothes. What's not to love?

When I first travelled to the continent I was amazed at all the little underwear shops selling smalls at what I thought were extortionate prices. I reasoned that there was nothing wrong with a pack of five knickers for the price of one bra-strap in some chichi shop. Up to a point I was right. There are days when those cotton no-frills knickers work well. But what is truly different about your average French woman, is that she will wear sexy matching bra and knickers every day. And she is prepared to spend around £60 on each ensemble.

Now that I live in France I have gone very French in my attitude towards underwear. My bra and knicker drawers are stuffed full of matching ensembles. And oddly enough, once I started on this gig, I found it hard to go back to the five-packs. There's something empowering about matching top and bottom and for this reason you should seriously consider buying at least two pairs of knickers with each bra. To make sure you don't suffer from the dreaded VPL under trousers always make at least one of these pairs a g-string, or try out French knickers or boxer shorts for girls – no VPL and damn sexy!

Sex appeal has a lot to do with confidence and there is nothing like good underwear to enhance your body shape and make you feel more attractive. For the flatter-chested among us, there is no more comforting moment than pulling a T-shirt over a new Wonderbra and seeing our body shapes totally transformed. For larger ladies, a good well-fitting bra is even more essential. If you want to minimise your bust under business suits, get measured by an expert to find out your correct cup size – you will lose 10lbs, I swear, immediately you put on the right fitting bra. And if you want to emphasise your cleavage, a right fitting bra does this stupendously well, besides being much more comfortable.

Here's an idea for you...

This expensive underwear is all very well, but a pain to hand wash. I take mine into the shower with me and wash it there, which is much easier. It also means you don't end up with that awful grey shade of white as your smalls get washed on a 60 degree cycle with all the wrong colours. Treat it well, and it will last much longer.

A sexy g-string can work wonders for your buttocks. Some people find them incredibly uncomfortable – I did to begin with – but once you get used to them you will hardly ever wear ordinary knickers again.

If you're wearing the right underwear, you feel like you can take on the world. It makes you feel so much more confident. You walk into a business meeting and although the others can't see what you've got on underneath your suit, you know, and it gives you a sense of superiority. I spoke to Chantal Thomass, France's leading underwear designer, on this subject. 'Lingerie is fundamental to the way a woman feels,' she says, 'if your underwear isn't right, nothing else works.' A friend of mine says it determines her whole mood for the day: 'It's the first thing I put on and it puts me in a good or bad mood,' she says. 'I have a very intimate relationship with my lingerie, after all it is the thing I put on next to my skin.'

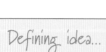

Defining idea...

'A lady is one who never shows her underwear unintentionally.'
LILLIAN DAY, American author

As we all know, for whatever reason, men adore stockings and suspenders. Just about every man I know is totally gone on them. 'I don't know what it is about them,' says one. 'They just drive me wild. Maybe it's because all the Playboy models I lusted over in my youth wore them.' Our job here is not to analyse, just wear them. Classic black suspender belts are the best but red can be good for a special occasion, adding an extra sex-vixen allure. The great thing about kinky or sexy underwear is that it enhances your sex drive as well as your partner's. You're hardly going to sit around feeling like a drudge in a pair of red crotchless knickers!

62. Enduring allure

It's not difficult to feel sexy at the beginning of a relationship. That first kiss is one of the most memorable things ever. Just the touch of your lover's hand will give you goose bumps.

But that sort of intensity doesn't last forever. Sadly it goes with time and with familiarity. What can you do to rekindle it?

I once read a story about a couple who had been together for years and got bored with one another. One night they both went to a party. For some reason she ended up naked in the host's bedroom. The lights were out, he came in and got into bed with her. They had fabulous sex and each only realised afterwards that they had slept with their spouse. Slightly far-fetched but what it highlights is the fact that great sex needn't stop. It's all in the mind. These people hadn't had sex with each other for months. Because each thought he or she was with someone else, that it was forbidden, they had a great time.

So, you need to get the fact that you are an old boring married couple out of your mind and start thinking about all the things that drove you wild about each other. You are still the same people, if a little older and more familiar – you just need to rediscover each other.

Here's an idea for you...

One evening sit down and reminisce. Go through your first date, what you wore, what you did, where you had sex. Talk about all the things that first attracted you to each other. Was it the way he talked, something he said? Was it a certain skirt she wore, the way she flicked her hair? This should bring back happy memories and rekindle lustful thoughts.

If you are married or living with someone and have children, finding the time to rediscover each other is not always easy. If you possibly can then go away together alone at least once every three months or so. It's not just the fact of being alone that's important, it's being away from all the chores and worries of home. It's hard to feel sexy when all you can talk about is a burst pipe, ill children and unpaid bills. You work all day, run the house, and collapse into bed exhausted at night. Not much time for sex. Try to think of sex as a priority and make time for it. Forget washing up, ironing or watching hours of television in the evening: slip into some sexy underwear and seduce your husband instead. What could be more important than that?

There are lots of little ways to make your everyday life sexier. Try to add spark to your life by thinking of each day as a day filled with sexy opportunities. Broaden your horizons: for example, don't just think of the bathroom as a place to shave but a place to rekindle your romance.

'Some people ask the secret of our long marriage. We take time to go to a restaurant two times a week. A little candlelit dinner, music and dancing. She goes Tuesdays, I go Fridays.'
HENRY YOUNGMAN, American comedian

Being sexy is of course not just about looking good. Some friends of mine recently got divorced. The husband is a workaholic with his own business while the wife didn't work. 'I just lost respect for her,' he told me. 'I couldn't bear to see her wasting time and achieving nothing. She seemed to have no ambition whatsoever, no respect for herself or her own status. In the end she also had nothing to talk about, apart from what to eat or what the kids had done at school.' He sounds harsh but I see his point. He didn't care that his wife didn't work, but he did care that she never used her mind. There are those among us who want nothing more than the luxury of staying at home and raising our children, which is great as long as you don't forget that when you got married you were an interesting person in your own right and you need to ensure you stay that way.

63. Spice up your life

Time to reinvigorate yourself with something completely different.

You have already taken an important first step by buying this book. It is jam-packed full of tips on how to improve your sexiness and life. Another major step is to make routine a thing of the past.

Think differently to the pack. Be your own person and do your own thing. I'm not suggesting you go awol, but I am suggesting you use a little imagination to spice up your everyday life and increase your sexy image. Be more aware of your surroundings, look for the positive in the humdrum and create sexy situations where you normally wouldn't.

For example, your alarm goes off at 7am, you get up, have a shower, eat something, trudge down to the underground or the train in the pouring rain and go to work. This happens most days. However, some days, something different will break the monotony: a busker playing your favourite song, a story in the newspaper that makes you laugh, a brief glance from a fellow-commuter that sets something off in the depths of your half-asleep psyche. But to notice these things you have to be receptive and ready for them.

Try to treat each day as an adventure. It's a terrible old cliché but live each day as if it were your last. Realistically you can't do that or you would never go to work but you get my drift? Instead of thinking 'God this is dreadful, I hate this commute' think 'I wonder what or who is waiting around the corner' or even if you're not so optimistic that anything remotely exciting awaits you on the 7.47 take something exciting with you like a novel full of steamy sex and adventure. Try reading Dangerous Liaisons or The Sexual Life of Catherine M on the train – it will at least get the imagination going of any commuter reading over your shoulder.

In terms of your sex life and your relationship, you should adopt the same approach. 'If there is a choice of what to do at the weekend, always go for the most

> Here's an idea for you...
>
> **Surprise him by offering to wash his car, wearing a short skirt and stockings and suspenders. The neighbours will be eternally grateful too. Use your imagination to surprise people, including yourself!**

Defining idea...

'Variety is the spice of life.'
Late 18th century proverb

eccentric one,' says a male friend of mine who has an above average success rate with members of the opposite sex. 'I find things like ice skating, a sandwich on the Millennium Wheel or a picnic in a boat on the Serpentine work better than a classic dinner out.'

Romance is something that often goes out of a relationship early on; try to keep it alive by making an effort to do things a bit differently. Think about how much it meant at the beginning that your partner had even agreed to go on a date with you. Try to recapture that feeling and hold on to it; at least for a night once in a while. Increase the sexiness and excitement of being together by doing something you don't normally do. Get on a bargain flight to a city you've never visited, spend all day in bed feeding each other strawberries or do something you've always wanted to do but have never dared try, be it bungee-jumping or dressing up in a nurse's uniform.

If you're not in a regular relationship then try to break out of your own pattern once in a while too. If you normally spend Saturday afternoons watching the football, get off the sofa and go to a museum for once. If you're single, it's an even better idea. 'Museums are a perfect pulling ground,' a 21-year-old male friend tells me. 'They're the one place girls often go alone and you can easily strike up a conversation by asking what they think of a particular painting. And they love the fact that you're there at all, it immediately says you're the sensitive, arty type.'

64. Getting it right

How do you get your lover to love you the way you want to be loved?

Just because you've been together forever, doesn't mean you press each other's buttons absolutely perfectly. Yet the man or woman who can tell their lover that they want to be touched differently from the way they've been touched a million times before is pretty rare.

There are ways to ask without embarrassing yourself and mortifying your lover. Here's how to get your lover to do something differently when they think they've been getting it right for years.

The WRONG way

Using phrases starting with 'Why don't you…', 'You never…' or 'That doesn't…' will cause offence and your partner will get defensive. Moreover, whining is deeply unattractive.

The RIGHT way

Step 1: Praise, praise, praise – your new resolution
From now on, you're going to be an appreciative lover. You're going to praise your lover's performance every chance you get and using every way you can think of. This will create a 'win–win' situation. Be especially appreciative during sex. Do it

with body language. Do it loudly. Spell it out: 'I love everything you do in bed', 'You're just so sexy', 'No one's ever done that to me the way that you do'. They should finish every session assured that you're blissfully happy.

If you're not an appreciative lover, make this your modus operandi from now on. For one thing, this technique will backfire spectacularly on you if it stops as soon as you get what you want – it will look like a cynical ploy. (That's because it will be a cynical ploy.) So wise up, there's nothing to be ashamed of in creating confidence in your lover. Their 'win' is that you're creating an atmosphere where they can't fail. They won't fear trying something different if they don't feel that your happiness is dependent on it. If they get it wrong or if they don't want to go through with it, they've nothing to lose because they know just how much you value them. Your 'win' is that besides being a lovely person you're also gearing them up for moving your sex life on to greater heights.

Step 2: Focus on the positive

Once you've created a climate of confidence, you can modify their technique by focusing on the positive. For instance, 'I love the way you do that, especially when you go slowly/quickly/hang off the bedside table while you're doing it.' The other great bonus of this approach is that within reason it doesn't matter if it's a complete lie. For example, your lover may go down on you with the speed of a rotodriver, but if you tell him how lovely it is when his mouth goes really slowly he'll probably believe you. He'll almost certainly start doing it slowly too. The payoff for you is that you'll get more of what you want.

This clearly can be overdone. He's obviously going to get suspicious if he never hangs off the edge of the bedside table while doing it yet you can't stop talking it up. Use discretion and be specific if possible. And you really need to use your hands to gently direct the action the way you want it.

Step 3: Suggest how they could change
Now you can suggest doing it differently. This has to be done with grace and it has to be done lightly, not as if your entire sexual happiness depends on it (remember they can't fail). Say that you've read about something you'd like to try in a book and ask if they would oblige....

Defining idea...

'The secret to telling someone they're the worst lover you've ever had, is...not to. Focus on what you want, not what you don't...Start by focusing on yourself, not your partner's [faults]. Make a list of ten things you want more of in bed, ten things you want less of, and ten new things you'd like to try. You have to know what you want in bed in order to get it.'
TRACEY COX, Supersex

65. Lust – it's all in your mind

Not as interested as you used to be? The easiest way out of a rut is to get sex on the brain – literally.

Researching this book has thrown up some surprises for me and one of them has been the effect on my own libido.

Always an 'average' on the sex-o-meter – in other words, I'm not the girl most likely to suggest a love-in with the neighbours – thinking, reading and talking about sex for three months has had an extraordinary effect on my sexual response. I don't mean that I've been tempted to give swinging a try, but having sex on the brain has definitely increased my desire for sex and I'll now advise people that the simplest way to ensure you have (and want) more sex is to think about it more regularly.

As time goes on, we become subsumed in the minutiae of our lives – the fetching, carrying, hunting, gathering. But as sex writer Ann Hooper says, 'You can try every sex position you can think of, including dangling from the ceiling, but if you don't bring your fertile brain into play, you may not manage to become aroused.'

The secret is to fantasise. But first you'll have to rethink your idea of what sexual fantasy means.

When did you consistently have the best sex you've ever had? Most of us would say in the first few months of getting it on with a new partner, hopefully the partner we're still with. Why? New love of course, or new lust at the very least. The principal reason that the sex at the beginning of a relationship is so outstanding is that it's fantasy-fuelled. New lovers spend just about every minute they're not in bed with their lover fantasising about their lover. Their minds are constantly running over what they got up to the night before and what they'd like to be doing next time they meet. They walk around in a fug of erotic fantasy. And this fuels their sexual encounters. The second they see their lover they're primed and ready to go.

> *Here's an idea for you...*
>
> **Read sexy romance novels or soft porn. Listen to music that makes you feel sexual – whatever it is, if it rocks your boat, play it loud and play it often.**

We tend to think it's the person that fuels our desperation for sex, but physiologically it's got just as much to do with the mind being constantly focused on doing the deed and the signals this sends to our body. So, if you've wistfully looked back on the way you used to feel about each other and if you firmly believe that you can't reconstruct that lust, try thinking about sex more. Any thoughts you have – no matter how fleeting – count. Think about sex during the day, and when the chance to have sex turns up you're far more likely to be enthusiastic. Just a touch will get the juices flowing. On the other hand, if nary a sexual thought has fluttered across your mind during the day, your lover is going to have an uphill and probably futile struggle to get you to even try.

> *Here's an idea for you...*
>
> **Count the number of people you meet in a day who actively appeal to you. Seek to get aroused by other people, but obviously don't act on it. That old chestnut about taking the energy back to stoke the home fires isn't an old chestnut for nothing.**

Counsellor Sarah Litvinoff says, 'Sex therapists often find that women who claim never to have been sexually interested or who have gone off sex, never think sexual thoughts. Many people narrowly define sexual fantasies as the mini-pornographic scenes you play out in your head, which might include, say, bondage or lesbian images, that are a mental turn-on, but which you wouldn't necessarily enjoy enacting for real. But, in fact, any sexual thought is sexual fantasy.' And any sort of sexual thought gets the job done.

Let your mind wander, look for the lascivious and feel the throb of sex that is lying beneath the layers of our sophisticated lifestyle. Find stimulation in your daily routine and you'll find yourself overspilling with erotic charge, which will translate into action. You will initiate sex and respond to your partner in a different way sexually. You'll be gagging for it.

Begin to make a habit of daydreaming about sex. First thing when you wake up in the morning or last thing before you go to sleep, think a dirty thought or two. When you're commuting, let the last time you made love run through your mind. As you're queuing or waiting for your train, relive your sexual greatest hits. Remember that every time sex flits across your mind it's a fantasy, and that those who fantasise most have the best sex lives.

NB Like faith healing, you don't have to believe in this for it to work.

66. Surprise!

Isn't it time you got in touch with your creative side?

Laura Corn, author of '101 Nights of Grrreat Sex', has based her considerable best-selling success on one simple concept: the importance of the surprise factor. Each of her 101 suggestions depends on the fact that your partner doesn't have a clue what sexual delight you're planning.

It's a clever gimmick and it works. Surprise your lover sexually every week for a year and you can bet your bootee you won't be collecting any 'boring in bed' prizes. Encouraging the element of surprise in your sex life will keep you young and playful, keep you feeling cherished and appreciated and keep your lover crazy for you.

A little bit of effort to surprise your lover with a new technique, seduction, outfit or behaviour reaps huge improvements. As long as it's something unexpected, the surprise can be whatever you like. It can be filthy, funny, sweet and romantic or it can be more embarrassing than karaoke night down your local.

Why surprise works

Some of your surprises will be easy to organise. Some will take more planning. You might spend an hour (or more) setting up a gorgeous seduction for your mate, which is a lot I grant you, but the end result (and this is no exaggeration) will be burned into the hard drive of their memory for the rest of their life. Great sex has that sort of effect on us.

But even more unforgettable for your mate than the great sex you'll enjoy is how loved they'll feel. Men, just as much as women (in fact, if the psychologists are to be believed, even more than women), are delighted by the proof that someone wants them so much that they'll put thought and effort into their seduction. All of us love to feel special.

> *Here's an idea for you...*
>
> **Do something slightly differen** **every time you make love.** **Throw in an element of surpris** **Mixing it up will become secon** **nature after a few weeks and** **the payoff will make it** **worthwhile..**

What does it take for it to work?

It takes both of you to commit to the idea. You will only want to put effort into thrilling your partner if you feel they're going to make the same effort for you.

I recommend Laura Corn's book (mentioned above) because she gives you lots of ideas and she gives you structure. The surprise element can't be spontaneous, at least not at first. If we don't plan, we just get lazy and don't bother. You're aiming to give your lover a 'guaranteed surprise', if you see what I mean. In other words, although they'll be able to look forward to being surprised, they won't know what they're looking forward to.

If you don't want to spring for Corn's book, then in the immortal words of Fleetwood Mac, 'Go your own way.' Or simply customise some of the following suggestions to get the ball rolling:

For her

❀ He's in the shower. Wait until it's good and steamy in there and then slip in beside him wearing your flimsiest, sheerest underwear. If there's one thing more likely to turn him on than you naked, it's wet, clinging wisps of material. (Blokes could try this, too, but it has to be silk boxers – soggy, cotton Y-fronts just don't cut it.)

❀ On your next date, you can keep your coat on. Well, you don't want the whole restaurant to know you're naked underneath. Just him.

For him

❀ Buy her half a case of her favourite wine (a dozen bottles is classier, but might be too much of a demand on your imagination). Around the neck of each, place a sealed envelope containing details of where and when you're going to drink it together. These are IOUs of pleasure. Let your imagination run riot.

❀ One night when you're getting amorous in a lovey-dovey sort of way, suddenly flip personality – change the whole atmosphere. From Dr Jekyll to Mr Hyde. Stop smiling. Get mean. Overcome her. Tie her wrists to the headboard and blindfold her. Now you can do whatever you like, but if you want to give her a night to remember (and especially if she's still really pissed off with you), go down on her until she stops cursing and starts begging.

Defining idea...

'We want to know how to turn our mates on. We want them to know what turns us on. We'd like more variety...more foreplay...more surprises...more interest...new tricks...and, once in a while, somebody else should do all the work!'
LAURA CORN

❀ Spend an hour or so pleasuring her sensually, such as oral sex, washing her hair, painting her toenails, applying body lotion to every inch of her skin or holding her and stroking her hair until she falls asleep. Don't allow her to do a thing for you in return.

67. Think kink

Remember: we don't always get what we want. But we can ask.

Your mission, should you choose to accept it, is to ask your partner to try something you're convinced has never occurred to them. This idea is a generic 'how to' on asking for this something, be it group sex, dogging, fisting, voting nationalist or whatever.

Stating the obvious

If you want to try something out of the norm, then you'll have to communicate it to your lover either verbally or physically.

1. Butter them up first by faking a midlife crisis. Tell them you're worried that they'll leave you – couples are splitting up everywhere (give examples). Do this in a light-hearted way over a bottle of wine or in a worried way after faking moodiness that has them wondering what's wrong. I recommend the former,

but hey, it's your relationship. Tell them that although your love life is fine, you feel you've been complacent and you don't want them to get bored. Modify this basic script depending on your lover's gullibility levels but you get the basic idea – you make it your problem, not theirs. And then you make some changes to your love life.

2. Once you've mixed it up a little and you're regularly trying new things, suggest a modest first step on the way to what you want. If you want them to whip you with a cat of nine tails, then suggesting you experiment with a little mild pain via dripping candle wax is a good start.

3. Work up to the real deal. Be patient. Six months' patient if necessary.

Here's an idea for you...

If you're still shy of asking for what you really want, remember that the taboo of today is the norm of tomorrow. Rejoice in the thought of being a sexual pioneer, and pity all those blokes who went through the fifties longing for a blowjob but who were too afraid to ask in case they were thought to be perverts.

Never forget

The secret in persuading your lover to do something kinky that you want and they aren't particularly interested in is to make it clear that it's them doing the kinky thing that you're interested in, not the kinky thing itself. Use imagination, tact and flattery to find a way to make this obvious.

Defining idea...

'[Kinky sex] is not about giving up "normal" sex, adopting a new "lifestyle", joining a "community" or becoming a "freak". It's about making sex hotter. It's about giving voice to your darker, maybe even slightly disturbing desires by exploring new sensations, playing make-believe and other mind games. It's about making kink a part of your everyday sex life...OK maybe just your weekend and holiday sex life.'
EM and LO, sex gurus on nerve.com and authors of The Big Bang

Right: 'Your bum looks amazing in rubber.'
Wrong: 'All I can think of is Michelle Pfeiffer in that Cat Woman outfit.'

Remember that the secret is always to make your lover feel special and to convince them how special they are to you. You'd be quite amazed at the things that some people can persuade others to do with this terribly simple strategy. But I've seen the police reports.

How not to do it

I received a letter once from a man who couldn't understand why his new girlfriend wouldn't join him and his five best friends naked in a sauna for a beer. It turned him on so much and his ex-wife hadn't had a problem with it. Letting his mates leer at her and compare her with his previous bird must have been an alluring prospect for the new girlfriend! He was clearly not as interested in women per se as in their willingness to get naked in front of his mates. Something told me that here was a man with a lot of disappointment ahead of him.

The last word: Most sex lives benefit from including a few of the minor elements from some of the major fetishes. So, give it a go and if it's not you, don't try it again.

68. Building bridges

How can a woman come just like a man?

Women – if you could come as easily as your man, wouldn't you want to have sex more often? Men – if she came as easily as you did, wouldn't you be grateful?

A ton of foreplay is, of course, vital. Oral sex is, of course, important. Candlelit dinners, lots of chat and making an effort for each other are critical for a long-standing, ever-loving relationship. But sometimes it's Monday night, you have an early start in the morning, you've had a long hard day and you just want for both of you to come with the minimum of effort.

As the Hite Report – the most exhaustive description of female sexuality available – tells us, the great majority of women need clitoral stimulation with either hand or vibrator if they're going to come during penetrative sex. Still the ideal persists that we should all be multiorgasmic by penile insertion. Frankly, it's rubbish. Thrusting the penis into the vagina is anatomically the same thing as pulling on a man's balls. You could make a man come eventually by this method – every tug would move the skin on the upper tip of the penis so eventually he might get enough stimulation – but boy, would it take a while. And for some men it would never work. The only hope for the vast majority of women is to get used to coming during penile penetration through clitoral stimulation.

Here's an idea for you...

Contract your vaginal muscles (PC muscles) as you approach orgasm. This will help bring on your orgasm and will also help you when you stop clitoral stimulation. Eventually, the contractions may be enough to power you into orgasm with no further clitoral stimulation. A few dirty words whispered in your ear won't hurt.

According to the irresistibly direct D. Claire Hutchins in her almost as irresistibly titled 5 Minutes to Orgasm: Every Time You Make Love, 'Millions of women enjoy orgasm during intercourse by using additional stimulation of the clitoris. The question should not be is this wrong? Can this be fixed? The question should be, why do we keep asking such a stupid question in the first place? Why resort to everything in the book, from scented candles and bubble baths, extensive analysis and sex therapy to make orgasm happen any other way. Ladies – let's move on. If the thought of touching yourself in front of your partner scares you, you'll have to get over it.'

Bravo D. Claire Hutchins. However, women and men do persist in feeling that they'd like to come from the same thrusting stimulation. And there is a way to do it: bridging. And what you're building is a 'bridge' between clitoral and penile stimulation. The bridge manoeuvre means simply using clitoral stimulation – which most women need to orgasm – to bring the woman to the very edge of coming, then desisting and the woman coming following a few thrusts more from the man. This is a three-step process that anyone can learn, although it takes practice. Personally speaking, if you get to step two and come that way, you'll still be in a good place.

Step 1: Adopt the position

Find a position that allows maximum clitoral stimulation. It can be the missionary position or any other as long as your hand stimulates your clitoris. Best is the big mama of quick female orgasm: you straddle your partner, pull aside your labia and lean forward so that your clitoris rubs directly against his pelvic bone or sit upright so that you can masturbate your clitoris while on top of him.

Step 2: Bring your mind into play

You're on top (or underneath, or hanging off the ceiling pendant, whatever rocks your world), writhing about, touching yourself. Feel yourself getting closer to orgasm? No? OK, time to bring fantasy into the act. With fantasy, you stop worrying about your stomach wobbling, the kids' lost homework, whether he's getting bored or not or whether you are. With fantasy, you concentrate on sex. With fantasy, you're the star of the show, the focus of the action – and you're gorgeous. Or as American humorist Nora Ephron put it, 'In my fantasy, no one loves me for my mind.' Concentrate on achieving your orgasm. Shut your eyes. Forget about your bloke if necessary. Don't stop until you come, if you want to bridge…

Step 3: Bridging

Take yourself to the very edge of orgasm and then stop the clitoral stimulation. Bring yourself off by grinding yourself against his body. This is partly a mental thing. When you believe you're going to come through penetration only, it's more likely that you will.

Defining idea…

'Women can't alter the physiology in order to conform to what is expected of us, so we adopt countless strategies to reconcile reality with expectations, including faking orgasm. But who loses? Women do, and so do men. Instead of faking it, let's just accept our bodies and move on. Let's adjust.'
D. CLAIRE HUTCHINS, American writer

69. Easy routes to a faster orgasm

Quicker, harder, faster? How to come more easily.

Tweaking your usual lovemaking pattern can improve your sex
life with a minimal amount of effort. We could have called this
chapter 'How to have a simultaneous orgasm', but we've always
thought that an overrated pastime. However, if you insist....

Squeezing

When you orgasm, your pubococcygeal (PC) muscles in the vagina contract rapidly.
Tighten your PC muscles as he withdraws, and relax them as he enters. It'll take a bit of
practice but this is a recommendation from the queen of the female orgasm, Betty
Dodson, who through her workshops and books has taught thousands of women how
to come, and how to come better. Squeezing will jump-start your own orgasmic
contractions.

Pressing

Downward pressure on your pubic area before orgasm can increase the intensity of
stimulation. Experiment with pressing down with your hand on your stomach just
above your pubic bone while masturbating or using a vibrator. Then try this during
intercourse. Another technique is to 'bear down'. This is pushing out with your PC

muscles, which may help force your G-spot closer to your vaginal opening so it's likelier to get indirect stimulation from his penis.

Stretching

Stretching your legs flat on the bed and bringing them together while in the missionary position will increase clitoral stimulation. It works even better when you're on top. Slide your thighs down so they are over his thighs rather than his hips. Arch your back so you're bending backwards. Forming an arc means you'll be putting maximum pressure on the clitoral area. Just be careful you don't bend his penis back too far – you have all the control here and being a gent he might not want to interrupt your obvious pleasure to tell you that you're in imminent danger of breaking it off.

It's also worth experimenting with other positions where you are on top and your feet are stretched down towards his feet. These tend to increase clitoral stimulation.

Hanging

Hang your head over the edge of the bed when you're having sex. The rush of blood to the brain increases sensations.

Here's an idea for you...

To increase your chances of simultaneous orgasm, let your partner know how excited you are and encourage the same feedback from him. If you want to minimise prosaic chat, whisper a number to your mate to let him know exactly where on a scale of 1 to 10 you are in terms of getting your rocks off. He can do the same.

Sexy special online offer with LoveHoney.co.uk

Get in touch with your inner sex goddess with help from **LoveHoney.co.uk**. When you spend £40 or more you'll get £10 off.

The **LoveHoney.co.uk** web site offers the UK's widest range of adult toys, lingerie, erotic books, romantic gifts and naughty games. **LoveHoney** is home to the Rabbit vibrator (as seen on *Sex and the City*) and an exclusive range of products produced in association with TV sex expert Tracey Cox, presenter of *The Sex Inspectors*. **LoveHoney** is also home to the iBuzz, the unique music-activated sex toy that plugs into your iPod and vibrates in time with your favourite music!

On your own or with a partner, **LoveHoney** has the products that can spice up your sex life. They offer free delivery, and security, privacy and discretion are guaranteed.

For details on how to take advantage of this fantastic offer please go to page 488, where you'll also find information on all the other great deals throughout *Goddess*.

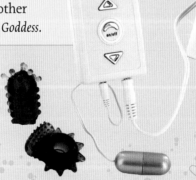

LoveHoney.co.uk
Sexy and Secure Adult Shopping

Make everybody love you

'It's easier to think about love than to live with it.'

JULIETTE BINOCHE

There are some people with a natural ability to make everybody they meet love them. The rest of us have to work at it. Whether it's finding a mate, keeping your partner interested or getting your colleagues to really appreciate you, here are the ideas that can transform you into Ms Popular.

How charming are you?

Some people sail through life. Some people are loaded with charisma. The ability to make people like you, love you and keep on doing so is one of life's great skills. So where do you fall in the charisma scale?

1. How many people do you greet with genuine pleasure in an average day?
- [ ] a. Your nearest and dearest and that's it.
- [ ] b. Just about everyone you come across.
- [ ] c. The people you see every day.

2. Are you ever found in the kitchen at parties, talking intently to someone who looks a bit of a wallflower:
- [ ] a. Never, you'd rather go home.
- [ ] b. Sometimes – you usually find people interesting when you get started talking.
- [ ] c. Only if you don't know anyone else there and are a bit lonely yourself.

3. You remember names:
- [ ] a. Easily.
- [ ] b. Most of the time.
- [ ] c. You're pretty rubbish actually – it can be embarrassing.

4. 'Mirroring body language' means copying, often subconsciously, the body movements of the person you're talking to. Do you mirror body language:
- [ ] a. Not consciously, sounds creepy.
- [ ] b. All the time, to put people at ease.
- [ ] c. Only when I want to get something out of them.

5. Do you generally find that most people are a little bit less interesting than you?

☐ a. Yes, often, if I'm being honest.

☐ b. No – some people are, some aren't.

☐ c. Not at all – I'm interested in most people.

Score

1. a 0, b 2, c 1

2. a 0, b 2, c 1

3. a 2, b 1, c 0

4. a 0, b 2, c 1

5. a 0, b 1, c 2

Your charm rating

A score of 6 or more, means you've mastered the art of charming others. The higher the score the better.

Any score under 6 is a bit of a disaster on the charisma scale. Read ideas 82–84 on making everyone love you all the time.

70. Learn from the masters

Everyone knows someone who is an incredible flirt, whose social diary always seems to need extra fold-out sections and who seems to be adored by all men, from infants to grandfathers.

Rather than make a voodoo doll of her, watch and learn: the good and the bad.

But she's so obvious!

Most women with these skills often seem transparent to other women; they seem to turn on the charm unashamedly and suck up to a man's ego without a second thought. Well: newsflash – men don't care. And more often than not, they usually don't even notice that she does it to every other guy in the office unless she is known as the 'praying mantis' and eats her partners after sex. This is because most people could do with a little extra attention in their lives. Face it, even if you know the guy in accounts flirts with every woman he meets on the stairs, it still makes your day less dreary – and that's because flirting makes life more fun.

Flirting also doesn't have to be about sex. It can just be about remembering to look up, crack a smile and not take everything so seriously. You may not have just made a connection with the love of your life but it's good to remember to keep things light; it's a great way to stop every date you do have from seeming like a full-scale interview.

Here's an idea for you...

Look at the people who make you feel good and consider which of their qualities you like. Maybe your grandmother is a very calming person to be around because she is a great listener. Maybe your best friend is brilliant at coming up with exciting plans and making things happen. Your brother might always know how to put nervous people at ease... think about how you can adopt these easy ways of being, and look for similar traits in yourself.

Recognising it in action

Most good flirts have a few skills in common. Firstly, they smile a lot. That is not to say that they could be extras in *The Stepford Wives*. They just keep things upbeat, a quality that draws people whether they are friends or colleagues. Secondly, they ask questions and remember details; any good networker will tell you that this is an essential tool in making good contacts. It makes people feel appreciated, understood and special, so try and make a mental rule to ask more questions than you answer. Again, this will not turn you into some 50s housewife; it's as useful a skill in big business as it is in personal relationships. And thirdly, they often use physical contact, sometimes with themselves, and sometimes with others. Touching your hair or face gives the other person a clear signal that you are interested in them. Touching their arm or hand as you chat, taking their elbow as you go through a door – these are all ways of making people know that you are comfortable with the idea of being in their body space: or of having them in yours.

Getting flirting right for you

That isn't to say these are all right for you. If every time you see the arch-flirt you want to lock her in the stationery cupboard for pretending she can't work the photocopier when she used to work for Xerox, then you know you need to modify her tactics when you use them yourself. Maybe you can emulate the way she remembers everyone's name or gets involved with after-work activities (you might not fancy Bob in IT, but his brother could be pretty hot). It's about knowing that you might need to sharpen up your skills consciously without coming into work the next day with a completely different personality. You can use what she does wrong to help guide you: maybe her whole conversation is about the other person, which is a great way to get attention but isn't going to help move things on to the next stage. Maybe the neckline of her blouse ends around her waistband; also not a winner with every guy in town. The wise girl looks for lessons everywhere…

> Defining idea…
>
> **'The mysterious is always attractive. People will always follow a veil.'**
> English writer and cleric BEDE JARRETT, from The House of Gold

What comes naturally

This is why you also need to think about how you already put yourself out there. Are you always coming up with wisecracks or reminding men you meet how smart you are? Do you find yourself joking about, like you did with your male friends at college or your ex-boyfriend? Whilst this might be a great place to *get to* with a partner, it's not necessarily ideal when you first meet someone. Most people have a limit to how much they can take in during one sitting and definitely to how much they want to know. You may think chatting about your ex, your eating disorder and your PhD just shows your openness, but is it possible that you might be scaring people off by showing what a handful you are? Revealing yourself as you get to know one another is a much better way of allowing space for both of you to get comfortable.

71. Being lucky at getting lucky

Got friends who seem to glide through life, people whom everyone calls 'born lucky', while nothing whatsoever seems to go your way?

Recent research has shown that there is a big difference between 'luck' and 'chance'. And you can work things out in your favour.

Chance covers things that happen to you without your input, like a hereditary illness or finding money on the street. But luck is something you can generate, by organising your life in a way that maximises every opportunity that comes along. So forget leaving your dating destiny to fate, and make sure that when good luck comes along the odds are already stacked in your favour.

Reset your mind

The first thing you need to do is change your perception of yourself as 'unlucky'. Most people can improve their chances by reprogramming their minds to think of themselves as fortunate; this means that you expect good things to happen to you and recognise opportunities as they come up, and it stops you from turning your back on chances because you believe things are too good to be true. The postman could be your perfect man but you might open the door without looking up every morning if you have decided that love is not going to come your way.

Start by resisting the temptation to relive your past failures and worries. It can dampen your spirits. Lucky people get things in perspective, look for ways to turn around disasters and expect that they will need to take chances to get what they would like out of life. When things do go right, even the little things such as finding a parking space, put that down to your skill: it will help you feel in control of your good fortune. If you find it hard to do, then jot them down on your calendar or on a notepad and see how quickly the good stuff adds up.

Become a social butterfly

Research shows that lucky people have much wider social networks, and are good at meeting new people. So get friendly; at weddings, for example, be the first to ask everyone at your table their names and whether they are friends of the bride or groom – not only will you make connections but they'll all be grateful to you for breaking the ice. You can make this easier by looking lucky. Lucky people are optimists who expect good fortune, which radiates from the way they carry themselves. If you don't do this naturally, then you can cheat: imitating their body language will fast track you to success. So avoid the folded arms, hunched shoulders, and lack of eye contact which ward people off. Be open, look up and around: how are you going to get lucky in love if you miss the opportunity to catch the eye of the handsome guy at the bar?

Here's an idea for you...

'Reframing' is a technique often employed by psychotherapists to help clients get a more positive perspective. You place the experience in another frame which fits the 'facts' of the same concrete situation equally well or even better, and thereby changes its entire meaning. It sounds a bit complicated, but it isn't, so here's an example. If you had a bad relationship that has crushed your confidence, rather than thinking you can never get over it, try thinking that you are glad to have the bad experience behind you so that you can make a better choice next time. It may feel unnatural at first, but soon choosing a better way of seeing things will become second nature.

Defining idea...

'How can you say luck and chance are the same thing? Chance is the first step you take, luck is what comes afterwards.'

AMY TAN, US novelist

You know you know

Learning to trust your instincts will build your confidence and help you believe in your ability to choose what is right for you. You learn to move between 'hard knowing', which is the facts, and 'soft knowing', which is the feeling those facts give you, and you can then base your decisions on both. If you feel like something is right but can't decide, then write down the pros and cons and see if the result matches what you feel. Trying will also help you build confidence, because taking risks is essential to getting what you want. Still find it hard to take the leap? Try reading a few stars' autobiographies or watching films of their lives and see how many 'successful' people have struggled for years before getting their breaks, and also that life has ups, downs and then some more ups again. The one thing you can rely on, with luck, is that it will change.

72. Dress for success

Clothing communicates, it's a simple fact. No matter how much we regard ourselves as able to look behind the façade, one of the first signifiers we read is the packaging.

And getting yours right is key when trying to attract the right kind of attention. So exactly what is the right kind of attention?

Basically, you need to dress for the kind of man you want to appeal to, and for the kind of relationship you want to establish. Looking for a playful fling? As long as you aren't wearing a bin bag, it almost doesn't matter what you have on as you know what you want. Looking for a fellow art buff for a meaningful, life-long relationship? A spandex off-the-shoulder, thigh-skimming tube dress with some plastic wet-look boots may make other viewers at the private view think you are a performance artist. Or whatever. But you might at least earn your bus fare home.

What happened to self-respect?

Dressing to attract a man might sound like the past hundred years of women's liberation never happened. But the fact is, wearing your favourite neck-to-ankle baggy jumper may make you feel secure but it does not, in any way whatsoever, say that you are available or interested in taking things to a romantic level. Sexual attraction is an important part of finding a partner and there is nothing wrong with it: so get with the programme, have a good think about your best bits and pieces, and get them out.

Think about how your outfits are received; you may think you are being the belle of the ball but actually be coming on like a train. Consider the type of event you are going to and not just the impression you would like to make. A Halloween house party might be more suited to a fun homemade tramp outfit than an expensively hired catsuit; nothing says 'Look at me, I'm desperate!' like a bid to be super-sexy at all times. One quiet Saturday afternoon, try on lots of clothes and find something that is flattering, a little sexy and comfortable; then hang it on the back of the bedroom door as your SOS date outfit, if you get panicked. If in doubt, default to a little black dress. These have served womankind well for a very long time.

Feeling fine

So how do you get the balance between what you feel comfortable in and what you think might attract the right man? Firstly, you must feel comfortable in whatever you wear, as that will help radiate confidence and an ease with your body. And don't try anything frighteningly new or too high fashion; lots of men don't care that your shoes are the latest catwalk chic, but they might care if you take a head-first dive down the club steps because you haven't mastered the art of walking in them.

A little bit of what you fancy...

It never hurts to advertise, and men are basically visual creatures, so a glimpse of a taut thigh, a crisp white shirt with a flattering neckline or a well-turned ankle in some killer heels are all great tools in your armoury. However, there is a fine line between being tantalising and being tarty. This is where the 'one or the other' rule comes into play. If you have a great décolletage, feel free to hoist your boobs up and dab some seductive scent in pertinent places. However, you may want to team that stunning, sparkly, low-cut top with some simple flattering black trousers, rather than a denim skirt the size of a belt. Even if you also have fabulous legs, too much of a good thing can slide into slut. So choose one good area and work it to its best advantage.

Now consider where you are going. A miniskirt with a black polo neck is a winning combination if you have devastating legs, but not if you have to hide all your assets under the table during dinner, with you now looking like a severe intellectual beatnik about to grill him on existentialism. The same miniskirt worn in the gods at the theatre might get the audience looking in the opposite direction from the stage. Be as objective as you can; you might love that skirt to bits, but if it's not going to work for you, put it back in the wardrobe.

> *Defining* idea...
>
> **'Put even the plainest woman into a beautiful dress and unconsciously she will try to live up to it.'**
> LADY DUFF GORDON, 20s fashion designer

73. What men want

OK, OK, let's keep it clean, ladies. Of course, all men want that, but there are some other qualities that men are looking for too.

And there are some universal truths about what men are after, just as there are for us women.

Love

Believe it or not, men are just as keen to make a connection as women are, they are just not as likely to confuse it with good sex. Someone to share things with, rely on and love comes high on many male lists. But don't confuse the desire to love with the desire to commit: that comes later.

Here's an idea for you...

As well as knowing a little more about the male mind, it might be a useful exercise to work out what qualities you would ideally like – and then try and make them a reality in your next relationship rather than hoping he's a mind reader.

Desire

They want you to want them as much as they want you: and, yes, they'll want you to think about embarking on any kind of relationship. You don't have to fit the standard-issue magazine model, but they do want someone who takes pride in how she looks and feels good about her own body. There's no bigger turn-off than someone waving their cellulite in your face and telling you how hideous it is – it's called negative marketing. Stop it. You can loll about the house in no make-up and your jogging bottoms and still appear attractive if you feel good doing it, but throw in greasy hair and some whining and you are on your own.

Happiness

Happy people are like luck magnets; everyone wants to be around them, learn their secret, get happy osmosis. And while no one can be happy all the time, your world view is pretty important. Only the creepiest of men want a depressed woman around, usually so they can feel superior. If you do have personal issues then take control of them yourself; while it's totally appropriate to share your woes with your loved one, he's not your therapist. He needs some lifting up too.

Friendship

This mustn't be confused with being like one of his mates. While men want the good stuff – loyalty, concern, fun, companionship – they don't necessarily want you outdoing them in a belching competition. And don't fake an interest in football if you haven't got any; they can always find someone else to go to the match with.

Support

Constant criticism is wearing, and an easy trap to fall into. Buoying up someone's spirits, being friendly to their friends or work associates, these are all ways of making someone feel treasured and supported. If you can do it without them having to remind you, this will also create more trust, a vital part of feeling valued.

Sanity

What once seemed exciting and off the wall soon becomes a hideous chore. A neurotic, clingy or shouting woman might be a sexy stereotype in a film but is a nightmare to have in your life as a friend or a partner. After all, the same qualities in a man would put you off, whereas a rational person, someone you can talk to and lean on at times, generates respect and trust. Being irrational shouldn't be confused with being a challenge. Mount Everest is a challenge, but no one wants to live on it.

Challenge

So what is a good challenge? A woman who stands her ground and knows her own mind, being sharp enough to know when someone is trying it on and not becoming so acquiescent that she becomes almost invisible. If someone lets you down be clear about your feelings; men respond to direct statements (hysterics switch them off), and it shows that you think you're worth more. So they will, too.

Consideration

Shockingly, men respond to the same stuff as women! Who would have thought it? Tea in bed, making sure he has something in the fridge to eat when he gets home if he has to work late and offering to pick up medicine when he is ill... It may all seem like some weird, 50s-throwback behaviour, but these are the little acts of thoughtfulness that make a woman go weak at the knees when shown to her. The rest of the world is indifferent to his minor personal crises, so you shouldn't be. Of course, these acts should be returned, but studies show that acts of kindness make both the doer and the receiver feel good, so if you get the balance right you can both be nurtured and nurture. I can feel world peace just around the corner.

Space

Finally, men want space (and emotionally healthy women should too). Men want the room to make their own decisions, have their own private thoughts and sometimes just not think at all. Part of women's lifeblood is to always try and work out where things are at; men don't want that constant pressure. If you call him constantly at work, expect him to remember the name and love lives of your thirteen cousins *and* their cats, then you are actually expecting him to be a woman. That is what your best friend is for. Only teenage girls expect to share every intimate detail of their lives with their partners.

74. And what do you do?

Small talk. Hideous. My idea of hell is standing around a drinks party while people ask me what I do. I know that it's a useful question for generating 15 further minutes of conversation. But it's right up there with, 'Do you come here often?' in the tedium stakes as a first line.

Being sexy is not just about the way you look, smell and dress. It's about your character. One word that people associate with sexy is 'enigmatic' so try to make your first line something a bit more unusual.

In the film *White Mischief* Charles Dance clocks Greta Scacchi as they walk down the stairs. There is an obvious magnetism between them. At the bottom of the stairs he turns to her and says, "Are you going to tell your husband, or shall I?"

OK, that's fantasy not reality. But it certainly beats, 'What do you do?' in the first line stakes. I remember my father telling me off when I was about 12 for saying I was hungry. 'Don't be so banal,' he said. 'Use your imagination. Instead of saying you're hungry say: "the people in the street seem to me transformed into plates of pasta coming towards me"'. OK, so he is Italian – and mad – but you get the idea? Think slightly eccentric, quirky and charming. Instead of coming out with a line people expect you to say, dare to be different. Try starting with something that happened to you recently, or something interesting you've read or seen in the news. The conversation will flow from whatever starting point you give it, but the person's impression of you will be different.

Here's an idea for you...

Jerry Hall once suggested wives should read something interesting every day so that when their husbands returned from work they had something interesting to talk about. Old-fashioned but we can all learn from the principle. If you don't do, read, see or experience anything new, you're not going to have much to talk about. So try to stay well-informed and alert, it's much sexier than ignorant.

I can't remember the number of times I have been stuck next to people at dinner parties and they have started talking about commuting or childcare. Deadly. At first I wondered whether it was me, was I really so dull that all people could find to talk to me about was that? But when I compared notes with friends they said they'd experienced the same thing. I resolved to counter-attack. Every time someone started to talk about either topic I would say, 'Isn't it extraordinary how as soon as we get to a dinner party we start to talk about nannies or commuting? I'd much rather talk about sex, wouldn't you?' Either they start to bore the person on their other side, or you can get stuck into a gritty sexy conversation. Marvellous! Changing the tack of the conversation is good practice and just as valuable as avoiding being a dull conversationalist yourself.

Most people like to talk about themselves and have something interesting to say, even if it's not immediately apparent. In other words, you need to bring this something interesting out of them. Remember that you can learn something from everyone. Even if they initially come across as the dullest person you've ever met, try to use the time with them to bring out their best side.

A good answer to the question, 'How old are you?' is, 'About your age'. This totally floors people and also means you can avoid telling them. Adopt this attitude when people try to make dull conversation. Conversation is a little bit like sport: you will play to the level you find yourself. If someone is deadly dull, you're more likely to be so yourself and dull is NOT sexy. Either walk away from them or try to change the subject matter. Most people are just as keen as you are to enjoy life. They will also want to sparkle and a good conversation will help them do that. There is nothing more infuriating than watching someone else have the crack while you're stuck next

Defining idea...

'Talking and eloquence are not the same: to speak, and to speak well, are two things.'
BEN JOHNSON, 17th century dramatist and wit

to great bores of today talking about trains. Now you've read this you need never go there again. Someone totally intent on talking about trains will not be keen to spend time with the new super-sexy conversationalist you're going to become. You need never be on the periphery of the party again.

How to impress...your lover

75. 'Let a woman be a woman and a man be a man'

There's a bloke in the States called David Deida who has some interesting ideas as to why sex goes off the boil.

There's nothing particularly new about his ideas, but the way he packages his theories is pretty compulsive.

We're equal, but we're knackered. Even long-standing relationships are crumbling under the strain of couples overworking. Latest figures show that the divorce rate is inching towards half of all marriages.

But according to Deida, life doesn't have to be this way. Deida says women aren't drudges, but passionate, vital, thrilling creatures who given the chance should be living a life of rich emotional complexity. In order to shine, they need the love of what Deida calls 'the superior man'. A strong, focused, individual striving towards his destiny. According to Deida, when men are strong and women can rely on them, passionate intensity isn't far away. What's wrecking our sex lives, he says, is too much equality. Yes, you read that right.

'The bottom line of today's fifty–fifty relationship,' Deida continues, 'is that men and women are clinging to a politically correct sameness even in bed and that's when sexual attraction disappears. The love may be strong, but the sexual polarity fades.' According to Deida, men and women have both a masculine and feminine side or 'polarity'. It's fine for men to get in touch with their feminine side (real men do cry), and women with their masculine (they're brilliant in the boardroom). She can be the breadwinner, he can look after the kids, but if they want fireworks to continue, he has to be someone she can rely on and trust, and she has to remove the shoulder pads as soon as she walks through the front door.

> *Here's an idea for you...*
> **David Deida has written several books, including The Way of the Superior Man (for men) and It's a Guy Thing (for women). You can check out www.deida.com to see if his ideas are likely to appeal.**

What's a superior man?

Deida's roots appear to be in the men's movement, the reaction to feminism, which tries to help men make sense of our crazy, mixed-up world, and their role in it. He believes that a man isn't really happy unless he's striving towards his goal, whatever that is. When he loses sight of his goal, he needs 'time out' – what in other cultures would have been called a 'vision quest' – sort of metaphorically speaking going into the desert and beating his drum until he finds his way again. Unless he finds his way he's no use to anyone, least of all his bird. This is why she has to understand the importance of his quest. She can also help him be a superior man by 'challenging him', i.e. not putting up with any shit. No lying about watching Sky

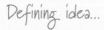

Defining idea...

'Both men and women are bisexual in the psychological sense. I shall conclude that you have decided in your own minds to make "active" coincide with "masculine" and "passive" with "feminine". But I advise against it.'
SIGMUND FREUD

Sports when he should be looking for a job, say. No nights down the pub to distract him from the fact that he hasn't written a word of that best-selling novel. Deida calls it 'challenging'. It sounds like plain old 'nagging' to me. Anyway, there's lots in his work about how a man can become superior, but here's a couple of ways he can be superior in direct relation to the woman in his life.

You'll know you're a superior man when you stop trying to control a woman's emotions and you listen to her. You do your best to understand her feelings and don't walk away from them. You don't offer useless advice when she wants you as a sounding board, but give her a hug. You make her laugh a lot. You're your own man. You listen, you take advice on board and then you do what you think best. You're trustworthy. You do what you say you'll do. And when you don't, you own up and take responsibility for it. You pay attention to your partner. You know that thirty minutes fully concentrating on her is worth four hours half-listening and fiddling with the remote. Got that?

Deida's ideas aren't for everyone, but I've met and interviewed couples for whom his ideas work well. The couples are equal, but they accept the sexes are different and that a man and a woman can't be everything to each other. Deida's ideas give a way of negotiating the contradictions of being a 'good bloke' and being a 'new man', which lots of men struggle with. If you can handle the New Age language, of course.

76. What's your Love Quotient score?

Imagine you're in the Mastermind chair and your specialist subject is your lover. What would be your Love Quotient (LQ) score?

It's a weird one. Ten years into our relationship and we know more about what lights the candle of the person sitting next to us at work than the person we've chosen to share our lives with.

Years ago I read something in one of John Gray's books that has saved me a lot of grief since. John Gray wrote *Men are from Mars, Women are from Venus*, and the point he made – directed at men – was simple: if your partner adores chocolates and sees them as the eternal proof that you love her, why on earth would you buy her roses? Yet the world is full of guys turning up with bunches of roses and wondering why they get thrown at their head. The moral is simple: if your lover needs chocolates to make them feel loved, give 'em chocolates. It's irrelevant whether you think a bunch of red roses is more romantic. You need to give your partner what they need or you might as well not bother.

Start looking for the 'roses instead of chocolate' trait and you'll start seeing people everywhere doing loads for their loved ones that's going unnoticed. I was quite stunned to discover that after a 'make or break' fight with my partner, all I had to do to appease him was cook him dinner. For whatever screwed up reasons of his psyche, what makes him feel loved isn't gifts of books, CDs, Thai prostitutes or weekends away – it's me getting my pinny on. And when I was upset with him, that's what he would do for me – cook me dinner. For a long time it got him nowhere, as what works for me when I feel angry is long extended conversations – and jewellery of course. Jesting aside, it wasn't until I read the John Gray book that I got it. Our LQs were low. But now when I need to butter him up I just throw a steak on the grill. And when he's upset me, he grits his teeth and gets prepared to bare his soul.

Broadly speaking, to successfully love the person we're with we need to understand what they need to feel loved. To keep their love we must give them what they need as far as possible. If you're reading this and wondering what this has to do with sex, my answer to you is, 'Duh! Just about everything.' Loads of couples are having indifferent or absolutely no sex, not because they don't spark off each other but because they haven't felt loved by their partner for years. The classic example is the bloke faced with a distraught missus, who will 'do' something practical for her – put up shelves, clean her car, pay the bills – when all she wants is a babysitter booked and a meal out.

When your lover's feeling insecure, stressed or worried, how do you make them feel safe and reassured? Does it work? If not, do you know what would? If yes, why do you withhold it from them? Do you like to play mean just for the hell of it? It might seem to work and it might keep you the 'superior' partner, but the price is high. Your partner won't be able to trust you and that sort of trust is near enough essential to keep sex hot between you when the first thrill has gone.

Would your lover rather have a romantic meal or a wild night out on the town as a prelude to sex? Do you occasionally indulge them, even if you'd rather do something else?

> Defining idea...
>
> **'Sex is a conversation carried out by another means.'**
> PETER USTINOV

Does your partner feel closer to you when you're laughing together or being upset with you? If the answer's 'upset', do you respond in a way that seems to satisfy them or are they disappointed in you? If the answer's 'laughing', when was the last time you went out of your way to make sure you had a good laugh together?

What's your lover's favourite way of resolving a fight (not necessarily the way you always resolve it)?

These are the kind of questions you have to know the answers to. And your partner, of course, has to know what works for you. Emotionally we have to be given chocolates at least some of the time or we start to shut off from our partner and get tempted by someone who appears to offer Milk Tray on demand. If you're with someone for whom chocolate equals love, all the roses in the world won't fix your relationship or help you get good sex.

77. Just say 'no'

There's saying 'no' and there's saying 'no' nicely. Two very different things.

Every relationship has its sexual deserts when sex is off the cards. Here's how to negotiate your way through them so no one gets too hurt.

Sometimes we simply want to say 'no'. We might be tired. We might be feeling sad. We might be preoccupied with something else. If your partner approaches you and you feel ambivalent about having sex, my best advice is to go along with it for a while and try to get yourself in the mood (with their help, of course). If, however, you fail to rise onto that wave of lust, all you can do is gaze into their eyes tenderly and say, 'Sorry, it isn't working for me tonight, but I promise that tomorrow we'll do the deed.' Sex therapists pretty much agree that rejection is easier to take if there's a definite date set for a retry. As a consolation prize and to give them the human contact that we all crave (and which probably instigated their shuffle across the bed in the first place), you could hold your partner while they masturbate to orgasm. (And if you're not comfortable masturbating in front of each other, maybe you ought to think about why not. It's a useful habit.)

But what if you know that tomorrow you're not going to want to have sex either? What if this one's going to run and run? A genuine sexual desert where it's been months and months and months, and you don't need so much to negotiate it as buy a map and a compass and start charting the unknown continent. First things first. Do you both want to emerge from your desert and find your oasis?

'Yes' to the oasis?

Is there a medical reason that one or both of you has gone off sex? Is it because one or both of you is having a mid-life crisis? Deal with that and do the following.

'No' to the oasis

Tricky one this. You've gone off sex. You don't fancy your partner anymore. You can't be bothered to try. When they approach you, you simply don't want to do it.

> **Here's an idea for you...**
>
> **If you and your partner haven't had sex for a month, sit down, look into his/her eyes and ask why. The longer you go without sex, the easier it becomes to do without it. The more you do it, the more you'll want to.**

Don't let sex be an *ad hoc* arrangement. Decide on a time when you're going to get physical and then do all you can to get yourself in the mood, such as a bath, delicious food, candles or a chat. Enjoy each other. Don't expect mind-bending lust – mildly being up for it is good enough. If it's been a long time and you're a bit nervous about having sex, go back to basics. It doesn't matter what you do as long as you're physically close. Being physically close without having penetrative sex can eventually kick start your libido. In fact, when you've been together for a while, you often need physical proximity to *start* feeling desire. In other words, you can' t hang around waiting for an overwhelming wave of lust to wash over you or you'll wait a long time. Start having sex and let Mother Nature take her course.

The bottom line is, if you can't be bothered to do all you can to get yourself and your partner in the mood for sex then you're a rotten lover. What's loving about a person who doesn't at least try? This is brutal, but it's true. Perhaps you're right to take your lover's constancy for granted even when you're not putting out, trusting that they'll stick by you. But they're almost certain to get depressed and unconfident – both traits are hell to live with and unlikely to endear them to you. Keeping your sex life extant is as important for your mental health as theirs.

How to impress...at work

78. Keep a lifelong contact book

Most people start networking when they are unhappy in their job or have been made redundant. Too late. Put your network of contacts to work on your career at all times. You never know when someone you used to know comes around again.

Bear in mind the endgame, now.

The endgame of a brilliant career includes some non-executive directorships. It's a good life. You are paid a modest sum of money a year for preparing for and attending a board meeting every month. If asked, you can always take on a one-off project on behalf of the board, to keep your hand in. And if it gets a little niffy or unpleasant, like the grandchildren you simply hand the problem back to the people who own it and just walk away. But to get these directorships you need to push.

There are many things I like about politicians but one thing above all. They wear their ambition on their sleeves. Seldom do they try to hide the fact that they are playing to win, and winning means getting more and more power. They expect us to think that. They seem to relish the battle and to pursue their careers even though they must be aware that almost all of them, when they eventually succumb to the people's will, are going to be denigrated and probably despised by their conquerors. Yet such is their vanity or their self-belief – or both – that they plunge into the fray. It is easy to use words like battle and war in this context, and when you come down to it, in the business environment as well. It's either you or someone else. One gets the glory and the other stays in a job that firstly bores them, secondly irritates them and finally embitters them.

Here's an idea for you...

Make a regular plan for staying in contact with a wide range of people in your address book. I don't mean a circular letter at Christmas; just a personal note asking how they are doing. This keeps your name alive, triggers thoughts and will give rise to all sorts of opportunities.

So, if you're in business you may as well join the mêlée and cut loose your ambition. You need to stand out in the crowd and get yourself noticed. If you want to join the board, people must see you as utterly unflappable and competent. They must notice that you are normally right and always confident. You will make them feel their own inadequacies. But how do you close the business and get the job? Well, you start now by keeping in contact with people you have worked with or for, with old customers and with suppliers. Henry Lewis, a former CEO of Marks & Spencer, was offered non-execs by many of his suppliers. One of them was so keen that it kept back a sizable chunk of shares so that it could offer them to Harry when he retired in exchange for his coming on to its board.

Keep a lifetime address book

Look at it this way. Some companies place such value on their database of knowledge of their customers and prospective customers that they quantify it and put it on the balance sheet as an intangible asset. Companies have changed hands because one bought another for its market information, and mergers have taken place where the only real synergy was complementary customer lists. Your version of this is your address book. Never take anyone off it. You never know when they might come in useful. Organise it in sections so that you have a reminder of where and why you met each contact.

A man who was on a training course that my colleague John ran some fifteen years ago rang him up recently. Since the man was in the delegate section of his address book John was able to demonstrate his remarkable memory. He also had recorded the opinions of himself and the other managers running the course on how good they thought this guy was at the time. All of this proved invaluable: now a senior manager, this man is currently one of John's prospective clients.

I have never met anyone who has kept a long-term address book say that it has been a waste of time. I have heard many regret that they didn't. I'm one of them, dammit.

79. Make good suggestions loudly

At any point in the chaos that describes your organisation, an opportunity can arise for you to make a sensible suggestion to the powers that be. Career people should grab such opportunities and actively seek them out.

The opportunities are legion. You've found an uncompetitive product feature, an outdated business process or an opportunity for new technology. Now's your chance to make sensible suggestions. Or think about publicity or sponsorship.

If you know the arts or sport preferences of the CEO, for example, you might just stumble across a local opportunity for sponsorship. If you make that happen, you can be sure the chief executive will be there for the event.

High-profile people get noticed, and the higher up the people doing the noticing the better. Form a plan for getting more than your fair share of senior management's attention, and then communicate your ideas clearly in a brief paper.

First make sure that your idea is in an area where the issues are being discussed at least two levels above you. Now put up your paper.

You'll soon realise how vitally important it is that your boss thinks you are top-notch, and that you help to make him or her look brilliant as well. And not only your boss, but also your boss's boss.

Make sure they can bear to read it

Here's an idea for you...

When did you last meet the most senior person in your building? If you are not based at the company's headquarters the answer to that question has to be at least in the last month. Take responsibility for this – do you know when you will next have an opportunity to meet senior people?

So, you have a good idea. Now think about the quality of the communication. Think through, for example, the level of detail your boss wants to read and hear. As you go up the organisation you find people who are capable of going into detail, but less likely to want to. In both written and oral communications, write clear, simple management summaries.

Once you have written your paper, try to shorten it significantly, say by half. Throw out anything except the essentials. Remember you want to have the opportunity to discuss it. If it is too comprehensive you may have given the thing lock, stock and barrel for someone else to dine out on. Release it effectively – in other words in the way that best serves your interests. After all, it was your idea.

A good paper may help in other ways as well. There are lots of conferences out there, and lots of organisers looking for people to read papers. Reading a paper anywhere abroad, for example, looks good on the CV.

Be creative in getting your ideas to the right people

To follow up your paper and for other reasons, there are many ways of communicating with the great and the good in your organisation outside the normal business environment. Volunteer for these. I don't mean volunteer for anything that has a low impact no matter how worthy. There is no point for the careerist in being a member of the St John's ambulance team at the local football ground. But there may be a point in being the fire officer for your floor. Check it out first. Does it get you in front of the Director of Logistics? Is there an opportunity to be a representative on the pension council? That's a high profile place.

Another promising area is promoting the company at sport by wearing the logo. If you are good at sport, senior managers will bask in your limelight. You will also come into contact with the people you are trying to impress if they come to the golf match you have arranged. Ask them to make a speech (and offer to help with some gags perhaps) and present the prizes.

Another good place to get your ideas known is the company newsletter, particularly if it involves interviewing senior people. Only speak at the Christmas party if you are really good at making people laugh. If being witty does not come naturally to you, speak at conferences where being amusing is a significant but secondary requirement.

> Defining idea...
>
> **'Think about the 4 C's, Continuous learning, Confidence in yourself, Care and attention to those you love and Communication – wherever you are, well-honed communication skills are highly important.'**
> Chairman, Scottish Power

80. Actions speak louder than decisions

If you have taken a decision and informed your boss of what you and your team are going to do, for your career's sake make absolutely sure it happens.

If you haven't started the action plan, you may as well not have made a decision.

I've a friend who's an elderly painter and decorator. His children have moved on and he now has no dependents. He does not want to retire altogether but he does want to have more time for himself; but he's finding it difficult to cut down the amount of work he does. Unfortunately for him he is brilliant at his job and a very nice chap to boot. This means that his old clients all turn to him when they want work done and he finds it difficult to say no. Plus, his relatives and friends have been used to asking him over, giving him good food and drink and getting him to do some decorating.

Over coffee one day he asked me what I meant when I murmured that a decision is not a decision until there is commitment to the action plan and the first steps are taken. I asked him what he wanted to do in the spare time he was trying to create, and he rather coyly admitted that he had decided to take up golf. He then tried to implement his decision. He resolved to take every Friday off to pursue this new hobby. Four weeks later he told me that he had not been able to do that once. I pressed him to commit to a lesson with the professional on the next Friday morning and another one that afternoon. We agreed that he would pay for the lessons in advance. This broke the deadlock and he started to play. He is now an addict and plays every Friday and quite often on other days as well – but it wasn't a decision until he'd gone into action.

Never disappoint the powers that be

Right, where is this stuff important? Most teams work with some operational targets that they need urgently to achieve. If your team is well organised you'll also have a strategic plan that includes a series of projects aimed at improving the environment in which you operate. If you implement these projects, life will become easier and performance will improve. Being career-minded you will, of course, have told your boss all about the changes the team is going to make – perhaps with a loud drum roll. But in the real world pressure is always on maintaining performance rather than developing new methods. In my experience a boss will ask three times how you are getting on with the new idea. The third time they hear your excuse that unfortunately there just has not been time to get it going, they will forget it and write you down as all mouth and no trousers.

Here's an idea for you...

Pick a team member who has difficulty with the 'do it now' concept. He tends to agree to a decision made by you, himself or the team, and then finds loads of reasons why he can't implement it. Sit him down and tell him the story of the painter. Now get him to take a decision he has been prevaricating over and put the actions into his diary. Phone him just before and just after he should have started to implement the decision.

Defining idea...

'Men of action whose minds are too busy with the day's work to see beyond it. They are essential men, we cannot do without them, and yet we must not allow all our vision to be bound by the limitations of men of action.'
PEARL S. BUCK, American writer

249

81. Don't talk so much

It is frightening how little listening goes on. Because of this, your boss's team meetings offer an excellent opportunity for appearing authoritative and getting your own way.

We all do it, we just don't listen. I did a small piece of research on key management skills. While not statistically valid, the response of some thirty senior business people showed a huge majority put listening at the top of their list of necessary skills. One of them called it 'active listening'.

Here is the art of listening going wrong for an architect. He had the job of advising a couple on how they should use the space and carry out the refurbishment of an old, run-down property they had just bought. Unfortunately there was a hiatus between the architect's survey and his first meeting with the new owners. He used the time to speculate on what they might want to do with the house. What did it lack, in his view, and what would they have to do to put that lack right?

The owners arrived for the first meeting with a list of their requirements for the property. Despite this, the architect went ahead and presented the ideas that he had already sketched. After all, that's human nature. We all want to show our original ideas off since they feel so right to us. The architect was in fact interrupting the customer to make a point. When the customer eventually tabled the list, it was very different from the first thoughts of their adviser. They now had a situation of the customer not wanting to make the adviser feel bad, and the adviser feeling the need to defend his work. Despite all that went after, the relationship never got over this appalling start. Please don't ignore this story because you think that you would never do that. Keep quiet at your next meeting and just watch people, even senior people, not listening at all.

Like all skills you get better at listening if you practice it. Here's an exercise I got from Penny Ferguson. Get yourself and a colleague, or if that's difficult a member of your family, to sit down in comfortable chairs facing each other. Now explain that you are going to listen to them for three minutes without any interruption. Then give them the topic. Ask them to talk for three minutes about things that they appreciate about themselves. Now settle down to do some active listening. Keep your eyes steady on them, although theirs will probably wander as they think about the question. For many people this is quite difficult. Normally we would be in there talking, advising and correcting, but that's not the point.

Here's another statistically invalid finding from my experience. Women in business are instinctively better at this than men. So women, be careful that your listening does not look as though you have no ideas. And men, for pity's sake don't talk so much!

Here's an idea for you...

At your boss's next team meeting don't leap in with your views. Listen until everyone has spoken, assimilate what has been said and eventually summarise the substance. By that time you will know where your interests lie and be able to steer the meeting towards them.

Defining idea...

'*If you know the enemy and know yourself, you need not fear the result of a hundred battles. If you know yourself but not the enemy, for every victory gained you will also suffer a defeat. If you know neither the enemy nor yourself, you will succumb in every battle.*'
SUN TZU, The Art of War

How to impress...everyone, all the time

82. The impact of appreciation

Everybody needs to know that they're appreciated. However, it's easy to forget this and simply criticise the performance of our team and the behaviour of our families and friends.

I came across a young lad who'd been expelled from school, had fallen in with a bad crowd, was smoking illegal substances and was generally behaving badly. His worried parents couldn't see how to change his behaviour. The lad's mother especially was always saying things like, 'Why don't you have different friends? These ones aren't good.' 'You must work harder or you won't get the results you need.' 'Keep your room tidy.' 'No, you can't ride a motorbike as it's dangerous.' 'You must do your share of the housework.' She said these things because she loved him, but nothing ever changed. I persuaded the lad's father not to criticise his son at all for one month, but instead to notice the things that he did well. So, when the lad's bedroom looked marginally less of a tip than usual, his father thanked him for making it look nicer. When the lad happened to hang his coat up rather than drop it on the floor, his father noticed and thanked him. And when the lad chatted happily at a meal rather than sitting in sullen silence, his father told him what a joy he was. At any given opportunity, his father appreciated his son for who he was and what he did.

Imagine how that lad might have been feeling up until that point – worthless, just one big problem. Under those circumstances, how could he see any hope for a way out of his difficulties? The new approach produced dramatic results and he's now doing extremely well.

Aim at 80% appreciation, 20% criticism

> **Here's an idea for you...**
>
> Telephone someone who's important to you and tell them what you appreciate about them. When they ask why you called, don't muddy the water by having domestic arrangements to discuss. Just tell them that the only reason you called was to thank them for their strengths and the value that they bring to your life.

When was the last time you told your partner that you love them and how much you appreciate their role in your life? How long is it since you pointed out to your children what they're doing well at school as opposed to what they're doing badly? And do you know who our worst enemy in this regard is? Us. It's said that an actor only remembers the member of the audience who didn't clap. We play a half decent round of golf and only remember the half that wasn't decent. If we do this to ourselves, how much more do we do it to others? When I ask people in companies what sort of feedback they get from their managers, they almost invariably start by saying that they're told when they're doing something wrong.

Can you remember a day when you woke up simply feeling good? About life, about yourself, about everything? When you feel like that, how do you perform? Everything goes well doesn't it? You handle the call to a difficult client better, that sale comes in more easily, you handle a sensitive conversation with a friend more effectively. So, if we know that we perform better when we feel good about ourselves, why do we then criticise people and expect them to be motivated to perform better? It really doesn't make sense.

I'm not proud of it, but this is exactly what I used to do with my children. Because I cared. I loved them so much that I didn't want them to make the mistakes that I'd made. So, I kept telling them where they were getting it wrong because I wanted them to be better next time. Now my concentration is different. I don't run away from issues. Instead I help my children to focus on their strengths and on what they're getting right. And because I concentrate on their strengths, they display their strengths more and more. If you focus on people's strengths, including your own, your life could change beyond recognition.

83. Show some trust

If we assume people are workshy, untrustworthy and lack commitment and then proceed to treat them as though this is how they are, they'll probably start to exhibit this kind of behaviour.

The following idea derives from some interesting business research. It can easily be adopted in our personal lives as well as our working lives.

Let's look at the business angle first. The motivation guru Douglas McGregor produced one of the most enduring pieces of management theory: Theory X and Theory Y Management. This has become part of management business vocabulary. According to McGregor, managers tend to make assumptions about the people who work for them. These assumptions fall into two broad categories.

Theory X managers have little faith in their employees. They believe that people dislike work and that money and fear are their only motivations. They also believe that employees can't be trusted and that they lack creativity except in finding ways round management rules. Theory X is, of course, a self-fulfilling prophecy. If you make assumptions about people and treat them as though that is how they are, then that is how they're likely to behave.

Here's an idea for you...

How could you be sending Theory X messages to your team or family? Talk to them about it and ask them to tell you whenever they get that feeling. How can you positively change how you deal with someone to demonstrate that you believe them to be Theory Y? Think hard about how you're communicating. Are you concentrating on getting your own ideas across and criticising other people's, or are you encouraging and supporting the ideas of others?

Theory Y managers believe pretty much the opposite. They believe that people need to work for psychological as well as economic reasons and that they're motivated by recognition and achievement, easy to trust, seek responsibility and so creative that they represent the best source of ideas in the business. This, too, is a self-fulfilling prophecy.

McGregor believes that people tend to be a mixture of the two theories, with Theory Y behaviour predominating unless external pressures, such as failing to meet targets, move them towards Theory X.

'People become motivated when you guide them to the source of their own power and when you make heroes out of employees who personify what you want to see in the organisation.'
ANITA RODDICK

Interestingly, if you were to ask any employee which of the two profiles most closely describes them, the vast majority will choose Theory Y regardless of what grade or level in the organisation the person is.

However, if managers are asked whether or not they agree that there are more Theory X attitudes and behaviours displayed by employees at operational levels than they would ideally like to see, the answer is nearly always 'Yes'. However, since all employees describe themselves as more Theory Y than Theory X, then if we accept the self-fulfilling prophecy principle it stands to reason that Theory X behaviour only arises as a result of the way managers treat their staff.

On the face of it this seems nonsense, since these managers have no doubt described themselves as predominantly Y. I have a theory about this. Suppose that every day at work the managers are unintentionally sending Theory X messages to their employees because of the way in which they communicate. If managers don't listen to their employees, tend to tell them what to do all the time and suppress their ideas because of their own seniority and increased experience, then they're probably sending a message that they don't trust each individual and their team to perform.

This can now be transposed into our personal lives. We trust our children, but do we really display this trust? For example, if we check every Thursday that our son has remembered his football boots, then will he bother to remember them? If we trust him to remember, he may be more likely to remember or take responsibility for the outcome if he forgets (which might serve as a reminder for next time too). More seriously, if we display an attitude that says, 'You don't want to do school work because it's too much effort', then children might adopt that attitude. If, on the other hand, we treat children as though they understand the need to learn and want to get on with it, then hopefully they'll develop Theory Y attitudes and behaviours.

84. How do I persuade them?

We all want to steer people towards our way of thinking. So, what's the most effective way of influencing people?

When we want people to follow our lead, we usually try to find as many different ways to get our thoughts across as possible. If someone disagrees, we just try to come at it another way. However, does this actually work?

A picture

Picture a pile of sand. If I pour a jug of water over the sand it's likely that some of it will be soaked up by the sand and that some of it will trickle down the edge of the pile making pathways as it goes. If I pour another jug of water on the same pile of sand, more may soak in and some may make new pathways. Most of it, however, is likely to travel down the original pathways and make these deeper. If I pour yet

For the duration of your very next conversation try not to use the word 'I' – I think, I suggest, I don't agree. Concentrate entirely on 'you'. Ask 'you' questions. What do you think about this? How might you handle this? Let me test what you are saying to be sure that I've understood you correctly. That is a great idea that you have just had. This way you'll see how much more people are able to contribute. You'll also notice how difficult you'll find it to not take over and voice your ideas.

another jug of water over the sand it will be virtually impossible for the water to do anything other than go down the existing pathways, making them deeper than ever.

This is almost exactly how the brain works. When you give someone a problem to solve they'll begin to think it through and pathways or traces will be created through the brain. You tell them you think they've got it wrong and they need to think it through again. This they do and they may possibly find a new pathway but it's highly likely that they'll go down the same pathway, making that idea deeper or more firmly entrenched. Ask them to think it through again and it'll be almost impossible for them to come up with a new solution. It's not that they don't want to, it's just that the pathways have now been created and the brain finds it virtually impossible to move away from those pathways.

When you look at this picture it's obvious that continually trying to change someone's mind by telling them, yet again, why you think the way you do, is likely to be less than useless.

'I' versus 'you'

When we run our Personal Leadership Programme one of the first things that we do is measure how well people communicate. We all have a perception of the way we communicate and most of us think that we're open to ideas, that we show caring to others and that we encourage others to come forward with their thoughts and suggestions. People are typically shocked and horrified by the results of the measurement. We absolutely do not communicate the way we think we do. I've as yet found almost no exception to this.

> **Defining idea…**
>
> *'To listen well is as powerful a means of communication and influence as to talk well.'*
> JOHN MARSHALL

Without even realising it, we usually communicate by giving our point of view, giving our suggestions and telling people why we don't agree with their ideas. What we don't do is support their ideas, ask for their opinions, test our understanding of what they're saying, summarise all their points of view, or take their ideas and demonstrate their value by building on them. We don't invite them into the conversation. In the first way, all our focus is on 'I'; in the second, it's all on 'you'. The thing I've discovered is that those of us in what you might describe as the caring professions are frequently the worst! Why? I suspect because we feel that we really need to give people the benefit of our wisdom.

Actually, if you really want to influence people the knack is to ask questions that allow them the opportunity to think abut something in a different way. In other words, allow the brain to come from a different start point. First, focus on helping them explore their idea. Then focus on developing their idea to incorporate ours.

Great offer with Grape Vine Social

Get even more people to love you with help from a **Grape Vine Social** evening. *Goddess* readers are eligible for a **£10 discount** on any event when booking online.

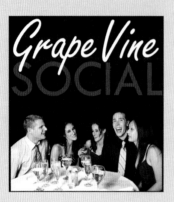

A **Grape Vine Social** wine tasting experience arouses the senses through the excellent blend of meeting other singles in a stylish setting while tasting great new wines and learning about the characteristics of each variety. You'll sound so knowledgeable when you turn up at the next dinner party, or when you want to buy the perfect bottle for your girl's night in or mate's house warming.

Grape Vine Social was created by four single professionals who wanted a more innovative way of meeting new people than going speed dating or standing in a bar. The unique concept of wine tasting dating works on the basis that a good night out requires a stylish venue, a relaxed environment, and a good crowd of social singletons with something in common to talk about. The wine tasting creates an instant ice breaker and tongue loosener!

For details on how to take advantage of this fantastic offer please go to page 488, where you'll also find information on all the other great deals found throughout *Goddess*.

Unleash your creativity,
stun with your sheer genius

'Think like a queen. A queen is not afraid to fail.
Failure is another stepping stone to greatness.'

OPRAH WINFREY (Athena)

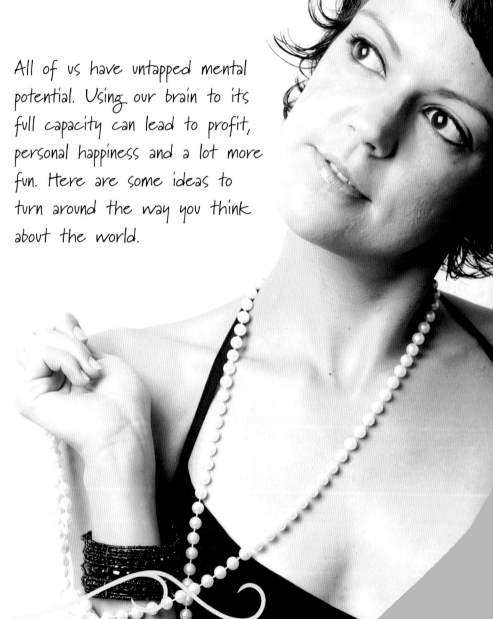

All of us have untapped mental potential. Using our brain to its full capacity can lead to profit, personal happiness and a lot more fun. Here are some ideas to turn around the way you think about the world.

Are you using all of your brain?

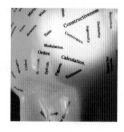

We tend to either use our left brain or our right brain. Which one predominates for you?

1. If you're going to visit a friend in a place you've never visited before you prefer

☐ a. Detailed instructions.

☐ b. The address – you'll use a map.

2. Which would be the greatest handicap to you?

☐ a. Being forced to speak instantly without having a chance to think out what you want to say.

☐ b. Having your wrists tied together so you can't use hand gestures when you speak.

3. How often are you conscious of being nervous and a little frightened at the prospect of some task?

☐ a. Once a year.

☐ b. Once a week, certainly once a month.

4. Your doodles are more likely to be

☐ a. Words.

☐ b. Pictures.

5. You would rather spend a Saturday
☐ a. Curled up with a book.
☐ b. Lying in bed daydreaming.

6. Do you find acting on your hunches yields better results for you than the problems you solve by logical reasoning?
☐ a. Hardly ever.
☐ b. Nearly all the time.

7. At work, are you more valued because
☐ a. You're great at seeing other people's point of view and then persuading them to your way of thinking.
☐ b. You have a maverick mind, suggest what no one else has thought of, and are valued for your straight talking.

Mostly 'a's: You're more likely to have a left-handed brain. Good with words and wonderful at detail and reasoning, logical is your middle name. You are good at finding the right persuasive argument. You find inspiration in being quiet and alone. But by boosting your right brain you could become more intuitive and that could make you more creative. Look at idea 88, Look at things differently, for some tips.

Mostly 'b's: You're ruled more by the right brain. Creative, daring and flexible, you are likely to consider your intuition as valuable as your IQ in making decisions. You 'see' in pictures not words. But by boosting your left brain, you could become more organised and that could make you more productive. Look at idea 87, Be organised, to find out more.

Get your creative juices flowing

85. Start anywhere, start now

How to start being creative with the things around you, right here, right now, no excuses, no prevarication.

Not knowing when or how to begin is a problem we're all quite familiar with. It may well be the reason why you're reading this. For many people, taking that first step is the most difficult aspect of any creative task. It's a declaration of intent and also an act of faith, since all too often we start a project without really knowing where to start or – worryingly – where, how or when it will end.

Sometimes, too, getting started can feel like the end of a lovely period of free and endless thinking. Giving shape and form to your ideas can feel like you're killing them a little, selling them short – or limiting them in some way that feels uncomfortable.

It's amazing, in fact, how creative one can be when it comes to finding ways of not starting. Perhaps you feel the need to clear your desk of all distractions, to have gathered together all possible source materials close to hand, and possibly even to have installed all the latest software upgrades before you can do anything. Or maybe you engross yourself in a series of seemingly urgent household chores, including laundry, washing up, gardening and supermarket shopping.

Here's an idea for you...

If you need proof of how pregnant with creative possibility 'found' objects can be, take a look at www.foundmagazine.com. You're almost bound to find something there that can become your jumping off point for a new idea.

These may look like avoidance techniques, but we are here to tell you that a fair deal of vital mental and emotional preparation goes on during this time.

To some extent, how you delay and prepare yourself for the task ahead may well help reveal the best way in to your work. Sometimes you really do have to sneak up on your ideas and view them from several angles before deciding on your point of attack.

It is not always the best approach to start at the beginning. Quite often, you need to get to the point where you can see the whole of the project and understand the style of the piece before you can deliver an opening that really sets it all off.

Sometimes you tackle the most difficult and challenging problem first. Usually this is because you've already sussed out how to solve it, or you're so bursting with energy and excitement that you need something major to attack.

On the other hand, peripheral matters can often be good starting points, because they can be done easily and quickly. There's a lot to be said for getting something done, even if it's small.

Quite when you start is a different matter – and usually depends on what your brief is. Much of the time, your creative work will be about addressing a specific problem within a specific time frame. That makes it easier to give yourself some deadlines to work to and a plan of action. But starting with a completely blank canvas and no particular brief changes the rules (a bit), and much depends on the resources you have to hand.

So pause from reading for a moment and take stock of all the things that are lying around you right now. If you're an organised person, you may well have a whole heap of really useful research material and tools ready and waiting. If you're not organised, you probably still have a whole heap of really useful research material and tools ready and waiting, but you just don't know it yet. So don't ever think that you have nothing to get started with. Just use what you can find.

> *Defining idea...*
>
> **'The brain is a wonderful organ; it starts the moment you get up in the morning and does not stop until you get to the office.'**
> ROBERT FROST

86. Do your research

When studying any new subject it's important to learn when to skim and when to take the plunge and dive in deep.

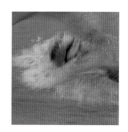

Over time you can develop the kind of instinct that will help you effectively sift and sort everything that comes your way.

When we talk about research here, we don't just mean long hours in the library or on the internet, boning up on a specialist subject like the history of liquorice or advanced bauxite mining techniques. That's the kind of research that happens when you already know what you're doing creatively, and you're attacking your interest in an organised, methodical way. If you're genuinely interested in a single

Here's an idea for you...

Cross-referencing and linking your research – either deliberately or at random – is a fantastic way to get started with new ideas. Ask yourself: 'What links the last three books I've read?' Or pick three areas you've looked at quite separately – say, cooking, code and collage – jam them together and see what kind of relationship your imagination can forge between them.

subject area, the best thing to do – even in these days of the Web and multiple information sources – is get hold of a couple of authoritative books.

But what research should you be doing when you don't know what you're looking for? The fact is that creative people are always curious, always on the lookout for new stimuli and therefore always researching in one way or another. It's therefore important to develop a sense of curiosity about everything that confronts you. Be vigilant. Ask 'why' a lot. Don't accept anything at face value.

One easy way to engage in this process of constant research is to keep a camera handy (preferably digital) and take photos of everything and anything that catches your eye. Another is to squirrel away little bits of information (and intriguing bits of rubbish!) as you find them, building up a personal collection of seemingly useless and unrelated factoids, newspaper cuttings, URL bookmarks, postcards, brochures, food packaging... anything that catches your eye. This process is sometimes referred to as 'jackdawing'.

Be careful, though: unless you are wise to the next great trick of good creative research – knowing when to ignore something you come across – you'll end up with a house full of rubbish or more photos than you could fit on Mount Fuji.

So how do you know when something you've stumbled across is worth keeping, exploring or even incorporating into your creative output? And how can you tell when the rubbish you're rifling through is just that – rubbish? Frankly, you probably don't, not right away. You simply have to develop your own instinct and work on hunches.

Always ask yourself whenever you're picking up on something for the first time: how confident am I that the effort I'm investing in this X is going to be rewarded with some kind of creative output? In short, how excited and stimulated do you feel about the creative possibilities of X?

> Defining idea...
>
> *'I find that a great part of the information I have was acquired by looking up something and finding something else on the way.'*
> FRANKLIN ADAMS, writer

Some intriguing items only need to be looked at once to be logged. You don't need to take things any further. You've simply picked out a nugget from the dross. But other sources of inspiration may require further inspection. You've simply uncovered the first signs of a rich seam that you now need to explore more thoroughly.

At this point you may need to consider your prospecting/mining techniques. Do you sift through things in fine detail or blast away at big chunks of the research landscape with a stick of dynamite? Both approaches are valid. Sifting gives you a good chance of picking up even more nuggets that you weren't expecting to find (and which may take you off on a tangent into a completely different area of research). Blasting may expose not just one seam, but many, thus encouraging you to keep digging and not curtail your research at the first sign of success.

What's important here is that your collection can become an inventory of the things that interest you; and consequently you are defining to some extent the scope and range of your work. Don't feel hemmed in by this. You'll still be able to synthesise your research materials in any number of ways, with magical results.

87. Be organised

Keeping a tidy desk and writing out long, neat to-do lists are all very well. But how can you be sure that you're going to end the day having really done something?

A big part of being creative is not simply about being 'inspired', it's about getting things done. So join the art and graft movement.

Since we all became 'knowledge workers' of one kind or another – and increasingly time-poor as a result – time management has become a whole industry in itself. The world is infested with time-management devices, theories and techniques to make them work. But don't be fooled by this. Above all, don't panic-buy the latest newfangled kit and associated manuals that will ultimately do you no good. We're here to tell you that at the core of all of this time-management mumbo-jumbo lies just one essential device: the good old-fashioned to-do list.

Whatever you use to create your to-do list – be it a piece of scrap paper, post-it notes, a white board or a PDA – the basic principles are the same. You need to concentrate on three things.

1. smart and realistic prioritisation of the tasks

2. the breaking down of big tasks into smaller, more achievable ones

3. the making of a new list for every new day

When it comes to prioritising, remember Pareto's principle, or the '80/20 rule': 80% of all results come from 20% of all efforts. This means that roughly one in five of the items on your list are truly essential and you should concentrate on completing these. Everything else may be useful, but the world won't end if they don't get done.

Don't confine yourself to simple A, B, C-style rankings of importance, however: you also need to recognise that some tasks take longer than others. For example, one 'A' category phone call might take just five minutes while an equivalent writing task could take as much as five hours.

If you have one big important thing that needs to be done by the end of the day ('Send hard copy of manuscript to publisher'), be aware that a dozen smaller tasks are hidden within that one bald statement ('Check the printer works, check there is

Here's an idea for you...
Write a list of impossible tasks. Put it away somewhere safe and only get it out at the end of a day if you're completely overwhelmed, or you feel you haven't really achieved what you set out to do. Looking at it might help you regain a sense of perspective and become re-energised for tomorrow.

Defining idea...
'Failing to plan is a plan to fail.'
EFFIE JONES, author

enough paper, print out the manuscript, proof-read, make revisions, print out fresh copy, bind/staple, write covering letter, buy large envelopes and stamps, check and write address, check time of the last post…and send!'). Each one of these smaller tasks needs to be itemised and allocated time. If you don't do this, how can you ever be sure that your one big to-do item of the day is really achievable?

Sometimes, your list will become just too cluttered with tasks, big and small. To combat this, make two separate lists: one of things you absolutely need to do today and another of things you might get round to if you have the time or inclination. Don't even think about looking at the second list until the first has been dealt with.

The end of each working day is an important time. It's then that you should compile your lists for tomorrow. Don't wait until morning and find that the first task on your new to-do list is writing a to-do list. And don't just re-edit today's list – start afresh each time.

Quite often people use up the last half hour of their working day tidying up and 'clearing the decks' for the next day. Don't. It's much better to greet the new day with a messy desk and a clear head than the other way round.

88. Look at things differently

Changing your point of view rearranges your physical relationship with everything around you. And brings a whole new meaning to 'hanging around' at parties.

It can also force conceptual changes – like thinking about a door as a 'portal' instead of just a door. Or thinking of it as 'a jar'. Or even imagining yourself being the door.

You've probably already been told several times to 'consider the bigger picture'. But how do you get yourself into a position to do it?

The next time you want to get a better handle on a situation, try and inspect it from on high: either literally, by standing on a chair or climbing a ladder (best not to do this in meetings too often), or metaphorically by imagining yourself looking from very far away at all the things that are currently up close and personal. This will help you gain some mental and emotional distance from the things and people you work with, and help you think more clearly about the possibilities open to you.

Changing your point of view needn't always be about looking – you can use your other senses too. Instead of concentrating on what things look like, make a note about how they feel (rough, smooth, warm, cold, soft, hard) or smell.

Here's an exercise you can try in the privacy of your own desk. Take a relatively small object, such as a cup, stapler or bulldog clip. Now subject your object to a series of experiments that will force you to look at things in a different way. Keep a notebook handy and write down all the thoughts that occur to you.

> Here's an idea for you...
>
> **Another obvious way to change your perspective is to 'rescale'. Imagine big things as small, and vice versa. For example, take a big thing and treat it like a little thing (like a new Lamborghini).**

First, turn your object upside down (if you picked a full coffee cup, that's your look-out). Think about how its shape has changed, how it might look like something else, how its function may be impaired by being upside down, how it might become useful as something other than what it is.

Draw it roughly with your non-drawing hand so that you have a deliberately naïve and scruffy sketch. What does it look like now?

Now put it outside and look at it through a window, so that it looks abandoned or 'not yours'. Does it look comfortable outside? Does it look like it belongs there? If not, why not? If you can bear it, leave the object outside for a few days and see how it weathers. Does it change colour? Does mould or rust form? If you can't bear it, pluck up courage to abandon it in a public place for 20 minutes anyway and write down how you feel about its potential loss.

Now bring it back indoors. Put it behind you and look at it through a mirror. What you're looking at now is its reverse image. Reach out and try and touch that image. How do you feel, being able to look but not touch? Shine a torch on it and see how light and shadow play upon it, both directly and via the mirror image. What shadow shapes can you create?

> *Defining* idea...
>
> **'Cinema, radio, television, magazines are a school of inattention: people look without seeing, listen in without hearing.'**
> ROBERT BRESSON, French film director

Now it's time to abuse your object a bit. Put it on a turntable and watch it spin around; put it under water; or suspend it on a wire and swing it. Feel free to play with it like a cat plays with a mouse. Don't be afraid to break it. And when you're done, hide it in a place where you think no one will ever find it (like a dog with a bone).

If you're enjoying this relationship with your object, take it further. Give it a name, or write a caption or slogan to go with it. Wrap it up and give it to someone as a special present. Photograph it as if it were a supermodel. Write a song about it. Wear it. Cook it. Probably best not to eat it.

The important thing is always to challenge yourself about how you perceive the object, how you use and abuse it, and what it could potentially become given your changed perspective.

89. Don't do lunch

Drink too much, stay up late, take the morning off, get up at 4 a.m., do all the wrong things and then start being creative.

In the middle of the day you should either be working obsessively or recovering from a night on the tiles.

By avoiding all the usual times for eating and sleeping, you can learn to step outside the normal social timetable. One of Bruce Mau's statements in his inspiring Incomplete Manifesto for Growth is: 'Stay up late. Strange things happen when you've gone too far, been up too long, worked too hard, and you're separated from the rest of the world.' Certainly it's important to be persistent when attacking a creative problem and to keep working even when you and everyone else feel like giving up. If you push yourself – don't bother having that break, going to lunch or heading for bed – eventually something will happen.

Working alone at night can have strange effects. The combination of silence, the dark and a sense that the rest of the world is asleep can definitely throw you in on yourself – and give rise to thoughts and feelings that you might not have access to during the day. Charles Dickens was a notorious night-owl, but instead of sitting in his room working on the next great novel, he'd actually get out and about in the wee small hours and walk for miles. Many of the characters who inhabited his fiction are drawn from his encounters with strange folk miles from home in the middle of the night.

Night-walking can allow you to see your local neighbourhood in a very different light. You meet a different type of person at three in the morning, and probably a few animals you wouldn't see during the day. Obviously, there's the fear that you might be mugged or find yourself in a difficult situation with a complete stranger – but that's part of the creative exercise. You can use that fear to take you to places you wouldn't otherwise go. And working your way through a strange and difficult situation is always going to give rise to creative material and memories that you can draw on later.

Staying up late, drinking too much and then sleeping in is, of course, another great way of missing lunch. It's amazing how many great artists were also piss-artists (Francis Bacon, Dylan Thomas, Kingsley Amis, Richard Burton…). In the case of French intellectual Guy Debord (co-founder of the Situationist International), drinking actually became a key part of his art: 'First like everyone, I appreciated the effect of slight drunkenness. Then very soon I grew to like what lies beyond violent drunkenness, when one has passed that stage: a magnificent and terrible peace, the true taste of the passage of time. Although in the first decades I may have allowed my self have slight indications to appear

Here's an idea for you...

Instead of being at your desk at 9 a.m., bright eyed and bushy tailed, try drinking all day instead, staying up until four in the morning and behaving quite badly (and yes, we are being serious). Obviously there are consequences in adopting this creative strategy. First, you'll have less time for work, because you've wasted it arsing about. You'll also be challenging social norms – your employers may well disapprove of liquid lunches. The good news is that the periods that you do work should have a furious intensity about them. By leaving things to the last minute and generally disrupting your usual working pattern, you'll inevitably start looking at the world in a different way. You'll also have to deal with the hangovers and feeling less than good. But strange things will spring to mind when you're in that tired, fuzzy state.

Defining idea...

'Always make the effort to take things one step beyond.'
MICHAEL IAN KAYE, designer

once or twice a week, it is a fact that I have been continuously drunk for periods of several months; and the rest of the time I still drank a lot.'

90. Drift

Learning the gentle art of going nowhere in particular and bumping into things can help spark your creativity – wherever it is you find yourself.

Now this is the easiest creative exercise you're ever going to get: just stumble around in any direction and make it look like you really don't know what you're doing.

There's a fine tradition of this stumbling and bumbling within all forms of art, but this key idea of 'drift' or dérive has probably been best employed and explained by Guy Debord, French intellectual and founding father of the art movement Situationist International. Dérive for Debord usually involved bouncing around Paris drunk, following some deliberately vague rules.

These included:

❀ Drop your usual motives for movement and action, relations, work and leisure activities.

❀ The average duration of a *dérive* is a day, considered as the time between two periods of sleep.

❀ The spatial field of the *dérive* may be precisely delimited or vague.

Although this sounds suspiciously like not doing much at all, it was highly political in its day, coming to the fore during the Paris riots of 1968.

By deliberately not having any specific creative aim or output in mind from the outset, Debord and others were attempting to remove themselves from the 'madeness' of modern life, the capitalistic urge to always turn creativity into product and experience life only as consumption (or shopping). By avoiding the manufactured elements of your experience (your schooling, your class, your job) you can perceive something more authentic and 'real'. This idea has roots in surrealism, and several other French '-isms' besides. As such, we're not recommending you take it too seriously. (For Debord, it led to links with international terrorist groups, alcoholism and suicide.)

Here's an idea for you...

Go for a walk online. Use an arbitrary system of clicks and links to lose yourself entirely in the Web, and confront yourself with loads of thought-provoking online material along the way.

Defining idea...

'The idea is to have no idea. Get lost. Get lost in the landscape.'
MALCOLM MORLEY, painter and sculptor

But there are two basic concepts that you might like to experiment with. The first is the idea of spurning the straight and narrow for the playful and lateral. Learn to love the free associative wander. The second is to play with the idea of useless maps and dabble in a bit of psychogeography: 'the study of specific effects of the geographical environment, consciously organised or not, on the emotions and behaviour of individuals'. Debord's example of a psychogeographic excursion was to use a map of London as his means for navigating a region of Germany. By doing so, he didn't really know where he was going, so his route would be random and his response to the geography of the German town would be spontaneous.

The British artist and musician Bill Drummond also likes to play with these ideas (you can check his work out at www.penkiln-burn.com). He once planned a tour for the band Echo & the Bunnymen based on the idea that their route would draw out a giant pair of bunny ears across the map of the UK.

Another group of artists, the Boyle family, threw darts randomly at a map of the world and have been travelling to these places ever since, taking photographs of the corresponding portion of land – be it pavement, wasteland or beach – and then creating an exact replica of it from resin and fibreglass.

We're not expecting you to go that far, but you could try a different kind of journey around your home, following a trail that's based not on a normal function (e.g. 'I need to brush my teeth so I'm going to the bathroom') but on some other sense of direction. For example, get hold of an audiotape guide of a gallery or your local town and use it to tour your home: 'In front of you is a marvellous sculpture from the nineteenth century,' says the tape, while you're stood in front of your TV in the living room. 'Turn left and enter a beautiful park,' says the tape. You turn left and you're in the downstairs toilet. This should help you look at your world in a very different way and make connections between different geographical spaces.

Alternatively, you could make your own audiotapes that describe a favourite walk in general terms and then apply it to other walks in places you don't really like.

Scott Paterson has been experimenting for a number of years with ideas about using mobile technologies to map out big cities in terms of personal experience and emotional reactions – rather than just checking off where the nearest shoe-store is. Check it out at www.pdpal.com

91. Familiar paths

Change your journey to work, go home a different way – or don't go home at all.

Many of us have rat-runs and desire paths that we follow every day without really thinking about it. If you're a regular commuter to and from work, you'll know all about this. And quite often it feels like you're operating on autopilot. You know the best route to the train station, you know exactly what time you'll arrive at work to the nearest 30 seconds, you know already which coffee shop or café you're going to stop in at on the way. This is not good for a creative person – in fact, it's like the creative equivalent of anti-matter. So you should always be looking for ways of disrupting your routine, and therefore jerking yourself out of your habitual thought patterns.

The simplest way to make a familiar route a bit strange would be to travel it by means of another mode of transport. Instead of driving, take the train; instead of the train, take a bus; instead of a bus, ride a bike.

Try also to mix up the media that you associate with different modes of transport. For example, a lot of people read newspapers on the train and not a lot of chatting goes on. On a bus, chatting is very much allowed (why, we don't know) and there's a lot more staring out of the window. In cars, there's a lot of staring out of windows, but reading newspapers is generally regarded as a bad idea, especially if you're driving. If you're travelling underground, mobile phone conversations are nixed and space is confined, so often people read paperback books or listen to personal hi-fis. These are all things to notice and react against. Try chatting on the train and staring out of the window on the underground.

All the little rituals of a typical journey also require your scrutiny. Why do you always buy the same coffee from the same vendor, or always read the same kind of book by the same kind of author? Why do you always buy the local newspaper on the way back from work, but never on the way there.

Check out other people's rituals too. If you haven't noticed already, there's a whole load of other people travelling along the same paths as you. What do they get up to? What are they doing with their journey time? What are their habits? Make notes. Maybe go as far as writing down the times that all your 'regulars' appear and disappear. They will become characters. Tiny fluctuations in their habits will form big significances in your mind. You can invent reasons for changes in their travel times, general behaviour, hairstyles, and before you know it, you've got yourself a story. As long as you're not intrusive, you could even play at surreptitiously following them. Follow, say, a person with red clothing until you come across

Here's an idea for you...

Go up to various people and ask them for directions to the same place. Note how each person has a different way of describing the same route, focusing on different landmarks and shortcuts. How does the way they see things compare with your own?

Defining idea...

'The creative approach, the right approach, is deceptively simple: avoid the commonplace; try something different. Trying change for the sake of change isn't a meaningless exercise for the creative person; it's a systematic method for achieving better results.'
MARTIN HOLLOWAY, designer

Defining idea...

'Be like the fox who makes more tracks than necessary, some in the wrong direction.'
WENDELL BERRY, farmer and writer

another, then jump from person to person. There are some great movies that concentrate on this idea – Richard Linklater's Slacker, Robert Altman's Short Cuts and Tarkovsky's Stalker. If this sounds a bit creepy, well, hell, that's because it is. People watching can be creepy, especially if it veers into stalking – so please be careful out there, and do respect other people's privacy and personal space.

92. Limbering up

Looking down at that blank page can send tsunami-sized shivers down your spine, but don't give in to the temptation to run for cover screaming, victory is just a scribble away.

The blank page is a monster, far worse than any Hollywood nightmare.

The blank page wages a war of fear and ridicule. It taunts you, it tells you it will never be filled, that anything you write will be a mere shadow of what's gone before. But be brave, take the plunge, and remember that this villain can be vanquished with a simple stroke of your pen.

First Steps

A common mistake when facing up to this immense white expanse is to believe that you can decorate it with a masterpiece straight away. The blank page wants you to think like this, as it's the first step to obliterating your confidence and self-respect. If you try to go for the big one first time, if you think you can wipe the smug expression from that blank with an instant work of sheer genius, then chances are after a few lines you will surrender and spend your days as a remorseful prisoner of war.

A Little At a Time

Most successful writers will tell you that a conflict with the blank page must be a war of attrition, not a full-on nuclear strike. The only path to victory is to gradually convert that white expanse into a page of words, your words. They don't have to be a masterpiece. In fact, they don't even have to be a story, or a poem, or a screenplay, they just have to make sense to you. Begin with random words and convert them into sentences – let them lead you. Before you know it, the blank page has shrunk, its taunts are fainter, mere whispers, and then it's gone. Don't think about what you're writing – nobody but you is ever going to see it – just keep that pen moving or those keys tapping until your old adversary has

> ## Here's an idea for you...
>
> **Do this every day. Take a blank sheet of paper, and just write for a set time at a set time. With each passing day your sketches should become more solid and less hesitant, as your confidence builds. Pick random subjects to write about and make sure you include the details, however small. When you feel up to it, start to put the bits and pieces you have been writing into a short story or a poem. You should find that the details you thought were unnecessary enable you to paint a vivid picture of something you've always taken for granted.**

> *Defining idea...*
>
> **'Writing is easy; all you have to do is sit staring at a blank sheet of paper until the drops of blood form on your forehead.'**
>
> GENE FOWLER, writer and director

vanished. Those stuttered fragments will become paragraphs, then pages, and after a while you'll wonder why on earth that innocuous white sheet of processed wood was giving you the cold sweats.

Get Off Running

OK, it's easy for me to say 'just write', but if you are still sitting facing the first page of your notepad or that virgin screen, then it may not seem so simple. The first thing to do is to get rid of the idea that you are about to start writing a finished piece. Don't try and carve out a first line of absolute genius, or write the beginnings of an epic tale you've had in your head for years, as you'll be putting yourself under an unhealthy amount of pressure. Instead, start writing a few words about the last relative that visited, your most memorable holiday, the state of your neighbour's garden, the last great argument you had.

Take practically any topic you like – if your mind is still blank, make a note of any sounds you can hear or sights from your window, or just open a dictionary at a random page and pick the first recognisable word. And once you've got that subject just start writing. Don't stop, don't edit, just gear yourself towards writing as much as possible in four or five minutes. Once you've started charging forwards, you'll find the words come more and more easily.

93. Taking the plunge

You may think your muse has passed you by, but it might be that she's the kind of girl who whispers rather than shouts. Ideas are everywhere, you just need to learn how to spot them.

So, you've cleared your desk, opened your notebook or a blank document on your computer, and are ready to write.

But suddenly your mind is devoid of inspiration and you begin to panic. What on earth are you going to write about? While there is more to being a writer than just a good idea, without an inspirational seed for your novel, screenplay or poem you are like a knight in armour with no monster to slay and no sweetheart to rescue.

Buses

For many of us, ideas are a lot like buses. You wait ages for one to come along and when it finally does it breaks down. Then, when you're walking home in the rain, three more turn up and everybody else jumps on board. Of course you may be one of the lucky ones, and already be nurturing the seed of an idea. But for the majority of writers, it's a difficult truth that it takes more than motivation alone to produce a masterpiece.

Here's an idea for you...

Stuck for something to write about? Open your eyes and look around you. There is material everywhere. Read old diaries or browse through your notebooks. Read newspapers and magazines for fascinating stories. Sit in a café and gaze out of the window. Listen to conversations, invent stories for the people who walk past and write them down. It may take a while, but if you pay attention to the world around you, then inspiration will come. The trick is not to go looking for the idea of a lifetime. Sit back, relax, soak up your surroundings, listen to the scraps of thought that flutter through your brain and before you know it you'll be running round the block screaming 'Eureka!'.

Don't Ignore It

If you have been inspired, don't ignore it. A great many writers turn away the ideas that flit around in the back of their head, begging to be put on paper. Why? Because the idea may not fit in with the self-image they want to nurture, or because they would like to write something more 'literary'. If you do this, you may be passing up a good thing. Don't ignore that persistent tug; take the bull by the horns and see where it leads.

The ideas that flutter in the half-light of our conscious mind are those that make us think, that make us laugh, or cry, or scream. Otherwise you would have forgotten them long ago. These ideas may be nothing more than a scene, a single character, perhaps something as small as a phrase. Or they might be an entire plot line, an epic journey that you have been mentally planning for years. But whether large or small, these threads are important to you, and because of this you have the ability to weave them into a work of art.

The writers I have known who have passed up these faint cries for attention have often gone on to pen strained and sterile work because the ideas they eventually work with don't engage them. Chances are, the ideas you may already possess, even if they are barely visible, have a personal significance. If you give them a chance, you will be able to draw on a wealth of personal emotion and experience in order to produce a literary work that truly connects with its readers.

> Defining idea...
> **'Experience is one thing you can get for nothing.'**
> OSCAR WILDE

But...

But what happens if you are champing at the bit and raring to go, but have nothing to write about? Don't worry. Ideas are the product of your experience, bits of your life, inspiration from books, films, plays, all mingled together in a turbulent alchemical mix. This bubbling cauldron of images, words, sounds, smells and thoughts is constantly generating tendrils and strands that appear as random ideas or dreams. Occasionally these strike a chord in our mind and germinate to become inspiration. This isn't always a flash of pure genius, so learn to watch out for the little things, the tentative thoughts, the shy visions – chances are the smallest of seeds will grow into an idea if properly nurtured.

What this means is that although you may not have an idea per se, you do have a vast wealth of experience to draw upon. This bank of material is unique – the people you have loved, the places you have visited, the games you have played – nobody else has lived the same life. Start to peel back the years and look at the vast web of activity that is your life, and the ideas will begin to roll in.

94. Playing games

Down at the English faculty, creative writing is a serious business for serious people.

But writers don't want to work all of the time. Some simple game play can be fun and inspirational.

Get your notebooks out, it's time for a few games...

I know you're here to write, and for many of you that will be a serious venture not to be undertaken lightly. Good, I'm glad you're committed; but no matter what you want to write about, or how spontaneous you want to be, it's always a good idea to practise some training exercises first. Even Miles Davis started off with scales before finding jazz.

Far From Amusing

How often have you stared at the ceiling appealing to your muse to pop down and bless you with inspiration? When I first started writing I was doing it all the time, spending afternoons alternately begging her to show up and cursing her for never doing so. I eventually realised that the poetic muse is shy. She likes to remain in the wings, out of the limelight. She'll wait until you're engrossed in other things, until your attention is elsewhere, then slip an idea into your head and disappear before you even know what's hit you.

Like her dental cousin, the poetic muse will sometimes appear when you're asleep: don't ignore those ideas that cling on after dreams – some excellent poems and stories have had their grounding in the weird world of sleep. If you want to encourage her to turn up more often, however, try playing games. And remember, inspiration isn't always an explosion. It can be a phrase, an image, even a word looked at from a new angle.

An Exquisite Corpse

Yes, it sounds creepy and disgusting (it was designed by the surrealists), but this oddly named game is one of the best tricks for developing your powers of expression and picking up strange new ideas. Get together with a few friends, not necessarily all writers. Now write a single line of poetry down at the top of a sheet of paper, fold it over so it can't be seen, and hand it to the next person who does the same thing. If you get a lot of people taking part you can end up with some fascinatingly surreal poems, but as long as there are at least two of you the results will be worthwhile and hilarious.

One variation on this is for the first player to write down an article and an adjective (the skinny) and fold the paper, the second person then writes a noun (marmoset), the third person writes a transitive verb (runs up), the fourth another article and

> ### Here's an idea for you...
>
> **Try playing detective. Spend a day giving in to your most curious urges, your most nosy habits. Pretend that everywhere you go is your crime scene, that everyone around you is a suspect (although try not to follow people around, it could get you arrested). Look for the unusual in the everyday, the surprises in familiar landscapes, the unusual snippets of conversation from the people around you. When you find something fascinating, probe it, question it, interrogate it and imagine it. From this seemingly random bundle of information can be pulled the threads that form a poem or story.**

adjective (the bleeding), and the fifth one last noun (sock). You end up with some rib-tickling sentences. They may not make much sense, but by playing around with random ideas you often find yourself tapping into your unconscious and finding inspiration.

English Lessons

Obviously there won't be many of you who don't speak English, unless you just bought this book for the pretty cover. But no matter how well you think you know your mother tongue, don't take it for granted. Those twenty-six letters may seem innocuous but they have the power to create anything you want, anything you can imagine, and your job as a writer is to make the alphabet speak in an original and surprising way.

Think of a child's abecedary (A is for Apple, B is for Bee,...). Now try writing one for grown-ups, thinking of unusual words for each letter, concrete or abstract nouns, verbs or adjectives. Focus on creating a particular tone: light-hearted, sinister, condescending – it's up to you. After each entry, write another short phrase based on whatever the image conjures, so you end up with something along the lines of 'A is for absolution; asked for but never given'. Another interesting game to play, based on a poem by John Updike, is to use 26 adjectives, each beginning with a different letter, to characterise 26 people. Use as many different words as you like, but the central description has to be based around that adjective.

Defining idea...

'Anything is fit material for poetry.'
WILLIAM CARLOS WILLIAMS

Is habit hindering your brain?

Smart people aren't necessarily cleverer – they just do things differently from the rest of us. Their brains are flexible and they will try something new to achieve what they want. To get an idea of how hard it is for you to think flexibly, tomorrow do the following:

- Brush your teeth with the opposite hand from normal.
- Take a different route to work.
- Buy a newspaper with a different political persuasion to your usual.
- Listen to talk radio if you normally listen to music.
- Smile at five people you'd normally not acknowledge.
- Answer the phone with the opposite hand from normal.
- Remain serious with three people you'd normally be especially 'smiley' with.
- Read ten pages of a novel you would normally run a mile from.
- Take a different method of transport home.
- Leave your mobile off if you use it a lot. Answer every call if you usually use 'call divert'.
- Eat food for dinner that you would normally avoid.
- Get into bed on the 'wrong' side.

OK, add up how many of these you actually did. Less than four and you find it pretty uncomfortable to move out of your normal pattern. The higher your score, the more flexible your brain is likely to be. The lower it is, the more you need this entire section on creativity and thinking smarter.

Get creative with this special offer from The Pink Toolbox Company

With a special offer **of £5** off, there's no excuse to leave those little DIY jobs untended.

Ready packed for use in **The Pink Toolbox** are a set of standard tools, all in pink: hammer, 4-in-1 multipurpose screwdriver, multiway spirit level, 5m tape measure, set of allen keys and adjustable wrench, all of which will make you the mistress of any unhung pictures, flatpack furniture or loose nuts and bolts around the home.

Apart from these indispensable tools, that would retail at around £40 if bought individually, also included are some items to complete your basic home kit such as scissors, disposable craft knife, string, picture hooks and wire, fuses and a bottle of general purpose oil.

The tools may be pink, but they're not lacking in strength and quality. For more information visit www.pinktoolbox.co.uk

For details on how to take advantage of this fantastic offer please go to page 488, where you'll also find information on all the other great deals throughout *Goddess*.

Terms and conditions
This offer is valid until 31 December 2007 and is subject to availability. The £5 discount will only apply if bought via telephone with The Pink Toolbox Company and cannot be used in conjunction with any other offer or promotion. Postage and packing is £2.95 per order.

95. Questions, questions

The key to quality thinking is asking quality questions. If you fancy giving yourself a mental stretch by tackling some testing questions, here are some real doozies.

Unless you're a politician or a criminal (or possibly both), good incisive questions are to be absolutely cherished. Answered honestly, they can propel our thinking in new directions, generating fresh insights and understanding on the way.

A good question unlocks or clarifies our current thinking. Although we can answer almost any question – no matter how brilliantly formed – with banal platitudes if we so wish, a good question has the potential to shake us out of any mental complacency.

The following is a list of questions I have found over the years to be productive. I've voiced them in the first person so that you can ask them initially of yourself, but they work equally in the second person, asked of others.

The questions are in no particular sequence. Nor would I recommend that you tackle them all in one go. Cast your eyes over the list and see what's catches your interest. OK then? The clock starts…now.

Here's an idea for you...

Sometimes when people are answering questions their initial response doesn't go far or deep enough. In case this happens, prepare some supplementary questions to keep to hand. Asking 'Can you be more specific?' or 'Do you have anything else to say on this subject?' can help to keep the exploration of the question going in a productive manner.

What do I want to achieve with my life?

What should I want?

What matters to me at this time in my life?

Why do I want what I want?

Does it really matter?

Who am I living my life for?

What don't I know?

What do I not question about myself?

What can I learn from this?

What are my plans for the next year?

What support do I need in order to...? Who can help me?

How ambitious am I these days?

Am I still learning and growing?

What needs my attention today/this week/this month/this year?

If I died tomorrow, what would be missing from my obituary that I would like to see there? What can I do about it?

What am I afraid of losing?

What am I afraid of gaining?

What would I like to overhear people saying about me?

What would I not like to hear said about me?

Why is my best friend my best friend?

Would winning the lottery be a blessing or a curse?

What would I do if I knew I couldn't fail?

Is that all there is to this?

How do I know this to be true?

In what way am I causing or reinforcing this behaviour?

If I had a year to live, what would I do with the time?

How do I feel when I get up in the morning?

When have I felt most alive?

Does my reputation work for or against me?

What would I like to be able to do in one year's time that I can't currently do? Or five years from now? Ten years? Twenty-five years? Fifty years? One hundred years? (You never know)

What action can I take rather than worrying?

What am I prepared to give up in order to...?

What's the best outcome in this situation? And the worst?

What could affect my plans?

What do I need to do to make sure that I get what I want?

What do I need to find out before I go any further?

Why not?

What's the best thing I've done in the last year and why?

What aspects of my life do I enjoy the most? And the least?

What could other people learn from me?

So how did you get on? Of course, you asking yourself those questions might feel like a slightly stilted experience. For that reason, it can be worthwhile to get somebody else to put the questions to you. For one thing, that gets you to speak your answers aloud, and that in itself can be quite instructive. Sometimes it's only when we hear ourselves say something out loud that we realise how true it is for us (or occasionally how wrong we are!).

96. Improve your memory

How the memory works, and what you can do to improve yours.

The last thirty years have seen tremendous advances in our understanding of how the brain works. Scientists can pinpoint with increasing confidence which parts of the brain perform which specific function.

However, as far as memory improvement is concerned, there's not a lot of new advice out there. There is some interesting research emerging from America (where else?) into the use of pharmaceutical pick-me-ups called ampakines as a tool for boosting mental performance, but it's still early days in the clinical trial process.

When it comes to recalling information more readily, the basic techniques for enabling this have not changed substantially for decades. Back in 1956, psychologist George A. Miller published a paper that helped to spark the cognitive revolution. The paper was called 'The magical number seven, plus or minus two: some limits on our capacity for processing information'. Miller's research revealed that the average human can hold only about seven items in mind at any one time. Some can hold only five items while others can comfortably manage up to nine.

This natural limitation on our capacity to remember has been with us for centuries and it helps to explain why we have needed to develop methods and techniques to help us extend our capacity to remember information.

The word 'mnemonics' originally meant the study and development of systems for improving the memory. Over time, the word has come to be commonly used to describe the systems themselves. Here are some examples of mnemonics:

Spelling mnemonics: these help us remember how to spell tricky words by creating memorable sentences with words whose first letters 'spell out' the word in question. For example, RHYTHM: Rhythm Helps Your Two Hips Move.

Numeric mnemonics: these help us to remember numbers via sentences whose words have the number of letters corresponding to the number itself. Example: a sentence to help us remember that the value of pi = 3.141592 might be 'How I wish I could calculate pi.'

Acrostics: this entails using the first letter of each word you are trying to remember to make a sentence. For example, My Dear Aunt Sally would help us recall the

---

Here's an idea for you...

On the basis that practice makes perfect, simply repeating the information is a good memory aid. Remember the children's game 'I'm going on a picnic and I'm bringing...' As each new object is added, the old objects are repeated. People can often remember a large number of objects this way. When remembering a list of things, you might try a similar concept, maybe 'I'm going to a very important meeting and I need to...'

mathematical order of operations – Multiply and Divide before you Add and Subtract.

Rhyming mnemonics: e.g. 'Thirty days hath September, April, June and November.'

Chunking: a method for remembering long numbers by breaking them down. So 04711998 might break down to 04 71 19 98. If there are combinations of numbers which are meaningful to you, so much the better. You might want to recast the number as 04 71 (the month and year I was born) and 1998 (the year our first child was born).

Number/rhyme: typically used for remembering up to ten items. For the numbers one to ten, you first come up with a rhyming word. Common rhymes are One: Bun, Two: Shoe, Three: Tree. You then assign the word you want to remember to a number. So you might assign the word 'burglar' to the number one. You then come up with a visual image associating 'burglar' with your rhyming word for one, namely 'bun'. (Hope you're keeping up with this.) The more memorable the image the better. You end up with a set of images which feature the word you want to remember, and because you've created a memorable association, you're more likely to recall the word.

Number/shape: a variation on number/rhyme, but instead of using One: Bun, you come up with a shape to represent the numbers. So the number 1 might be a pencil or a poker, 2 might be a swan. You then associate the word with the shape. So our burglar has to be

Defining idea...

'A memory is what is left when something happens and does not completely unhappen.'
EDWARD DE BONO

Defining idea...

'The two offices of memory are collection and distribution.'
SAMUEL JOHNSON

associated with a poker in this case – shouldn't be too difficult to come up with a visual image for that one.

The story method: similar to number/rhyme, except that the images are linked together as part of a story. This makes it easier to remember the order of events and create a memorable mnemonic.

97. Make it happen

Making it happen is about the desire to get on and take action, and to do so to a high standard. There's much more to life than giving yourself a gentle cerebral massage.

Let's confront a necessary if uncomfortable truth: knowledge without action is sterile; action without knowledge is blind. If the old enemy was mindset, the new enemy is inertia.

A friend of mine has a favourite four-letter acronym – JFDI – which, in the Parental Guidance version, stands for Just Flipping-well Do It. It's a call to arms of sorts, a recognition that there comes a point when the thinking and talking need to stop, and when ideas either turn into actions or regress back into mental mush.

So what's your track record like when it comes to making things happen? Are you an ace implementer who always follows plans through? Or are you somebody who's infinitely better at the talk than the walk – to use a phrase much loved by a colleague of mine, are you 'all mouth and no trousers'?

Most probably, you're selectively dynamic, i.e. sometimes you take effective action, sometimes you don't. If that's the case, you're welcome to join a not particularly select club sometimes better known as 'the vast majority of us'.

Let's look at what's probably a familiar example. Think back to an occasion when you bumped into an old friend or acquaintance in the street that you hadn't seen in a while. Chances are that you had a perfectly pleasant, if brief, chat and then parted with both of you saying that it would be great to meet up for a coffee or a beer sometime soon. Assuming you weren't lying through your molars about wanting to see them again, did you take any kind of responsibility for ensuring that the follow-up latte took place?

Here's an idea for you...

Once you have decided on a particular course of action, share your plans with somebody else. Declaring our intentions to others can lend real impetus to the process of making them happen. This probably works best when you're sharing plans face-to-face (it's pretty squirm-inducing having to tell your friends and colleagues you haven't done something you said you would). Increasingly, though, people use the internet as a means of sharing plans and supporting each other (I know of a group of people who operate a very successful weight loss club via phone and email).

If you're the sort of person who does habitually make sure that the next get-together happens, then you probably have the willpower, the energy and the organising skills to pick up a good idea and run with it. If, on the other hand, you find that those get-togethers never seem to get it together, you're one of the many amongst us whose good intentions sometimes get swamped by having too many other priorities clamouring for our attention. A friend of mine calls this phenomenon 'life overload'.

To make something happen in our lives, we need to have two particular things going for us – focus and energy. By focus, I'm talking about the ability to apply concentrated attention to a particular task. Energy is about our readiness to take action in pursuit of a chosen outcome. You need to have both in place to be able to pursue a goal in a purposeful manner.

Here's my advice. When it comes to making changes in your life, don't succumb to a rather insidious twenty-first-century condition called action-listitis. You know the sort of thing. For example, it's the start of a new year and so you resolve to get fit, lose weight, be nicer to people, learn the bassoon, take up macramé, sort out your finances, mend your bike, redecorate a bedroom or two, write a novel, give up booze, get more sleep, go to the movies more often, get to grips with Sudoku, etc., etc., etc.

Drawing up a list with twenty-three action points on it is almost certainly doomed to end in failure. If we manage to achieve four things from the list, the other nineteen stare back off the page at us in silent disappointment.

So rather than create a huge shopping list to take to the self-improvement superstore, pick just one thing to do. Pick the one change you would most like to make and then really apply some focus and energy to making sure it happens.

How do you pick that one thing? You need to decide what the most important criteria are for making the choice. For example, it could be the thing that inspires you the most, or it might be something that currently makes you really angry about yourself.

Whatever your choice, remember the words of Doctor Seuss: today is your day! Your mountain is waiting, so...get on your way.

98. Maintain your brain

Here are some tips for keeping your thinking gear in fine fettle.

What I'm about to say shouldn't come as any kind of surprise: your brain is a lifelong work-in-progress.

There's so much we all can do to develop our potential. Take it from me: given the amount of change we can expect to face over the coming decades, lifelong learning is not a trendy concept dreamt up by the human resources department, it's a survival necessity.

So, with an eye to the future, there are a few attributes you might want to consider working on if you're planning to go for more brain upgrades in the years to come. Here are a few suggestions:

Commit to lifelong learning

Here's an idea for you...

Open yourself to new experiences and insights by experimenting relentlessly (but legally, of course). Become a creature of un-habit: go to a Peter Gabriel concert; take a different route into work; try a different option off the menu; look for one thing, find something else; start a journal or an audio diary; buy a magazine you've never read before; check out a Girls Aloud gig (oops, probably went a bridge too far there).

Recognise that the skills, knowledge and experience that got you where you are today won't be enough to get you where you want to be in the future.

'Learning' does not always have to equal 'courses'. Read a book; talk to an expert; surf the net for information; just practice; take a secondment to another part of the business; go and do some work in the community.

Become a fluent communicator: Verbally and in writing

Feel confident that you can give a prepared talk that has style, substance and clarity.

Aim to be 'media-friendly' at all times. It's now pretty much impossible for a politician to succeed without being a skilled communicator. People who are capable at their work but who don't come across well on TV or in person will struggle to move into senior roles in the future.

To polish your writing skills, try reading The Pyramid Principle by Barbara Minto, to my mind the best book around on how to present complex ideas in writing.

Work and re-work your CV – it's your career calling card.

Embrace technology

Fewer than half of Britain's senior directors can send and receive their own emails and 60 per cent are unable to log on to their company's website without help. There may be something faintly comical and endearing about the greybeards struggling to find the on/off switch. However, if you're a thirty- or forty-something with a disdain for new technology, be warned. You can run, but you can't hide.

> ### Defining idea...
>
> **'Stay hungry, stay foolish.'**
> STEVE JOBS, CEO of Apple and Pixar

Be opportunistic

When you're given the chance to try something new, make 'Why not' your default response.

Be spontaneous.

Don't think yourself to a standstill

Upgrading your brain involves a mixture of thinking and action. You need both – thinking without action is sterile, action without thinking lacks direction and mindfulness.

As Richard Pascale once put it, it's easier to act yourself into a new way of thinking than to think yourself into a new way of acting.

You've made a good start in picking up this book (and an even better start if you've read this far!), but in itself it means little. To tweak a cliché: today is your first day with your upgraded brain. So what are you going to do about it?

Stay curious

For a few nights back in June 2005, the moon appeared to be larger than normal in the night sky. Generally acknowledged at the world's largest optical illusion, even NASA couldn't explain the phenomenon. There's so much we don't know, so much we have yet to experience. Life can be just as entrancing whether you are eight or eighty.

Develop your goals, pursue your dreams, go out and grab your life.

Compose the life you want but don't ignore opportunities to be spontaneous.

Of course, this is nothing like a comprehensive tip-sheet. After all, your brain is a lifelong work-in-progress. So now go off and develop six more ideas of your very own!

99. Develop your logic

Sometimes we know immediately what we have to do to tackle a problem. Here's a more structured approach you can adopt when the answer isn't so obvious.

Problems, problems. I don't know about you, but I rarely get through the day without facing more than my fair share of snags, mishaps and quandaries.

Whether it's my children wanting help with their maths homework, a doorknob dropping off or something else entirely, there's always something going on to test my problem-solving mettle. In most cases, the solutions are self-evident – setting up a project team to sort out the knobless door at home would be a solution-generating sledgehammer to crack a problematic nut.

Once in a while, though, a bigger problem looms. On these occasions, it's not always immediately apparent what should be done for the best. Indeed, sometimes it's not absolutely clear what the problem is. That's when I like to reach for the Xerox Problem-Solving Process.

In fairness, there are any number of problem-solving processes out there that you could use. Search on Google and you'll find five-, eight-, even ten-step versions. They all take you through the same essential process but break it up in different ways.

> Here's an idea for you...
>
> **After your brainstorming has generated lots of ideas for tackling your problems, whittle the ideas down to a realistic set of options by thinking about the most important criteria that your chosen solution will need to satisfy. For example, it might be most important to you that your solution saves money, or that it saves time or is accepted by everyone. Once you know your most important criteria, you can really get to grips with identifying and implementing the most appropriate solution.**

The Xerox approach isn't inherently better than most of the others, but it does provide a structured basis for tackling the decent-sized problems you're like to come across at home and at work. It consists of six steps, namely:

1. Identify and select the problem
2. Analyse the problem
3. Generate potential solutions

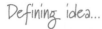

Defining idea...

'**All that is comes from the mind; it is based on the mind. It is fashioned by the mind.**'
The Pali Canon

4. Select and plan the solution
5. Implement the solution
6. Evaluate the solution

Let's have a quick look at each in turn:

Step 1. Identify and select the problem

What do we want to change? What's going on that makes you think there's a problem? Who is affected? When, where and how is it happening? Why is it happening? What's the point of this? Use the evidence you're gathering as a basis for coming up with a definition of the problem and what the desired outcome is.

Step 2. Analyse the problem

What's currently stopping us from reaching the desired outcome? What seem to be the key causes?

Step 3. Generate potential solutions

What are all the ways in which we could achieve the desired outcome? A brainstorming session (sometimes called a 'thought showers session' in the more politically correct environments) would be the classic tool to use at this point.

Step 4. Select and plan the solution

Of all the possible solutions, what is the best way to solve this problem? What are the benefits and risks attached to each possible solution? Do we have the necessary resources? Do we have enough time to implement the approach?

Step 5. Implement the solution

Are we following the plan? Is the plan working as expected or does it need tweaking as we go along?

Step 6. Evaluate the solution

How well did it work? Did it turn out as expected? If not, what happened and why? How well will the implemented solution bear up in the future?

As mentioned earlier, this is not the only problem-solving process around. There is, for example, another popular model that goes under the name of Fan Dance. It's an acronym describing an eight-step method – For, Against, Now what?, Definition, Alternatives, Narrow down, Check consequences, and Effect.

Whichever process you decide to go with, the benefits are the same. Any structured problem-solving process gives shape to your thinking, offers the key tools you need at every key stage, and – most crucial of all – enables you to focus on the problem at hand.

100. Make more mistakes faster

Working at speed with a high level of error can help you 'fail better'. Which means you'll get to something good quicker.

Creativity is often about speed of throughput. Believe it or not, making a hash of it at high speed may be the key to getting to where you want to go.

This idea is often attributed to Andy Grove of Intel, the processor manufacturing company that helped revolutionise the computer industry in the 1980s and 1990s. When your business is about crashing out millions of bits of finely etched silicon, it's easy to see why you might be prepared to keep the production line rolling even if a few batches get screwed up along the way.

For the sculptor who spends six months working one piece in stone, it may be less easy to write the resulting work off as a failure and start again. Nevertheless, for most of us, Grove's principle is a sound one. You have to keep scribbling and sketching, modelling and planning and thinking, setting things up to knock them down, scrumpling up bits of paper and throwing them in the bin, crashing and rebooting your computer, working continuously with enthusiasm and energy and wit, and above all without any embarrassment about the obvious cock-ups along the way. If you do this intelligently and energetically, other people will almost certainly be affected by your positive spirit and join you on your journey. Those who write you off as foolish and annoying – well, maybe hanging out with them is just another mistake and it's time to move on.

Also remember that mistakes are not always mistakes. Look at them another way and they become happy accidents. According to movie director Robert Altman, 'Chance is another name that we give to our mistakes. And all of the best things in my films are mistakes.' Mistakes, he is saying, are the stuff of life. And for him, they are also the stuff of art. (And according to chaos theory, they are also the stuff of stuff.)

> Defining idea...
>
> **'If I had my life to live over I'd dare to make more mistakes next time.'**
> NADINE STAIR, poet

This is the same attitude to life that Oscar Wilde describes when he writes: 'Nowadays most people die of a sort of creeping common sense, and discover when it is too late that the only things one never regrets are one's mistakes.'

Probably the most famous blunderer of them all is Alexander Fleming. Not only did he discover penicillin by accidentally contaminating some Petri dish samples and then not bothering to wash them up for a few days, he also discovered lysozyme when he didn't bother using a handkerchief and his nose accidentally dripped into a dish of bacteria. Are you creative enough not to wipe your nose for a week just to see what accidents might happen?

The true moral of this story might be: if it ain't fixed, break it.

Certainly, one of the best ways to understand how some things work is to break them apart. For your family's sake, it's probably best if you work out how to put them back together again as well, although this isn't critical (unless it's grandma's Zimmer frame). And if it turns out that you've broken something irretrievably, try and find a new use for what you've got left. Look at kids: they rarely throw old broken toys away, but remodel, fuse and repurpose them for use in another game.

And talking of small kids, it's as well to remember that we only ever learn to walk after a lot of falling over. In fact, if you want to get technical about it, walking is falling over. If you don't believe us, get up now and lean forward like you are going to fall – then stick your leg out at the last minute. Almost inevitably, your other leg will kick in and you'll take not one step but two in order to break your fall.

So now you see that even something as basic as walking is really just a controlled way for your body to blunder around the place.

101. Playing politics – and winning

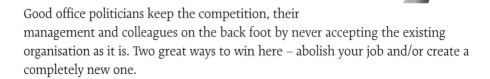

Show us someone who says they're not interested in office politics and we'll show you someone who's not going up the organisation as far as their talent deserves.

Good office politicians keep the competition, their management and colleagues on the back foot by never accepting the existing organisation as it is. Two great ways to win here – abolish your job and/or create a completely new one.

Promotions never come as fast as we want. The organisation settles down, your boss is comfortable with your performance but has no intention of promoting you because, you know, they'll have to find a replacement. And they certainly don't want you to get their job.

The time has come for you to play some office politics and make that new job happen. After all, you need to do more than survive in this area.

Job description, what job description?

One of the things you can do is to make your job redundant. This may seem a risky process, but it's a great mistake in career planning to assume that the current management structure is the one in which you have to succeed. Indeed the opposite is the case – and you'll probably get away with it.

Here's the reasoning. Many jobs exist because they have always done so, rather than because they represent the best way of getting things done successfully. If you go into a new job and do it the best way for your organisation to succeed, you'll probably find yourself going way outside the original job description. So, your way of operating gets better results. Now delegate as much of the job as you can in your new way of working and guess what. When you explain what has happened to your boss, he or she will realise that they need to change the structure of their operation. If you've done this ploy well, they'll also realise that your tasks are now handled much more efficiently and they don't need you in your old role. You've got away with it. Time to move onwards and upwards.

> *Here's an idea for you...*
>
> **Look around at how you and your colleagues work. Now ask yourself this question: 'If I owned this business, what changes would I make to my part of the organisation to make a big improvement?' This should give you loads of ammunition to put up a paper that suggests the changes which sensibly should be made. Now you're off and running towards inventing and then taking the new job that you really want.**

The fundamental lesson here is to use your influence and authority to get the best results possible without paying much attention to how things were done in the past.

Here's an idea for you...

'If the devil doesn't exist, but man has created him, he has created him in his own image and likeness.'
FYODOR DOSTOEVSKY

Oh, the obvious person for the job seems to be me
The corollary of abolishing your job, namely inventing a new one, also holds true. People who succeed are the ones who help the organisation keep up to date and help to prevent it ossifying.

It is easier to create a new job if the change helps the organisation achieve better performance, but it's possible to do it for your own purposes alone. Probably started by putting up an unsolicited paper, the creation of a new job is in two parts. First describe the new way of doing business that will ensure that the job of your dreams is going to exist. Then sell the idea. What you're doing here is showing what your new plan will do in business terms rather than in structural or people terms. Don't reveal your whole hand at this stage because it's too early. Don't give anyone the opportunity to say that what you're doing is for your own greater glory rather than the advancement of the organisation. Having sold the change, produce your implementation plan and, of course, include the new positions required.

Next, it's time to go for it. Do not at this stage play any kind of shrinking violet game; clearly show that you are the person for the promoted role you've chosen and defined. You have the business benefits behind you and they have been agreed, so tell people that you should have the job. Make sure, by the way, the new job description has all the elements needed for your next step – access to senior management and a high profile when required. The risk and return on getting away with this career procedure will be very good if you've got it right. After all, you've moulded a job where the circumstances and your skills will be a perfect fit.

And if all else fails...fake it

102. Faking being well read

Given that we're still judged by what we read, how do you fake being well read if you've flipped through nothing but Cosmo and Harry Potter since school?

A friend of mine gets very upset about the fact that, however bad the book, and however good the TV drama, you will always get more cred for having read a book than for watching the TV.

Victoria Beckham ('Posh Spice') once confessed to 'never having read a book' in her life and was immediately ridiculed by all and sundry. She quickly took it back. While it's fair to say that ridiculing Posh is fair game at any time, it's interesting that even bubblegum pop eye-candy can't be seen to be poorly read – it's an admission too far for anyone, it seems. So if your cultural tastes lean more to Spice Girl than Solzhenitsyn then this is what to do.

First off consider what your goal is in trying to pull this off. Are you attempting an all-round performance with a view to creating an aura of sophistication and culture, or are you trying to impress (or simply keep up with) someone who is themselves better read than you. Think carefully because the answer will define your strategy.

If you've never really read anything more taxing than cereal packets yet need to pass yourself off as the bionic bookworm then you're going to have to put in a little bit of legwork. You might even have to read something. Not much, though – that would be missing the point. For a start don't bother with any of the big fat ones (not that you were going to anyway). There are short cuts to cultivating your literary savoir-faire – reading a couple of short poems, for example, preferably in a foreign language, will go a long way.

If you realise you are expected to know a novelist then don't go for the favourites but instead find something short and obscure. Most of the big boys have written the odd short story or novella on the way to fame and the more weird and wonderful the better. Use this to head off any direct questions about the other books you've read. For example, if anyone starts talking about Hemingway's For Whom The Bell Tolls you need only nod and mumble something about the seeds for the novels being sowed early in the (satisfyingly) short stories.

A top tip for just-add-water intellectualism is to skim a copy of Schopenhauer's Essays and Aphorisms, which provides bite-size nuggets barely longer than the jokes in a Christmas cracker. Because they are philosophical musings on just about anything, they are also ripe to be brought out on almost any occasion. Use discretion when doing this, though; the person who insists on coming out with the same phrase over and over doesn't come across as well read, just well annoying.

Good phrases for the bluffer include lots of vague adjectives ('authoritative', 'entrancing', 'hypnotic') and a couple of equally vague themes ('alienation', 'timelessness', 'loss of innocence'). String these together and you're on a winner. Try it. You can sum up anything from Chekov to Charlie and the Chocolate Factory as a 'hypnotic study of alienation and loss'.

> Defining idea...
>
> **'Books . . . are like lobster shells: we surround ourselves with 'em, then we grow out of 'em and leave 'em behind, as evidence of our earlier stages of development.'**
> DOROTHY L. SAYERS

By the way, if you're pretending knowledge of books you've never read and it looks like you're going to be rumbled, don't forget that even those who really have read the work are unlikely to remember much detail. This is doubly so if they also read hundreds of other books and have been doing so for a long time. So a risky (but very satisfying) strategy is to infer that you read the entire works of an author years ago in your youth when devouring all the world's literature. This is harder to pull off if you're closer to sixteen than sixty but only literature professors can quote chapter and verse from books they've read. There is even a way to reverse this and head off the rumbling. When someone is detailing a precise scene or character, smile fondly and suggest that this freshness is because of their having only just discovered the writer. Then glaze over gently and nod as if casting your mind back to those days when you too were gauche enough to get excited about Gogol or Proust.

103. Passing an exam without revising

Spending hours and hours studying, wasting your life – social life at that – all for a piece of paper seems ludicrous, doesn't it? Well perhaps you don't have to.

Studying is, at the best of times, an exceptionally dull process. We use so little of what we retain in the real world that it hardly seems worth all the effort. The reality is, of course, we have no choice, unless we fancy ending up on the bap heap, at the bottom of the economic pile, flipping burgers for below-subsistence wages.

Why on earth do they make us study during the summer? When it's hot and sunny all you want to do is chase the opposite sex and frolic in the hay; the last thing on your mind is that all-important exam you have to prepare for. Perhaps it's a government-imposed mechanism for avoiding teen pregnancies. Or maybe it's the sadists in the exam system who want to make your life a misery. (We favour the latter.) So you find yourself in a bit of a bind. On one hand you know you have got to do at least the bare minimum to pass your exams; on the other, you want to escape the thin air of your bedroom. So what can you do to maximise the amount of time you get to play and ensure you do okay in the exams? Well, with the judicious use of a handful of techniques and tools you ought to satisfy your desires while still passing your exams. Of course, the balance you choose to place on both is entirely up to you!

Here are some favourite revision reducers:

❀ Subliminal learning – who needs books when you can have a few tapes with the key facts on them? After a day's lazing around in the sun, all you have to do is lie on your bed, pop on the Walkman and let your subconscious brain do the work. How's about that for an approach!?

❀ Use study aids – why reinvent the wheel when you can draw on all the advice and support you need from the experts? A lot of what you need to know for the exam can be condensed into a few pages of text contained within a study guide you can buy for a few pounds.

> *Here's an idea for you...*
>
> **Make a list of the exam techniques you can think of and decide which ones could offer you the greatest return for the least amount of effort. Certainly give question spotting a go – although it's a bit high risk, so is doing nothing. Once you have got your list, give each technique a try and focus on a small subset that allows you to maximise your frolicking.**

❀ Time management – if you can focus your efforts into a couple of hours a day, and we do mean focus here, then you can maximise the time you have for fun. It requires the self-discipline of a self-flagellant but without the scarring.

❀ Buy some time from someone else – if you are one of these lucky people who have plenty of cash or rich parents who would rather throw money at a problem than deal with it directly, then you are in luck. There are plenty of people out there who will prostitute themselves to get you through the exams: teachers, failed academics and smart-arses desperate for cash. Passing the buck to someone who knows the system is a sure-fire way to reduce the amount of time you need to be spending on revising.

> ## Defining idea...
>
> **'Learning is not compulsory ...
> neither is survival.'**
> W. EDWARDS DEMING

✿ Tune in to your natural way of learning – yes, we all have preferences, and sadly most of us are oblivious to them. You can waste literally weeks trying to get stuff into your skull to no avail. The simple reason why you fail is that you may have completely missed the way your brain prefers to learn. To absorb as much information as possible, as effortlessly as possible, means that you have to get to the root of how you learn, be it in pictures, words or feelings.

So there you have it, a collection of smart ways you can try out to limit the amount of study time. Don't get too carried away, though. This doesn't mean you can do nothing at all. And remember that spending too much time out in the sun shrivels your skin and gives you cancer, so maybe study is good for you after all.

104. Doing nothing at work

For run-of-the-mill workers, the key to loafing is to create an illusion of purpose and industry that deflects the scrutiny of superiors.

The late, great Spike Milligan used to tell a tale of his army years, during which one inspired loafer took to wandering around with a tin of DDT (insecticide). If ever anyone challenged him to explain what he was doing he snapped sharply to attention and replied 'de-lousing sir'. Nobody ever enquired further and he would be free to carry on doing precisely nothing in peace.

We're not saying that you should take to schlepping around large containers of poison (although this may still work in the military, prisons, and fast-food outlets) but the key points to this technique are as true today as they ever were. The first is that if you want to spend all day doing sweet Fanny Adams then you'd better have a cover story. The second is that whatever that story is you must be prepared to launch into it with conviction and the kind of enthusiasm that suggests nothing would please you more than to explain it in incomprehensible detail until your interrogator's ears bleed.

When it comes to a cover story there's nothing like a good prop and we've come a long way from the DDT tin. Today's loafers have at their fingertips an armoury of high-tech tools.

Here's an idea for you...

Get yourself a key friend in geekdom. Someone savvy on the systems side is needed to tell you crucial info such as whether the company has keystroke monitoring systems to record effort and detect games players. Bunking off to see a systems person is also a universally accepted ploy, even in the future. It's reassuring to note that in the high-tech futuristic vision The Island, Ewan McGregor regularly shouts 'computer down' and slides off to see his mate Steve Buscemi in tech support. Note also that the long-term result of this behaviour is that he gets to hang out on yachts and shack up in a playboy mansion with Scarlett Johansson.

Once the great trick was to always be seen with a clipboard. Clipboards speak volumes about business, importance, and those endless 'jobs' like 'stocktaking' and 'time and motion studies' that were always nothing more than the inventions of loafers looking to do as little as possible before knocking-off time came around again. The trusty clipboard (and its executive brother, the bulging file) can still come in handy but if you really want to get away with it these days it's time to go digital. Digital devices add a whole new dimension to loafing because their very presence intimidates the Luddites and their multi-tasking flexibility makes it hard for even the initiate to call your bluff. Proof positive of this is the evolution of the uber-loafer – the king of the freeloading food chain. Posing as 'systems administrator', 'network engineer' or any one of a dozen similarly meaningless monikers, these geek gods have reached the noodling nirvana where they can face down anybody from line managers to the CEO. This is done with nothing more than a withering look and a sarcastic outpouring of gobbledygeek. A typical example would go as follows:

Baffled CEO/MD/HR exec: 'So what exactly have you been doing for the last three weeks?'
Uber-loafer [sighing at the pathetic inadequacy of the question/questioner]: 'Patching the Unix kernel.'
CEO/MD/HR exec [even more baffled]: 'Patching the colonel?'
Uber-loafer [with the exaggerated patience normally reserved for small children]: 'Upgrade, protocol, security, TCP/IP, parallel-processing, cluster, hacker, hexadecimal, three-speed, cupcakes ..." [the final words of which are normally delivered to the back of an already retreating questioner].

You don't have to be an uber-loafer to take a leaf from their book. Even the humblest warehouse worker, if wielding one of those brilliant, handheld data input devices, is in a position of strength because nobody, not even the person who bought them, really knows all the things you might be doing with them. Other examples include Blackberries ('of course I'm not skiving; can't you see I'm emailing?'), laptops ('Fragfest? All-out Hover Tank war? Certainly not; it's a 3D graphic representation of next-year's projected margins'), or any kind of spreadsheet (make sure you can bring up an elaborate diagrammatic representation with a triumphant punch of the button).

> *Defining* idea...
>
> **'Look at me: I worked my way up from nothing to a state of extreme poverty.'**
> GROUCHO MARX

This outstanding offer from Olan Mills will make you smile

Whether you're looking to relax and unwind, or wanting to strut your stuff in front of the camera, this **free** Elegance make-over and photo session from **Olan Mills Photography** is your chance to get the full supermodel treatment. You'll look and feel like a real goddess with this outstanding offer (normal price £24.95).

This ultimate pampering session will take around two hours and starts with a professional make-up artist working closely with you to make sure you get the look you desire. You'll feel positively spoiled by all the attention and you'll get a make-up tip sheet to take away with you so that you can re-create your look time and time again.

What ever look you choose, your photographer will create a stunning series of images in a variety of styles and poses so don't forget to take 3–4 outfits with you! Straight after the shoot you can view the dazzling results, and purchase your photographs should you wish.

For details on how to take advantage of this fantastic offer please go to page 489, where you'll also find information on all the other great deals throughout *Goddess*.

OlanMills
photography

Simplify your life

'I don't understand people who work and talk about it like it was some sort of goddamn duty. Doing nothing feels like floating on warm water. Delightful. Perfect.'

AVA GARDNER

Life doesn't need to be complicated. It gets a whole lot easier when you have the fundamentals — home and hearth — sorted. These ideas will streamline your life, turn you into the perfect hostess and help you create a home that supports and nurtures you, so you have more time to play, pamper yourself or write your best-selling opus.

Clean up your act

Does your life need a makeover?
Tick all the statements that apply to you.

- ☐ My drawers are tidy and ordered
- ☐ My receipts are filed immediately
- ☐ The only clothes in my wardrobe suit me and I wear them regularly
- ☐ All the equipment and appliances in my home work efficiently
- ☐ If something is broken or damaged I deal with it within a week
- ☐ I recycle regularly – I can't bear piles of paper lying around my home
- ☐ My car is clean and well maintained
- ☐ If a friend called unexpectedly to say she could be with me in 10 minutes, I'd never have to put her off because the place was such a mess
- ☐ The area under my bed is well ordered and dust-free
- ☐ There is only one 'glory hole' drawer in my home for all those miscellaneous items
- ☐ I don't hang on to children's clothes or toys. Except for a few sentimental items, most are given away when the children have outgrown them
- ☐ There are no mysterious boxes and bags of unknown 'stuff' lying around my house

This isn't hard – a lot of ticks means you are pretty well on top of your life. If you ticked less than half the statements, turn to ideas 105–108 to start decluttering your life.

105. Blitz your home in a weekend

Decluttering. Space clearing. Majorly destressing.

Get rid of your clutter and you're free to redefine yourself.
Life becomes a lot simpler.

Everything I own fits pretty neatly into the average living
room – and that includes my car. I started decluttering about ten years ago, and I
haven't stopped since. It's addictive, it's life affirming. Nothing makes you feel so
serene and in control of your life as chucking out stuff you don't need.

Smug? You bet. Life wasn't always this way. For all of my twenties and most of my
thirties I had all the furniture, plants, ornaments, designer clothes and bad taste
costume jewellery you'd expect of someone who reached her majority in the 80s.
Then in the early 90s I thought I'd write about this new gimmick I'd heard rumours
about – feng shui (remember that!). And that's how I ended up inviting space
clearer Karen Kingston into my less than fragrant home. She told me to clear out
the wardrobe, clean out the junk under my bed and get rid of my books – 'let new
knowledge in'. Then the magic started to happen.

Life picked up a pace. In the three years following my meeting with Karen, I moved
out of the home I'd lived in for years, travelled extensively and reorganised my
working life so I earned enough from working half the hours.

My job is to research and write about what is called self-help or 'mind, body, spirit'. I've done it all from meditation to colonic irrigation. But nothing transformed my life like decluttering or to give it its esoteric name, space clearing.

Chuck it out, lose the guilt

How does it work? Most of us live among piles of ancient magazines, defunct utensils, clothes that neither fit nor suit us. The Chinese believe that all these unlovely, unwanted things lying about haphazardly block the flow of energy – the chi – in our homes. My theory is that by losing them, we lose a ton of guilt – guilt that we'll never fit into those hellishly expensive designer jeans again, guilt that we spent all that money on skis when we only go skiing once a decade, guilt that we never cook those fabulous dinners in those two dozen cookbooks. You get my point. Just about everything in your home probably engenders some sort of guilt. Cut your belongings by 90% and you do the same to your guilt.

> ### Here's an idea for you...
>
> **Try the 'one in, one out' rule. For instance, if you buy a new pair of shoes, then you must get rid of an existing pair. An added bonus is that this system protects you against impulse purchases of stuff you're not really fussed about as you have to focus your mind on what you'll chuck out when you get home.**

The big clear up

'Useful or beautiful, useful or beautiful' – that's the mantra. If any single object doesn't fulfil one of these criteria, bin it. Cultivate ruthlessness. If you haven't worn it, used it or thought about it in a year, do you really need it?

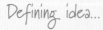

'If more of us valued food and cheer and song above hoarded gold, it would be a merrier world.'

J. R. R. TOLKIEN

Have three bin bags to hand as you work. One for stuff to chuck out, one for stuff to give to charity, one for things you want to clean or mend. Visit the charity shop as soon as you can – make it a priority. Give yourself two weeks to tackle the 'mend or clean' bag.

Something neither useful nor beautiful, but that you don't like to get rid of for sentimental reasons? Put it away for a year. Time out of sight makes it easier to get rid of.

Do this little but often. Try a couple of one-hour sessions per week. I operate the 40–20 rule: 40 minutes graft followed by 20 minutes sitting around feeling virtuous. You get better at decluttering. Soon it's second nature. Do two to three sessions a month.

Find a home for everything you own. You're allowed one drawer that acts as a glory hole for all the odd items.

106. Hug your home

It's hard to feel unstressed when your home is filthy. And even if it's clean, keeping it that way is often a major cause of stress.

There is no secret to having a fragrant, immaculate home. It takes time – either yours, or your cleaner's.

But even if you have a cleaner, at the end of the day we all have to do a bit of cleaning – unless we've got the luxury of a housekeeper 24/7.

So here are some ideas for making housework stress a thing of the past. It will benefit two groups of people.

✿ The owner of a messy home – your house will be cleaner.

✿ The owner of an already immaculate home, but the price for it is you find yourself polishing kitchen units at midnight. Believe it or not, you can benefit too, but you can skip through the first bit snorting with derision.

I am not a slob, but neither am I a perfectionist. So given that I'm busy, domesticity is way down on my priority list and my house gets dirty – certainly far below the standards acceptable to my grandmother. It used to upset me until I found www.flylady.com. I urge anyone domestically challenged to seek it out. A bit hokey, but sweet, it's a support group for those who have felt overwhelmed by the ceaseless round of domestic duty and fed up struggling with it alone. They have rules. One of

Here's an idea for you...

When cooking, fill the sink with hot soapy water and dump stuff in as you go along. Yes, even if you have a dishwasher. It helps you keep surfaces clear and then you enjoy yourself more too.

them is that the minute you get up, you make your bed, get dressed (including shoes), wash your face and get your make-up on. Try this and you'll be amazed at how much more productive you are. I have adapted some of their other rules to suit me. (Hint: the first tip here changed my life.)

Always have a clean kitchen sink

With a shiny sink, you feel you're in control. Wash dishes by hand if necessary (yes, shocking, but it's a skill you won't have forgotten). A shiny sink reflects back a vision of yourself as a domestic goddess in stunning control of your world. Don't leave home or go to bed for the evening without clearing the sink area. It really is best to clear your kitchen straight after the evening meal – or get your kids to do it. Before bed you can't always be bothered and it sets the morning off to a bad start.

Adopt the laser beam approach

Divide your home into clearly defined areas. You will clean one of these areas thoroughly every week. No area should take more than an hour. This could look like: hallway and bathroom; kitchen; reception rooms; bedroom and spare bedroom; children's bedroom(s). Now make a list of what you need to do to each area to get it cleaned to your satisfaction. Keep a master list for each room in a file. The reason for this? With a list you get to tick off items and that's immensely satisfying. First thing Saturday morning is a good time to clean, not least because if you have children they can get involved.

Bless your home

The flylady website calls it the Weekly Home Blessing hour – and this is the superficial cleaning you do to keep your home bearable. It takes an hour a week – or you can split it up. I do 10 minutes morning and evening, three times a week That on top of the hour a week I spend on one area is usually enough to keep my (small) home bearable. You may have a larger home and need to put more time in. During my 10-minute sessions I do one of these activities: sweep and mop floors; vacuum; dust; clean bathroom; polish all reflective surfaces; get rid of all rubbish – purge magazines, empty contents of recycling bins.

107. Zap those piles

No, not those kind of piles. We're talking about the avalanche of paper, magazines, unpaid bills, flyers for pizza houses – the general detritus of 21st-century life that threatens to overwhelm you.

Not to mention your kitchen surfaces.

This idea is very personal to me. Following it has reduced stress in my life by a factor of 10. When my daughter, then three, was asked what her mother did for a living she said 'My mummy tears bits of paper out of newspapers.' Which is actually quite an accurate description of what I do for a living – it's called 'research'. I spend hours tearing out, but it's never enough. All my working life, piles of paper have dragged down my spirit and proven to be a stressor in my domestic life. My partner objects to hefting piles of magazines off chairs before he can sit down.

This is the system that works for me, culled from reading and interviewing just about every organisational guru on the planet. The only drawback is that it takes time to set up. But if you have a day to spend or ten free hours, give it a go. Ten hours can work magic. You will probably have to make a few adjustments to suit your life.

Step 1

Gather together everything that you will need to create order in your world. For me that's cardboard magazine holders, folders, pens, labels, stapler, a couple of hard-backed address books (personal and business) and a huge industrial-strength binbag. I also keep the family calendar and my diary at hand so I can put dates directly into them as I reveal the invites and school dates in my pile.

Step 2

Work systematically. You are going to go from one side of your desk to the other, or one side of the room to the other. Gather together one pile of paper and assorted junk and place it bang in the middle of the room or your desk. Start sorting. Every single piece of paper that you touch must be actioned.

❀ If it contains a phone number that you might need in the future, then put the number straight into one of your address books.

❀ If it is a bill that has to be paid, or anything which must be acted on immediately, then create a file for urgent and unpaid bills. (I carry this file with me, in my handbag and work through it every day when I have a down moment.)

> *Defining idea...*
>
> **'We can lick gravity but sometimes the paperwork is overwhelming.'**
> WERNER VON BRAUN, rocket engineer

❀ If it is an article or piece of information that you might need in the future but which is not urgent, start creating files for these (named files) such as 'pensions', 'holidays', 'general interest'.

❀ If it is a piece of information that you need to act on or read or make a decision on but not now, put it in a file marked 'To Do' and make an appointment in your diary sometime in the next week when you'll deal with it. This file should be somewhere accessible and you should clear it not less than once every two weeks or it gets out of control.

Keep a tickle book. Tickle as in 'tickle my memory.' Mine is an A4 hardbacked notebook. In it I note down the names of anything I might need in the future: the idea of an article I might write or a savings account offering a good rate of interest. The point is that I don't have to hold on to endless bits of paper just in case I ever want this information – there's enough in the tickle book to help me trace it. I also keep the tickle book by my side at work and if anyone calls me with a piece of information I may need but don't know for sure, then I scribble down their number and a couple of explanatory lines so that I can follow up later. Same with my emails. The tickle book means I have been able to throw out dozens of pieces of paper almost as soon as they reach my desk.

108. Never lose your keys again

Often you can't remember where you left the car keys. Sometimes you can't remember where you left the car.

Here's why stress eats your memory – and what you can do about it.

Memory lapses aren't necessarily the first indication of Alzheimer's, so don't worry. But if they're increasing in frequency it could be that your memory is a casualty of a multi-tasking lifestyle.

Juggling a hectic schedule can have a disastrous effect on your memory. The 'fight or flight' response actually sharpens our cognitive abilities. But chronic stress over long periods of time is a different matter. If your mind is bustling ahead to deal with the day's problems it's concentrating on other things and you're not noticing what's going on around you. Not surprisingly you can't retrieve memories of what you did today because your mind was actually living in tomorrow. This in itself is deeply stressful.

What the hell's his name again?

The only answer is to be aware that when you're busy and stressed you're not taking in information in the same way and you're not going to be able to recall it. Make like a boy scout and be prepared. For example, on a busy day when you meet

someone new, be aware that you are more likely to
forget their name. Make more effort than usual during
introductions. Repeat a new name inside your head.
Use it again in conversation as soon as you can.

This repetition is important. When learning anything
new during a stressed period, repeat it to yourself and
if possible say it out loud three or four times,
increasing the amount of time between each
repetition. This 'repetition, pause, repetition' pattern
strengthens memory.

This technique also works for items or tasks that you
have to remember – and always forget. If you're fed up
going to the supermarket to buy tomatoes and coming back with everything else
but tomatoes, try the above. If it doesn't work, then make allowances and leave
notes in your purse or on your toothbrush, places where you will certainly check.
Don't rely on your memory.

> Here's an idea for you...
>
> **Try a supplement. There's some
> evidence that the herb gingko
> biloba improves blood flow to the
> brain and hence memory in the
> elderly, but it's likely that it will
> be proven to help younger people
> too. You can buy supplements
> containing gingko at chemists and
> health food shops. Sage is also
> good for memory.**

Where are my keys?

What few people realise is that most routine actions will cause memory problems
if you do them differently every day. The very fact that we do some things over and
over again can make them easy to forget. That's because when you put items you
use frequently in different places from one day to the next, you have to block the
memory of what you did with them yesterday and the day before in order to find
them today. Which is why it seems you've spent a half of your lifetime looking for
your keys and wallet.

Defining idea...

'Happiness is nothing more than good health and a bad memory.'
ALBERT SCHWEITZER

The answer
The easiest thing is to create a memory pot – a bowl or basket near your front door where everything goes as soon as you get home, and which you check before you leave the house. This is not as simple as it sounds – it takes about two or three weeks before it becomes second nature. And even then, it makes sense to keep a spare set of keys somewhere separately.

Did I switch off the iron?

The phenomenon of worrying endlessly if you've done something that you've done a hundred times before is down to something called 'social misattribution', the fancy name for recalling the action but not realising that you performed it on another occasion. Again, it's because you're not focusing on the action while you're doing it.

The answer
No matter how tied up your brain is with problems, take the time to check what you're wearing. As your arm reaches out to switch off the iron, note 'Oh yes, blue shirt.' When you get the doubt that you've done an action, recall what your arm was wearing when you did it. Look down. Blue shirt. Check. On you go with your day. Again, just like the above habit, it takes about two or three weeks for this to become second nature when we're undertaking all those activities that we do on automatic pilot – locking the front door, switching off the oven, picking up the children...OK, scratch the last one.

Perfect parties

109. Children's parties

Throwing perfect parties for children can be really complicated, so here are some suggestions to make them run smoothly.

Kids expect more than a game of Pass the Parcel and a party dress these days.

I'm talking about events for children who still require adult supervision. Some parents might suggest that this is the case even at an eighteenth birthday bash, but I am thinking more of children of about six to twelve. Dealing with this younger age group, I don't need to get into the rights and wrongs of alcohol or the possibility of a sneaky joint being passed around...

I will come clean at this point and tell you that I don't have kids of my own so I have never had sole responsibility for hosting my own children's parties, but there have been plenty of occasions when I have been roped in. When I was little the prospect of playing Pin the Tail on the Donkey or Musical Bumps was enough to guarantee that I'd have my hands washed and my party frock on in plenty of time. Maybe I'm being cynical about this, but today children have much higher expectations of what a party should offer.

Here's an idea for you...

If you're hosting the party at a venue, check and see if they can offer you somewhere to store presents. When you are trying to ferry children around and keep to a specific timetable you may not have space in the car or time at the event to gather together all the gifts and get them home. If the venue can supply a safe storage space, you can return and retrieve them once everyone is home safely.

There are two options. Pick a location where you can take the children for their special day or put in some extra effort to host the event at home. Here's a simple list of what you may need to consider whatever you decide:

✿ Numbers – how many children can you accommodate and how many adults can you drag in to help out?

✿ Invitations – shop-bought invites featuring favourite cartoon or TV characters will appeal to your child.

✿ The cake – consider how many slices you will need to get out of this. A tray bake is much easier to cut into a specific number.

✿ Decorations – how much are you going to dress up your home, or if you are using a venue can you leave this up to them?

✿ Food – sandwiches and plenty of crisps used to satisfy me, but pizza is a possibility for today's more demanding youngsters and can be fine for small vegetarians without the others feeling deprived.

✿ Games or activities – are you going to hire an entertainer or make up your games? Do you want to have a mini-disco (in which case a couple of chart-topping compilation discs are a must)?

✿ Party bags – as any child will tell you, these are how the party will be judged, so budget for some exciting treats for the guests to take away.

The budget is up to you. Bear in mind that it may be better to invite fewer children and bring in an entertainer, so that you can afford something really special, rather than have loads of kids and find that you have very little money left over once the essentials have been taken care of. One piece of advice when the birthday child is very young – keep the numbers down; too many people and too much excitement can lead to tears. Don't forget, that if parents are going to stay at the party (and when children are small this is the best way to ensure things run as smoothly as possible) you may want to include some wine for them on your shopping list.

> Defining idea...
>
> **'The essence of childhood, of course, is play.'**
> BILL COSBY

If you decide to have the party away from your home you'll need to ask some questions about the facilities and party packages on offer. The earlier that you get this organised, the better. There are a few points that should be up for discussion:

- Is there a defined area for your group or are you just another table on the day?
- What is the price per head? Don't be afraid to negotiate on this and remember there may be adults who need to be catered for.
- Do you have to leave by a particular time?
- Where are the toilet facilities?
- What sort of activities can they provide; how are they supervised?
- Are there any specific safety requirements?

A children's party is potentially a stressful affair, so take the worry out of the occasion by getting everything in place and you too can enjoy yourself.

110. Get your home guest-ready in an hour (it's a messy business)

Entertaining for the time-challenged person.

Surprise, surprise… some friends have just rung to say that they are in your area and would love to stop by.

How delightful, how inconvenient, how the hell are you going to be able to entertain them with just an hour to get your house straight, give yourself a wash and brush up and have some food available should they decide to stay on?

Panic now and all is lost. You will be wasting precious minutes which could be used much more constructively.

My first piece of advice is to prioritise. If the house is a tip, a quick clean up is essential; if there is a dish in the freezer, which you can take out to defrost, do this now. If you are going to put together a few appetisers from scratch, now is the time to check the fridge, the cupboards and the vegetable rack and start to think about which snacks can be quickly assembled. As for your appearance – could questions be asked about your personal hygiene? You are going to have to fit in a quick shower before they arrive. Now here's how.

House-proud

Decide in which areas you are going to entertain. Go round these rooms with a big bin bag and fill it with anything that isn't breakable but that needs to be cleared away, such as newspapers and magazines, half-done homework or stray items of clothing. Put the bag in the bottom of your wardrobe – you can sort it out once your guests have gone.

Now wipe down any surfaces that show ring marks or are very dusty. Work through every room (except the bathroom, but I'll come to that later). Lastly, run a vacuum cleaner across the floor. Remember to clean up any area through which your guests might pass: the hall, corridors and landings that lead to the bathroom are probably on the list. Check for anything that is very dirty. It is easier to remove a rug that is covered with dog hairs or a candle that is coated in candle wax than to try and clean them up in the valuable minutes that are available to you. Light a scented candle; an appealing smell will always detract from a few minor horrors. If your friends are arriving at dusk or later, dim the lights. This can help to hide a multitude of sins.

Looking good

Once you have finished your clean up, jump in the shower. Make sure that you use a scented shampoo or body wash, as the aroma from this will linger and leave the bathroom smelling wonderful long after you have finished in there. While you are in the bathroom use the opportunity to tidy it and give it a quick wash and brush up too.

> ### Here's an idea for you...
>
> **When you answer the phone and someone suggests dropping in at the last minute, stall them. If they say that they will be free in an hour, then respond that it would lovely to see them but you have to run an errand and will only be back in two. That should give you ample time to sort everything out.**

Defining idea...

'Time is nature's way of keeping everything from happening at once.'

WOODY ALLEN

Put clean towels in there, so use the existing ones to wipe down all surfaces, including mirrors. Throw any messy bottles, gunked-up tubes of toothpaste or half-used toilet rolls into a carrier bag (making sure that the tops are firmly on the bottles) and again, hide it in the bottom of your wardrobe. Put in a fresh toilet roll and clean fluffy towels. Dress in an outfit in which you feel comfortable but know that you look good. If you are going to pull on jeans, then team them with a slightly dressy top.

Sneaky treats

I know I will sound smug if I tell you this, but I am going to share my secret with you anyway. I keep partially cooked French loaves in the freezer; you can buy them from any supermarket and they are perfect for emergencies. I always have a couple of bags of tortilla chips and jars of salsa tucked away at the back of the cupboard. When I use up my supply of tinned tuna and chopped tomatoes I always replace them instantly. How does this help with last minute entertaining? Here's how...

You can empty the tortilla chips out of a bag and into a beautiful bowl in seconds. You can decant the salsa from the jar and into a stylish dipping bowl in minutes. It doesn't take long to mix tuna with mayonnaise and put it next to a glass filled with breadsticks for a quick treat.

Now, if you have time, put on the kettle or open a bottle of wine and sit down in the lounge. When your guests arrive you will look amazingly relaxed.

111. Throwing the perfect dinner party

Here's a foolproof guide to planning a dinner party at home.

There is one truism about most forms of catering in your own kitchen...

Whether it's a large birthday bash or a small select dinner party for six, there is an easy way to do things and there is a hard way to do things. The easy way is to be organised and plan the whole thing. The hard way is to throw everything together at the last minute. Please try and follow the first!

Think about the type of dinner party that you wish to give.

Here's the first option. You plan to produce a full, five-course affair complete with perfect table settings, the correct wine glasses and a selection of china for every dish. You will be looking to prepare a really special meal, so you'll need plenty of preparation time and will be in and out of the kitchen making sure that the food is just perfect. This will involve you planning and practising the dishes and possibly even printing up a menu that will be presented on the table. The plan is to have a formal meal, so guests should understand
that they are expected to dress up. However, you are looking at it as an opportunity to socialise, so while the food will be carefully prepared, you won't be spending most of the meal flitting in and out of the kitchen getting the various courses ready. You'll present some tried and tested dishes that are the staples of your culinary art.

Then there's the second option: a relaxed and casual affair designed so that everyone can sit around, quaff some lovely wine and chow down on a simple dinner that may only consist of two courses. The table settings will be casual and the mood relaxed. For example, people may hang onto their cutlery after eating the starter and use the same ones when the next course appears on the table. The ideal food here would be something like an avocado, mozzarella and tomato starter with some garlic bread and then a lovely spaghetti bolognaise, presented in huge bowls, from which guests will help themselves.

Your decision about which type of event to host will be influenced by how much time you want to spend in the kitchen during the evening. If you hate the idea of everyone else gossiping while you are slaving over a hot stove, then you should be looking at the more casual approach, the second option. If you have only recently started to take cooking seriously but would like the opportunity to practise certain stylish dishes then you might be looking at a blend of the two. And if you really want to show off, are completely confident and know you can set the scene, it's got to be the first option.

Here's an idea for you...

There is a huge difference between cooking fillets of sole for two and having to prepare the dish for eight or ten people. Here's another example: unless you have the skills of a Michelin-starred chef, and all the equipment and staff of a professional kitchen, the chances are that you will not be able to prepare fillet steaks to suit the desires of eight different people: blue, medium rare, medium well done, etc. It is much easier serving some kind of casserole.

Next there are just a few other points to consider:

✿ How many courses? (Fewer for casual and more for formal.)

✿ What type of food? Do you have to build in provisions for a vegetarian, for example? If you want to spend most of your time at the table, then you have to decide on dishes which can be mostly prepared well in advance.

✿ Do you have all the right cutlery for the dishes that you want to create? Proper soup spoons, for instance, make all the difference if you are planning soup as a starter.

✿ How much time will you have beforehand to prepare the food? Unless you are going to take time off from work, choose a Saturday or Sunday night when you have a full day to prepare.

✿ Do you have both red and white wine glasses? Do you have water tumblers?

✿ Can any of the courses be served in oven-to-tableware so that people can help themselves from a central pot?

Once you have planned your menu, write a comprehensive list of all the ingredients, even if it is just a sprinkling of salt. Then go through your cupboards and group together any ingredients that you already have in store. Don't take the easy way out and head for the supermarket: find a butcher for the meat, a fishmonger for the shellfish and a deli for the cheese. One tip: before you head to the shops check out food suppliers on the web. If you have never bought food this way, it is a real eye-opener to discover just how many ingredients can be delivered fresh to your door.

Now assemble your ingredients; get your knives, pots and pans at the ready and go to work!

Defining idea...

'A man seldom thinks with more earnestness of anything than he does of his dinner.'
SAMUEL JOHNSON

112. Cheat's cuisine: how to host without skill or effort

Special occasion looming? Naturally, the smart move would be to serve up a cordon bleu foodgasm but (a) you haven't got the ability and (b) you can't be arsed. Time to cheat.

So you eat ready meals – who doesn't? Except that this time you've got someone coming round for dinner, or it's a romantic occasion, or there's a growing feeling that you're just a loafer in the home. Fraudulent cooking is one of the finest arts for the aspiring cad or caddess to master (mistress?). Skill with food conveys an air of worldliness, an understanding of the finer things in life, a practical ability in the kitchen and it can get you out of all kinds of scrapes by suggesting simultaneously that you are pulling your weight in the household and of course you love him/her.

The bottom line is that you are going to go out and get that supermarket ready meal because it's cheap and easy and even you know how to heat up lasagne. It's where you go from here that decides whether you are going to be hero or zero come suppertime.

Presentation is everything. Slap your pasta down on the table in its tinfoil package and you might as well pack your bags. Instead make a big fuss of needing to be left alone in the kitchen (this is why chefs develop their melodramatic flair) so no one can see what you're up to and remember to dispose of the wrappings very carefully indeed. The rest of the devilry is in the detail.

Lay the table with side plates for bread and butter. Have the butter itself in a ramekin (those little white bowls you always thought were ashtrays) and remember to lay out separate (larger) glasses for water as well as those for wine. Remember the candle – not only does it look romantic but it hides a multitude of sins when it comes to your food. Big white plates always work best and all food that's brought to the table should be in a serving dish (the plastic microwave tub doesn't count).

Garnishes are by far the easiest way of making dull grub look like haute cuisine. Fresh herbs are the best and favourite recommendation is Delia Smith's tip of throwing a handful of fresh Basil leaves over any pasta dish – tastes great, looks pro.

If you're really pushing the boat out and trying to make up for major misdemeanours then get hold of some edible flowers for a garnish. Cheese shavings (reach for the vegetable peeler) or ground nuts also work wonders. A swirl of cream (or yoghurt if weight

Here's an idea for you...

Check online for gourmet delivery companies that deliver the ingredients and instructions. Leaping Salmon blazed this particular trail by delivering top-quality ingredients to culinarily challenged Londoners. The meals come in kits, already washed, sliced and measured, just waiting for you to throw together, heat according to instructions and then emerge triumphantly to general applause (as long as you remember to hide the instructions afterwards). The idea has caught on and similar outfits are offering the meal kit approaches at mainline stations and on the Internet. Don't forget that all the above tips are still applicable, even if you've craftily ordered out.

conscious) will transform even tinned soups, stews, and curries, especially if you then dust it with a bit of ground paprika. Judiciously placed olives will do the same for hummus, tsatsiki, and pretty much any other dip. If you're going to have good old veg, then remember that baby versions of the corn, carrots, cabbages et al. not only look exotic and cute but also cook faster (result!).

A few easy touches can transform the simplest of things. Shop-bought meals are usually quickly recognised so go for the fancy premium versions available from the more up-market supermarkets and then slice mozzarella on top, melt it and garnish with fresh herbs so it looks different. A baguette or piece of pitta is bread but slice it diagonally, toast it and pour a little olive oil on it and it becomes cold-pressed, drizzled crostini. You didn't know you had it in you, did you?

Create your dream home

113. You've got the look

Settle on your style to create a room that's pleasing to the eye.

There is no way that you could or even should stick to every single rigid design rule when putting together your home. However, if you're happy to work with some guidelines in place, you'll reap the rewards in terms of creating an appealing and desirable space.

It's all about putting together the furniture, soft furnishings and accessories that match a certain mood.

I'm a minimalist, modernist, neutral colours kind of person and that means I have certain requirements in setting my style. There has to be plenty of storage in a room to keep it free from clutter. (I have serious storage issues but I do try to keep them behind closed doors.) The window treatments have to be simple. I have never contemplated curtains at any of my windows – it's always Roman blinds because of their clean lines. Fabrics are, in the main, natural: linen, wool, cotton and canvas. My vases are plain, clear glass and my flowers arrangements are always uncomplicated. And that's how to set a style.

> **Here's an idea for you...**
>
> Sit down and make a list of all the elements that you need. Break it down into the following: furniture, soft furnishings, flooring, window treatments, lighting and accessories. Now estimate a price beside each item on your list. It doesn't have to be exact, just a ballpark figure. Total this up and consider whether you can spend more or need to cut back. You can take away a chair and save some money or add an elaborate chandelier if you have the cash. Once you have a list that matches your budget, go to work on that room.

Think about spaces that you are drawn to. These could be a good indication of your personal style. (I loved the old Saatchi gallery in London's Westbourne Grove because it was just a vast, open, clutter-free space.) If you find yourself drawn to grand stately homes or always book a cosy country cottage for your holidays, these could be a starting point for tailoring a room to suit. Use a mood board to help you put together the look, incorporating a picture of your ideal room to inspire you as you work.

So what else influences your style?

Taste in music? You might worship at the feet of Elvis and so employ a retro approach to your interior.

Love of gardening? Cultivate a collection of floral prints that will give a theme for your scheme.

An historical period? Look for reproduction – or if you have the bank balance original – antique furniture.

Another country? Source sumptuous silks from the Orient, porcelain painted in China or hand-carved accessories from Indonesia.

This should be polarising your thoughts. So now consider the practicalities of putting your plan into action.

Give yourself a budget: some looks are less expensive to achieve than others. What about structural alterations? Will knocking two rooms into one give you the space you need to make a dramatic statement? You might also give some thought to the future. If you are planning to stay in the house for only a couple of years, should you tone down the colour scheme so that you won't have to redecorate when you want to sell? Last but not least, will your style work in the space that you have? Light-drenched loft style is difficult to achieve in a basement flat.

> *Defining idea...*
>
> **'To me style is just the outside of content, and content the inside of style, like the outside and inside of the human body – both go together, they can't be separated.'**
> JEAN-LUC GODARD

If you set a style and get all the elements right, then you'll be happy to live with the look for years.

114. Work that colour

Find the shades and tones that suit your home. The pick 'n' mix approach is all very well at the cinema sweetie counter but. . .

Colour scheming your whole house may sound like a huge challenge but by breaking it down room by room it is simply a matter of application. And in order to create a harmonious environment, it's really the only sensible approach.

Here's an idea for you...

You may already have a room that is wallpapered and it can be fag or just a downright waste of time to strip the room in order to match your overall scheme. Choose a colour from the paper, it may be a touch of blue in the print, for example, and then use that in an adjacent room to link the two together.

Oh good grief, do I have to be sensible?

Well yes, if you want to end up without colour clashes and disharmony as you move from room to room. Imagine when all the doors in the house are open being able to see a little bit of purple to the left (lounge), some green to the right (dining room), and walking through yellow (hallway), as you head for the blue kitchen. It's a quite a prospect isn't it?

(On a very practical level, if your room colours complement each other, then furniture, furnishings and accessories should work in a number of different places. This means that you can move pieces around your home when you want a change of scene, or to swap dining room for living room or guest room for master bedroom for example.)

I'm not the colour police. This approach doesn't mean that you have to be all white at every turn (apart from woodwork on which I would very rarely use any other paint). My advice is to stick with colours from the same broad family spectrum across most of your home or at least introduce the same colour in some form or another in each room. But there are three alternatives for successful colour scheming so take your pick from the list below. And if you decide to break the law in the odd space (hopefully just the box room) then you can live with your own guilt.

Take a look at a colour wheel and consider adopting the red and orangey siblings. Move around the wheel and introduce yourself to the yellow and greens or opt for the blues and purples. Each of these groups can affect your mood and effect changes of perception of the shape and size of the room. At the most basic level, for example, a red dining room will stimulate, a yellow dining room will cheer you up, and a blue room will engender a sense of calm.

> *Defining idea...*
>
> **'Colour possesses me. I don't have to pursue it. It will possess me always, I know it.'**
> PAUL KLEE

The size of rooms should have an influence on your colour choices. If you have a series of small rooms you'll need to stick to a lighter palette. Where there's the luxury of generous proportions you can afford to move to the darker colours in the spectrum.

Here are your choices:

- ❀ **A tonal scheme:** This is where you pick just one colour but use it in varying tones. With purples, for example, you might combine the palest lavender and lilac, magenta, plum and wine. For greens, you might use eau de nil, olive, sage and pine.

- ❀ **A harmonious scheme:** Choose colours that are closely associated. The best way to do this is to look at a rack of paint charts and take three or four adjacent to each other. Start with red, next to it you'll find terracotta, copper and then chestnut.

✿ **A complementary scheme:** This uses colours that are opposites of each other. Orange versus blue, green versus purple, yellow versus scarlet. You will need to decide which one of the two colours will be more dominant in a room; indecision here can cause infighting that will wreck the scheme.

Whichever of the above you choose, one simple way to unify the rooms in a house is to stick with the same colour for your woodwork throughout.

You may have heard this a thousand times but listen again!

Start out by buying tester pots. Then paint large pieces of white paper in your chosen colours and pin them up around your home. Leave them for several days. Watch how the light affects them in different rooms and swap them around to see how they may alter the perspective of a space. Make notes. Let someone else have an opinion (within reason). But do not paint a wall until you have lived with them for a least a week.

'Fools rush in' when it comes to making colour choices, so take time and take care and you won't 'fear to tread' in any of your rooms.

115. Perfect hallways

Seen first and frequently passed through, your hallway deserves more attention than you may think.

There are certain spaces that we often neglect. It is lack of thought more than a deliberate disregard, and the hall all too often falls into this list. In fact it could well be at the top.

Which is ludicrous when you think that this is the first space that you see when you get home and the last area that you pass through when you leave. Think about all the trips that you make through this space. You probably go through it in the morning to get tea from the kitchen and then you traverse it again on your way back upstairs to have a shower. Later on, you retrace your steps downstairs to make breakfast and then you nip into the hall to pick up the post. Are you getting the idea? You spend more time in the hall than you think. So it should, above all other rooms, deserve careful attention and a loving touch.

✿ **Make it welcoming:** A chair or reclaimed church pew that is tucked against the wall allows people to rest for a minute after they walk through the door.

✿ **Keep it useful:** Coat hooks, umbrella stands, a mat to wipe feet on and a table to dump the post on make it a functional space

✿ **Light it right:** Make sure that you have switches at the bottom and top of the staircase. If it's very dark, consider replacing a solid wood front door with a design that has glass panels.

A decorative chimney pot or length of earthenware pipe, placed in a stylish bowl, makes an alternative umbrella stand.

✿ **Make your home secure:** Add as many devices as you want: bolts, chains and a spy hole are all advisable.

It's more than likely that this area leads into other spaces so choose a colour scheme that won't clash with adjacent rooms. It is also probable that there is a lot of empty wall space and you could easily use it to hang a collection of prints. Are there areas that you could use to create extra storage space or redefine for another purpose? The space under the stairs, for example, might be used to house a desk or utilised as a laundry. These are all details that will enhance the look and functionality of your hall.

Defining idea...

'There is room in the halls of pleasure
For a large and lordly train,
But one by one we must all file on
Through the narrow aisles of pain.'
ELLA WHEELER WILCOX,
American poet

Step by step

Give plenty of thought to your staircase. What seems to be an immovable feature can be replaced or dressed up according to your budget. Accepting that wood is the material that most of us will inherit when we move into our home, it's a revelation when you think about the other materials that can be used to construct a staircase: glass, concrete and steel are all utilised in new builds and conversions to fit in with the overall scheme of an interior.

Consider one of the following options:

✿ If you need to bring more light into the space, then choose a glass balustrade and beechwood treads.

✿ Should you want to continue an open plan theme, commission a hanging wire system where the treads are seemingly suspended in space.

✿ Do you live in an industrial-style loft? Add rubber treads to the edge of each step.

✿ Want to be decorative but can't afford a runner (and they can be pricey)? Then leave the central half of each step in natural wood and paint the quarter each side to match the balustrade.

✿ Modernising an old building? Cover the steps with flexible zinc sheeting.

If you take the time to pay attention to your hallway you'll be rewarded with a welcome every time.

Defining idea...

'I have heard that stiff people lose something of their awkwardness under high ceilings, and in spacious halls.'
RALPH WALDO EMERSON

116. Perfect bathrooms

Washing, primping, bathing or refreshing – a well-designed bathroom is a versatile space.

I inherited a particularly hideous over-the-bath shower with elaborate shower rail system to allow the curtain to be pulled all the way around the bath. It was totally unnecessary, and the poles suspended in a mish-mash from walls and the ceiling made it look like an elaborate industrial mess. By simply taking away the curtain and associated poles and putting in a neat screen I made the room seem instantly bigger, and it's now definitely more pleasurable to lie in the bath and gaze at the ceiling, or my navel.

If you are going to revamp a bathroom, you need to decide whether you want to keep the existing layout and replace fixtures where they are, or move things in, out and around to get better use of what is often a spatially challenged room.

Suite pieces

I am a bidet fan and not ashamed to admit it. Let me give you some uses (other than the purpose it was designed for) to explain why, if you have the space, I would recommend that you fit the fourth piece into your suite of bath, basin and WC.

❀ There's always somewhere to leave the hand-laundry soaking.

❀ It is the perfect place for washing feet pre-pedicure.

❀ If you can't use the loo to be sick you have another receptacle.

With both bidets and toilets always opt for wall-hung designs, for one simple reason: cleaning around pedestals is a pain, and they are a place where dirt tends to gather. The joy of being able to mop across a floor unhindered by the usual obstructions has to be experienced to be really understood. (If you are now worried that I am slightly obsessive about fluff on the floor, I'd like to point out that I have a dog whose hair tends to get everywhere.)

It's a frequently overlooked issue that cast-iron baths weigh a ton (give or take a few pounds). If you are looking to recreate the look of a period bathroom, check that your floor will take the weight. Also remember that with a freestanding bath the amount of water that splashes over the edge will increase considerably (more sides for the bath water to slop over) so you do need flooring that will withstand regular soakings. While the idea of picking up an old fashioned piece from reclamation yards may have a romantic appeal, don't bother. Brand new is easily affordable and reproduction designs are so good that I would buy new every time.

> *Defining idea...*
>
> **'Colour is incredibly important to me, but in the bathroom that means the opposite of what you may think – everything's got to be white. When you're trying out every colour of every item in a make-up range, it's essential to have a neutral background. So the idea of coloured lights and fancy tiles is all well and good, but it's just not for me. And no, I never had an avocado suite.'**
> BARBARA DALY, The Independent Magazine

Sinking in

If you live with a partner or have kids, fit in a double sink wherever possible. There is great pleasure in having your own sink. I once stayed in a glorious hotel in Edinburgh for New Year where the bathroom had 'his and hers' sinks. My contact lens solution, make-up, body lotion, electric toothbrush and cotton wool pads all had a space, and didn't get shoved aside when 'him indoors' wanted to shave. Now translate that into your own home. Kids' stuff on one sink and adults' on the other for example – it's a cleansing experience.

117. Perfect bedrooms

Design your bedroom with comfort in mind. While buying a house may be the biggest financial investment we make, buying the right bed is one of the most important.

Really. Sleep deprivation caused by a crying baby, pressure of work or a snoring partner may not be easy to resolve, but if it is a direct result of an uncomfortable bed, then the solution is in your own hands.

But more of beds later. Let's consider just how you want your bedroom to look and how to achieve that before we get into the specifics of furniture. Start with the style, which will dictate colour choices, fabric types and furniture design, and bear in mind that there are endless variations on these themes.

Rustic living

Bring the comfort of the country into your bedroom. Yellows and greens or rosy pinks can form the basis for the scheme. Keep a light touch when decorating. Opt for wallpaper with a delicate print, and if you can't face papering every wall, then just use it in alcoves or on the wall facing the door. Choose carpet for the floor and reflect that cosy mood with wool blankets on the bed or a patchwork quilt that matches your colour scheme. Indulge yourself with a curvy wrought iron bedstead and plump for painted or pine wooden furniture for storage. Lamps with pleated fabric shades would be apposite for the bedside table, as would a blanket box positioned at the end of the bed.

Contemporary rooms

The art of Feng Shui and the influence of the Orient have had tremendous impact on interiors, and nowhere more so than in the bedroom. Work with a colour scheme including white, shades of grey, cream and brown. The mood is minimalist so hide or disguise clutter in the room. Opt for a laminate or real wood floor that you can dress up with rugs for extra comfort. Select natural linens to deck out the bed, calico or cotton pillowslips, for example, and put wooden Venetian blinds or shutters at the window. A low-level wooden bed would suit this style, and fitted wardrobes would contribute to the clean lines of the space.

Here's an idea for you...

Some notes about buying beds...
- Buy the largest bed you can fit into your bedroom. That way you and your partner will have your own space to sleep in.
- If you and your partner have different requirements, then consider investing in two different mattresses that will zip together.
- A hard mattress is not necessarily a good mattress. What you are looking for is the right amount of support. Lie on your choice for a good few minutes before you buy.
- Turn your new mattress every time you change your bed linen.
- Forget fashion – is the height of the bed you are buying right for you?

Defining idea...

'The bed is a bundle of paradoxes: we go to it with reluctance, yet we quit it with regret; we make up our minds every night to leave it early, but we make up our bodies every morning to keep it late.
OGDEN NASH

Classic living

Consider a muted yellow or duck egg blue as the starting point for your scheme. It may be appropriate to pick a patterned carpet so you will need to choose your bed linen to co-ordinate accordingly. Curtains are a must. If you want to add a dressy pelmet at the window then echo this look with a canopied bed and be lavish in your use of fabric. Feel free to introduce a gilded mirror or arrange classic prints across one wall. It suits the mood to display a collection of perfume bottles or perhaps have an antique set of brushes and hand held mirror on display. A slipper chair, fabric-covered ottoman or chaise longue will add the finishing touch.

Next consider how you will layout the room. Can you create a focal point with the bed or will you rely on architectural features such as a fireplace to draw the eye? Maybe you have invested in a magnificent old armoire that you are going to use for storing clothes and linen, or have a dressing table that will sit in the bay of a window. Where are you going to put the mirror? Don't leave it out but don't just stick it on the wall. Consider a freestanding design or a large framed mirror left on the floor to lean against the wall. Where are the lamps? A reading light mounted at either side of the bed or lamps positioned on bedside tables will add symmetry to the space.

Given that we spend up to a third of our lives in the bedroom, it is worth getting a style that works morning and night, summer and winter to fulfil every requirement.

118. Illuminating ideas

Get the lighting right and it can be the making of a room; skimp on this essential design detail and you may end up in gloom.

There's a good, a bad and a downright ugly way of lighting any space. Look at it this way: if lighting is an ingredient in the recipe of putting together a room, then it's the icing on the cake or the exquisite sauce on the steak. If it's good then it's Michelin starred.

If it's bad you may have perfected the main part of the dish but the overall meal will be just average. And if it's downright ugly then you have ruined the meal. You waste all the effort of putting together a lovely interior if you fail to pay attention to how the space is lit. Lighting ties quite neatly in to how the area will be used. Every room in your home serves a variety of purposes, so allow for an assortment of lighting options to fulfil each and every need. Lighting also has a role in drawing attention to specific features in a room, and the reverse of that is that it can be used as a means of disguise by leaving certain areas in darkness.

Sorting the styles

You can reduce lighting to three basic types, and to create a successful scheme you need to layer all three: ambient, task and accent lighting. Ambient light is designed to offer an all-over well-lit room. This is the starting point to any scheme and the most basic type of lighting. Task lighting, as the name suggests, works to illuminate specific tasks. These might be working at your computer, applying your make-up or cooking. Its purpose is to provide enough light for the activity concerned – enough to prevent eyestrain. Accent lighting is the type that can often be neglected but brings out the best in a room. It will highlight the best features such as works of art, pieces of furniture or a particular area – a dining table in a kitchen/diner is a classic example.

Room by room

The first space that you come to in a home is the hall. Do something different on the stairs. Position a recessed spot light or low-level wall washer beside every second or third step, making sure you have an on/off switch at the bottom and top. Moving into the lounge, why not avoid an overhead light altogether and have an electrician put two or three lamps on a circuit that is operated by a single switch? If you have shelving in alcoves either side of a chimneybreast, then use down-lighters to highlight the items that are displayed. Through to the kitchen, make sure that you include lights that run underneath wall-mounted cabinets as well as your overhead strip or spots. Have the different lights on separate circuits so you can use as much or as little light as you need. This will also mean you can transform a practical and functional working area into somewhere appropriately lit for an intimate dinner party.

Jump up the stairs to the bedroom, and you must have lights at either side of the bed. Move to the bathroom and make sure that you can see to cleanse your face. An illuminated mirror is a must.

When dressing up your home, lighting is an essential tool in creating the right look and style for every room.

> *Defining idea...*
>
> **'It is not economical to go to bed early to save the candles if the result is twins.'**
> Chinese proverb

119. Streamline your kitchen

Take the fitted approach to streamline your kitchen. The beauty of investing in a fitted kitchen is that it can be tailor-made to suit all the quirky corners or awkward shapes that exist in most homes.

It's also a way of maximising space and can provide some brilliant storage solutions, designed to make your life that much easier.

With the luxury of starting from scratch you can make sure that the light is right, that the power points are in the correct places for all your gadgets, and that your day-to-day use of the space is a joy. After inheriting a kitchen that had clearly been built by the previous owner's DIY-mad husband, I rejoiced when my kitchen had to be ripped apart. Oh the joy of a new beginning!

I have to say at this point that when you move into a new home, budget often precludes you from investing in a whole new kitchen however much you might hate the previous owner's colour scheme or layout. By using paints, replacements doors and perhaps a new floor, it's possible to give the room a facelift that might make it more bearable. You'll just have to live with the layout, but buying a freestanding kitchen trolley is one way of getting an accessible work surface if that is what you lack. However, we are dealing here with the extravagance of a whole new design so be clear about your budget before you start. Costs can easily run away with you and a cheaper option is always available for most things.

The triangle principle

This is an age-old device that kitchen planners have been promoting for years when they start to lay out the room.

It goes like something like this: the cooking area, preparation area and storage should each be at the point of a triangle so that you can move efficiently between the three work areas. I choose to ignore it because everybody cooks in a different way. While the sink may be one of your three important areas if you don't own a dishwasher, if you do it means your priorities will be different. And with microwaves replacing ovens for a lot of people who reheat

Defining idea...

**'Some of our most exquisite
murders have been domestic,
performed with tenderness in
simple, homey places like the
kitchen table.'**
ALFRED HITCHCOCK

ready-made meals, that lovely high-tec fan/gas/electric combi-cooker may only be used at the weekends. You want a layout that suits you for more than two days a week. I like space in my kitchen so have fitted everything along one wall to leave the rest of the room free of cabinets. It's a simple 'line' design with the cooker, sink and fridge positioned along the same side of the kitchen in a run. That way I can move easily and 'crablike' along the work surface and between the three – take potatoes out of the fridge, wash them in the sink and put them on the hob to boil. I predict I will save myself (over several years) hours and hours of running backwards and forwards across the kitchen. Well, quite frankly, if I needed that much exercise I wouldn't be cooking with real cream and butter.

Making plans

If the number of people hanging around the Ikea kitchen department on a Saturday morning is any indication, you'd think putting together a kitchen required a degree in design. It doesn't, but the sheer volume of options for cupboard doors, work surfaces, appliances, etc., can be intimidating. It does help when you are planning a kitchen, probably more than any other room in the house, if you can make a decision. If you are the kind of person who takes half an hour to choose which toppings you want on your pizza, give yourself a year to put your room together.

Considering that cooking, eating and even watching TV all take place in the kitchen, it's worth spending time to put together your perfect room.

120. Small but perfectly formed

Simple solutions for pocket-sized spaces. With clever use of colour and careful planning, even the smallest space works as a fully functioning home.

If it's true that our possessions expand to fill the available space, then give me a studio flat every time. Not an expansive loft-style studio but a well-designed and compact home.

It has to be said that if you are hopelessly untidy then you are going to have to work harder at this than if you were born with that elusive neat and tidy gene.

However, there is something very appealing about a space that works as a kitchen to cook in, a dining room to eat in and a bedroom to sleep in. It presents a challenge whether you are a slob or impeccably neat. How do you divide the different areas to define the disparate uses? How do you maximise the look of the space while creating different zones?

That's studio living. But what about a house conversion where each floor of the building was originally designed as one-third of a functioning home and is now divided into three separate units where the rooms seem very small?

For both situations, let's start with an illusion. In any situation where your floor space is limited you need to decorate and design it so that the area seems larger than it is. In the first place, choose a light colour to paint your walls. In the second place choose a light colour to decorate your ceiling. In the third place choose a light-coloured flooring. (You will bring in other details later so that this isn't as bland as it sounds.)

Now let's be realistic. You can't have a massive sofa, you can't have a king-sized bed. Apart from the style issues that need to be considered, they probably won't go up the stairs or get through the door. In the same way that a doll's house has pieces that are miniaturised versions of the real thing, you are going to have to sit on a diminutive sofa and sleep in a moderately sized bed. (If you can't bear the thought of that, a wall bed might be the answer; a design that folds away can be huge because it won't take up floor space when shut away.)

Just as a jug can also function as a vase and a mug might be the place where you keep your pens and pencils, so when you buy furniture for small spaces work on the principle that, where possible, you want to get two uses out of one item. A coffee table doubles up as a dining table if you have floor cushions to sit on while you eat, a storage chest functions as extra seating when covered with lovely blankets or throws, and a set of shelves can also become a room divider. Once you start to work on this principle you'll find your own ways to adapt things in your home.

Colour is a useful tool in defining spaces. Variations on the walls and in the floor can be a great way to signpost a change of use. While I have said, and stick to the idea,

Here's an idea for you...

You can use light, both natural and from fixtures and fittings, to manipulate space. In a small room, make sure that your window treatment doesn't obscure any of the window – you need to let as much sunshine in as possible. If part of your home is in the roof, keep the skylights clean and clear. One useful tip in small spaces is to use lights at floor level to lead the eye. Spotlights installed just above the skirting and running away from a kitchen area and towards the lounge will draw the eye away from the kitchen if you have extinguished all the lights in that area.

that everything should be kept light, you can still use a slightly darker paint in two different spaces. If your kitchen is pure white, then decorate the adjacent designated dining area in a shade of stone. And you can change the flooring – if the lounge area in a studio is covered in wood laminate, then choose seagrass to cover the space that you use as a study.

I would also urge you to consider investing in vertical blinds or sliding panels to screen off spaces. These can be fitted to run from floor to ceiling and are easily pulled out of the way when you want to be open plan, and drawn back into place when you wish to separate off your sleeping area for example.

(Just another quick note about decorating – your use of patterns should ideally be kept to a minimum in small spaces. I'm afraid you would be unwise to use a boldly patterned wallpaper even if you have fallen in love with the current trend for retro-style bold designs that seem to be used in every designer home in the magazines.)

> *Defining idea...*
>
> **'Room service? Send up a larger room.'**
> GROUCHO MARX

Much as I hate to state the obvious, storage will be a priority in your compact home. You need to take an uncluttered approach to living in any small space so have a good look around your home and pinpoint any areas that are completely clear. You can look at the floor for starters but then include the walls all the way up to the ceiling too. There is an area above every doorway that can be used to house a set of shelves. You'll find space beneath each set of stairs that might be ideal for hanging hooks. Invest in clothes bags that fit under the bed in the bedroom, inset a basin into a cabinet in the bathroom and use the plinth space in your kitchen for extra drawers, and you'll be well on the way to making the most of any dead space.

Create your dream garden

121. Sort out your soil

Not knowing what sort of soil you have in your garden is like guessing between sugar and salt in the kitchen – a recipe for disaster.

Hands up who knows what pH stands for? No, we didn't have a clue either but apparently it's vital to how your garden grows.

The old saying 'the answer lies in the soil' is invariably true. Get to know your soil and you can add the right stuff to improve it, and grow the types of plants that will enjoy it. Hardly anyone gardens on rich, light loam but each soil type still has its own distinct merits.

The acid test

To find the pH (read on, dear reader, read on) of your soil you need a soil-testing kit, available at any garden centre. This will help you find out what kind of soil you're gardening on. And with this small yet vital snippet of information, you'll know how to feed your soil and what plants you can grow.

Here's an idea for you...

Raised beds may be a solution if you have particularly difficult soil and want to grow a range of vegetables and herbs. Build them approx 1.5m square so they can be worked from the sides without standing on the soil. Edge the beds, to a height of 30cm or more, to keep the soil in place. Use old railway sleepers, woven hazel, reclaimed bricks, galvanised steel, whatever takes your fancy. Fork over the soil to improve the drainage and then dig in as much compost as possible, adding a fresh layer of compost each time you replant.

It pays to take three or four samples from the outer edges of the garden as you may have more than one soil type, each favouring different plants and treatments. The test will show whether your samples are acidic (below 7), neutral (7) or alkaline (above 7).

Most garden plants favour soil that is slightly acidic at 6.5, but there's still a good selection of plants for neutral and alkaline soils.

With your pH sorted, discovering your soil type is even easier. Just pick some up. If it's tightly packed, squeezes into a sticky ball and hangs about on your boots – it's clay. If it feels gritty, and water runs through it easily – it's sandy. If you discover the white cliffs of Dover under the surface – it's chalk.

Clay soil is hard to work. It's wet and cloggy in winter and bakes rock hard in a dry spell. But it is full of good things and the nutrients your plants need to grow, so don't despair. You do need to improve its drainage though, so mix in some horticultural grit or coarse sand when planting. Clay soil is usually neutral to acidic too so add lime – ground down calcium – especially if you're growing brassicas. Turn unplanted ground over in the autumn and leave the frost to break up the big lumps.

Dig in or spread as much compost as you can, whenever the conditions suit. Timing is crucial but it's the soil and the weather that set the time, not you! As soon as it's dry enough to stand on without it turning into a mud bath, get to work.

Success on sand will depend on how you can help the soil hang on to food and moisture. Adding in compost will help retain water and fertiliser long enough for it to do some good. But this will need to become a regular chore so you may wish to just focus on parts of the garden where you are growing hungry, thirsty plants such as the veg.

Because any fertiliser will pass through the soil quickly, spread it a little and often. Sandy soil can be acidic and will benefit from a light application of lime (250g per square metre – half that for clay soils). A bonus is that the soil is easy to work on and quick to warm up in spring, so grow early crops that will mature before things get too dry.

Chalky soil can be stony, or sticky and thin, but it's well-drained and you can work on it most of the year. Bulk it up by adding organic matter. Horse manure, which tends to be full of straw, is good for sticky chalk. As it breaks down relatively quickly, spread it on the surface and leave the earthworms to do their bit. Dig in any left-over straw in the spring.

Remember, chalky soil is alkaline and certain plants won't like it a bit. You can give plants a helping hand at the start of the growing season by sprinkling in bonemeal

or blood, fish and bone, to compensate for the lack of
phosphate and to help roots develop.

Just to recap, most plants like clay soils, drought
tolerant plants are for sandy soils and plant lime-lovers
on chalk. This means that azaleas, camellias,
rhododendrons and heathers (except the winter
flowering Erica carnea) will not grow on chalk but
plenty of other plants, and most herbs, love it.

Oh and pH, that'll be potential hydrogen. Nope, I'm none the wiser either.

122. Maximise your blooms

**Why let your borders flop at the end of July when
with a bit of TLC and a sharp pair of secateurs
you could be enjoying a second show of colour?**

It stands to reason that you want to get as colourful and as
long-lasting a display as possible from your flowers, especially
given the effort that's gone into getting them to bloom in the first place.

Clipping plants back after flowering can seem drastic but in a week or two fresh
leaves will provide the perfect foil for other plants yet to perform.

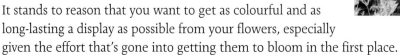

Cruel to be kind

The lungwort (Pulmonaria) is one of those harbingers of spring that gives you faith in the new season to come. Its blue and pink flowers (there are varieties that have just blue or white flowers too) are a welcome supply of nectar for early bees, but when they've done their bit be ruthless, and cut them off, together with most of the leaves. Water well and feed with a handful of bonemeal, and fresh dappled leaves with their 'spilt milk' markings) will soon appear.

> **Here's an idea for you...**
>
> Once they've flowered, shrubs and climbing roses could do with a bit of a lift. Plant the freely wandering, late flowering *Clematis tangutica* or some colourful climbing nasturtiums to ramble through and brighten things up.

You can be equally brutal with poppies (Papaver orientale) and also Lady's mantle (Alchemilla molis), once its lime green flowers show the first sign of browning (this will also prevent self-seeding, which this plant is particularly keen on). Hold back with the secateurs, and the leaves of these early performers will fade, rust and crumple by midsummer.

Plants that start flowering in the early summer can also benefit from a haircut to encourage a second flush of colour. Cat mint (Nepeta) and the pink flowering geranium (endressii) are two useful front-of-the-border fillers that respond well to this treatment. And if you cut them back just half at a time, you keep a succession of flowers and prevent the pudding-basin haircut appearance.

If you cut centaurea, delphiniums, anthemis and salvias back to ground level after flowering they may surprise you with a second flush too.

Defining idea...

'I uphold Beatrix Farrand's sentiment (Gertrude Jeykell's too) that the design should always fit the site; the site should not be bent to the design.'

ROSEMARY VEREY

Regular servicing

Midsummer is the time when you can really get to know and enjoy your plants, learning things about them that you can put into practice next year. There are often no big or laborious jobs that need doing – this is the time to potter. A bit of deadheading, a touch of cutting back and your border will keep its shape for weeks to come.

Deadhead once a week if possible – unless you want seeds for next year. Cutting off the spent flowers helps the plant put its energy into flowering again, instead of producing unwanted seeds.

When plants begin to look sad and need cutting right back, gaps may start to appear which can spoil the overall effect. While neighbouring plants may spread into the space, you can also strategically place the odd pot or container, submerging them out of sight. Alternatively, use some late flowering annuals, such as cosmos or lavatera. And, if you're organised, now's the time to send in the reinforcements, those spare plants grown from seed that you couldn't squeeze in early in the year but can now get in amongst them and play their part.

The real key to prolonging the border's display is succession planting. With a bit of thought and a season or two's experience, you'll soon become a dab hand. Try to think ahead. Group your plants together so that they not only complement each other in colour, height and leaf shape but also in flowering season. This simply means including some later flowering perennials close to your early performers.

Especially useful from midsummer until the first frosts are the Michaelmas daisy (Aster) and other daisy flowers (Rudbeckia, Helenium, Echinacea), the thistle-like Eryngium and Echinops, Japanese anemone and dahlias. Intersperse these next to plants that are in bloom in spring and you'll have a blooming border right through to late autumn.

123. Design without despair

You don't need a degree in landscape architecture to give shape to your garden – just a bit of inspiration and a rudimentary knowledge of elbow grease.

Starting from scratch is both daunting and exciting. You're about to invest a lot of time, and quite a few quid, into turning your weed-strewn plot into something with a little more structure, style and sophistication. So from the start it pays to have some vision or picture of how things are going to look when you're finished.

You need to get a feel for the site, thinking about what could go where and then working out whether it really should. Where are the garden's sunny spots? Where's the shade? Does anywhere tend to get waterlogged?

But at the same time don't get bogged down in detail because there's a lot to be said for seat-of-the-pants design. In other words go out and make a start. Keep standing back – even viewing from an upstairs window – and you'll soon get a feel for shape and proportion. The best advice at this stage of the proceedings is to leave the tape measure in the tool box.

Setting your sites

The first essential is to establish which direction your garden faces. On a suitable day follow the path of the sun across your garden noting the variations in light and shade, because while you may be basking in the reflected glory of a south-facing plot, it could sit under the canopy of the neighbour's spreading chestnut tree for most of the day.

Apropos neighbours, it pays to learn a little of their own gardening ambitions too. Is their newly planted leylandii to remain at a clipped 4 feet or allowed a free rein? And would neighbours on the other side mind if your clematis peeps over the top of their lapped larch fence?

Now, we all like our privacy but it's easy to become a bit obsessive about screening our gardens from the rest of the world. This is the difference between the British and Dutch gardening philosophies. We hide behind walls, fences and the densest hedges known to man, while the Dutch open their gardens for everybody to view as they pass by.

OK, now the fun really starts. Armed with small stakes or pegs mark out certain areas, such as the herbaceous border, rose bed and vegetable patch. A hosepipe is a great help in doing this. Being both light and flexible it will give you an immediate outline on which you can pass judgment.

At this stage, don't even think about any permanent structures like brick walls – their role and positioning will become more obvious as the rest of the garden takes shape. Shifting a few barrow loads of misplaced soil is one thing – reconstructing a wall or concrete path is another.

Off the straight and narrow

Unless you have a plot the size of Versailles, try and upset the symmetry of your garden, or at best confine any rigid formality and straight lines to the vegetable plot.

If you want a water feature, fine, but remember it doesn't have to be a lake if you only have a few square feet to play with. You could always confine yourself to a mini fountain or birdbath while the children are young and unaware of the potential dangers of a pond.

No matter how small your garden, you can still make use of existing rises and falls too, or create new and different levels. They help give the impression of more space and give you the opportunity to make a new patio or seating area.

The idea should be to create mystery! Try not to open everything up at once. Add fences, a winding path, a trellis or pergola smothered in climbers, which will tempt visitors to find out what's going on behind.

And treat permanent buildings as assets too. Cover garage walls with a cotoneaster; grow a wisteria on a south facing house wall; take advantage of a porch with a climbing rose. Even log stores or coalbunkers can look aesthetically pleasing given the right treatment. Cover up manholes or drain covers with a pot.

124. How to get the most from your containers

Even the biggest gardens have pots and containers brightening up a terrace, bringing life to a plain brick wall, or even lurking in the borders, adding a bit of timely, seasonal colour.

'Gardening with pots and containers – not like the real thing is it?' a friend quipped when we mentioned this chapter in the book. Oh, such folly! Containers are not an easy way out. They depend on you for constant food and water more than anything you have growing in the borders.

Yet this is also the beauty of containers – you're in control. You can move them, replant them, and keep them out of the reach of slugs and snails. You can let your imagination run wild, moving plants round as they come into bloom. And you can even surreptitiously place a few in your borders if they need a bit of a lift.

Getting kitted out

Plants will grow in just about anything, from ceramic vases to old watering cans, wooden planters to your own 'mock' rock troughs. But, even in small gardens, bear in mind you'll always make more impact by using large containers.

Terracotta pots are the pot of choice for most people. They look natural, age beautifully and are heavy enough to stand up to blustery conditions. But they're also very porous and, unless you line them with something like a bin bag with a few drainage holes added, they will soak up water before the plants get a look in. And stopping this water leaching into the terracotta also means they're less likely to crack when it freezes (and that goes for the so-called frost-proof pots as well).

The first thing to check with any container is that it has drainage holes at the bottom – if it doesn't, get the drill out. Next add some crocks, stones or old bits of polystyrene from broken up seed trays, to stop those vital drainage holes clogging up. An old cloth over the crocks will filter the water and stop your compost washing away.

Now for the compost itself. Tempting as it may be, avoid using garden soil as you don't know what pests and disease could be lurking in it. Better to use a loam based compost such as John Innes No2, or a general potting or multipurpose compost – peat-free of course.

Here's an idea for you...

To speed up that aging process on your terracotta or stone pots, a liberal coating of natural yoghurt will give the mosses and lichens a helping hand. Make sure you've soaked the pots in water first and once 'painted' put them somewhere cool, damp and shady to let the bacteria do its work

However, despite its impeccable green credentials, the downside of peat-free alternatives is that they dry out quicker than peat, so add a bit of leaf mould or garden compost, and some water-retentive crystals too.

For acid lovers like rhododendrons, you'll need to use lime-free ericaceous compost.

Mix and match

If you're planting up a container with several different varieties of plant, make sure that they all enjoy the same growing conditions. Arrange the plants, in their pots, on top of the compost first, imagining how they will fill out as they grow.

Start planting with the plant in the tallest pot (and therefore the biggest root ball) first. Put this in place and then add more compost to achieve the correct planting height for the smaller plants. This will also stop them sinking and ensure that their roots are in contact with the compost.

Always try and keep as much of the root ball intact as possible, tapping the base of the pot rather than yanking the plant out by its stem. Keep firming them in as you go, making sure there are no gaps or air pockets. If the roots of your plants have wound themselves around the bottom of the pot (pot-bound), gently spread them out before planting.

Your compost should finish about 3cm below the rim to allow for ample watering, which should also be your next job. Finally, add a layer of gravel both for decorative and practical reasons – it helps to retain moisture.

Bulbs are perfect for pots and growing tulips in containers allows you to appreciate their magnificence close up, and increases the chance of a 100% success. But you can grow most plants in containers – annuals, perennials, grasses, shrubs, climbers, vegetables and herbs, even small trees will be quite happy – as long as you look after them. And that's the key.

Constant care

Plants in containers need regular attention and regular watering – rain isn't enough to keep them going (even in the winter you need to keep an eye on the dryness of the compost). Pellets of slow-release fertiliser pressed into the soil are a good idea too, although the plants will also appreciate a fortnightly dose of tomato feed in summer.

Deadheading, replacing plants that are past their prime and checking pots for any pests, such as slugs or weevils, that have had the audacity to climb in, should all become part of your maintenance routine.

125. Self-contained

Even a tiny garden – or an apartment with a yard – can be used to grow edible produce if you know what containers to use.

Containers can be used to grow a wide variety of tasty crops, so don't be put off by thinking you haven't got enough space – start cultivating!

Containers are a convenient way to grow many tender and specialised plants. If you have limited space, container growing is a must. No space is too small to grow food. It can be grown wherever sunlight penetrates. You can grow plants in pots on windowsills, in conservatories, on balconies, in windowed stairwells and in roof gardens. If you live in an urban area this is even more important, because you need to build yourself a green oasis of calm that you can slip into to slough off the stresses of the day along with the grey grime of city living.

You have to be inventive and adaptable to make the most of your limited area. Use all of your vertical spaces, by fixing trellises for growing peas and beans – they don't need much floor space. Use hanging baskets for herbs and tumbling cherry tomatoes. And build window boxes for herbs and salad plants.

The great thing about container gardening is that you can start small, adding to your collection whenever you are ready. Try to grow a small amount of a wide variety of crops until you find what works, and what your family enjoys.

Containers

You can use anything that will contain compost. Old plastic catering-size food containers are ideal and available very cheaply – look in classified ads for details. Avoid non-food containers in case they have been filled with anything toxic.

Recycled sinks – not just the expensive antique variety, gorgeous though they are – together with old dustbins and tyre piles can make fabulous yard containers. They are big enough for you to grow fruit trees. Basically, anything that is big enough for the plant you want to grow is fine. Look at growth charts to work this out. Use your imagination – family and friends will likely have containers they are finished with that will be useful too.

Wooden troughs are easy to build from rough wood and can be painted to add rustic charm. These can contain anything from salads to climbers such as peas and beans. Recycled plastic containers can be bought cheaply from gardening centres and they are light enough for use on a balcony or in a roof garden. Baskets lined with polythene are also useful and light, and they are decorative too. If you use clay or pottery pots, make sure they are frost resistant if you intend leaving them outside during the winter.

Be sure to clean containers thoroughly to make sure you do not transfer any diseases from year to year.

> ## Here's an idea for you...
>
> Make your own 'growbags'. Even though the commercial varieties are cheap, they are of variable quality and may not be organic. Fill strong rubble sacks (from a builders' merchant) with your own home-made compost, worm casts, rotted manure and leaf mould mixed with a little soil. Seal the end with duct tape – it's waterproof and strong. Lay the 'growbag' on its side in its final position and use a craft knife to make a slit or window in the side. Then plant your tomatoes, cucumbers or whatever you fancy.

Compost

If it is humanly possible, have a compost bin. These are often available at a subsidised rate from your local council, so check it out. Worms are also a great addition to your compost making efforts. You can buy special kits or alternatively you can buy brandling worms (Eisenia foetida) from a fishing supplies store and add them to a container yourself. You can use any container with a tap at the bottom – adapting old wine-making equipment works well. The tap allows you to drain the liquid (essentially, worm pee) from the bottom of the container. This makes a great feeder to spray on plant leaves. Dilute 1:20 with water and put it in a spray mister.

The container needs a shelf inside for the worms – a piece of wire mesh works well. The worms have to be kept out of liquid they produce or they will drown. Add about 1.5 to 2 kg (dry weight) of shredded newspaper to the bin after it has been moistened with water. Then add the worms. Give them kitchen waste to feed on and remember they aren't keen on citrus or spicy foods. Add shredded newspaper as necessary to stop the container becoming anaerobic and smelly. Keep a lid on the top to exclude flies.

Defining idea...

'There are no gardening mistakes, only experiments.'
JANET KILBURN PHILLIPS, gardener

The worm bin should be totally emptied twice a year, after leaving it for a fortnight without adding any new material. The worms will wriggle to the top, and are easily removed to a temporary pot whilst you remove the rich matter left in the bin. You then start again with fresh newspaper.

126. Home grown herbs

Herbs can be used to flavour food, make houses fragrant, dye cloth and 'doctor' animals – and humans! Every garden should have some.

It's little wonder aromatic herbs have been grown since humans first planted seeds – there are few pleasures more satisfying than a walk in the herb garden on a warm day.

Besides the flavours and heady perfume, a herb garden also supplies you with a natural pharmacy. As with any self-administered remedy, though, take advice from a qualified practitioner as necessary.

Herbs generally like warmth and a sheltered spot. They also like well-drained soil, so prepare your soil by digging in plenty of grit to make it free draining (particularly if you are gardening on a heavy or clay soil).

There are perennial herbs – those that come back year after year – and annual herbs, which need sowing every year. Biennials are herbs that are sown one year and grow to maturity the next year before dying off and needing to be re-sown with new seeds. Read on to find out what you should grow, and why.

Here's an idea for you...

Make your own teas and tisanes. Use a small bunch of fresh herbs (about 25 g) or a heaped teaspoon of dried herbs, and put them in a small teapot kept especially for the purpose. Add boiling water and leave the herbs to steep. Strain them carefully to avoid getting 'salad teeth'. An old-fashioned tea strainer works well. Alternatively, you can buy a 'tea ball' – a small, spherical metal strainer on a chain – that you fill with herbs and dangle in a cup of hot water.

Perennials

Mint is the thug of the herb garden. Be careful about where you put it because you will never be rid of it. For this reason, many people like to grow it in containers. Bees and butterflies love this herb when it is in flower. Mint is a good culinary herb – lovely on tiny potatoes fresh from the garden – and makes a soothing tea, which is especially good for upset or unsettled stomachs and pregnancy sickness.

Rosemary bushes grow best in light soils, but having dug lots of grit into my heavy clay soil they grow prolifically here. Rosemary leaves, rubbed from a fresh sprig, make a fabulous flavouring for tiny roast potatoes and Mediterranean roast vegetables. In addition, rosemary makes a good astringent – just make strong tea and wipe the liquid across your skin to tighten pores. Rosemary also makes a rinse for putting glints and highlights into dark hair, and is good for dandruff sufferers.

Sage is a downy leaved plant that grows easily. However, it can become 'leggy', with long woody stems. Rather than cutting back hard, and potentially damaging the plant, I tend to take cuttings yearly. Sage is great for sauces and stuffings and the tea is also good for throat infections, or used cold as a mouthwash. Strong tea, used cold, soothes insect bites and stings.

Thyme grows easily on light soils, but heavy soils need grit dug in. Bees love the flowers in summer. Thyme is a great culinary herb, and is also a fine tonic for the digestive system – not just for humans but also livestock. Thyme tea with honey also promotes sound sleep.

Annuals and biennials

Basil is a delicious culinary herb. It is perhaps grown best in containers inside to protect it from the weather. Apart from the green variety, you can now buy seeds of purple and ragged edged basil for variety. Home grown, organic basil makes the most wonderful pesto. Basil also has mild antiseptic properties.

Borage is a beautiful plant that I would not be without – not least of all because the flowers look so great in a jug of Pimms! They are also delightful when crystallized in sugar for dessert decorations. The tiny blue star-like flowers are irresistible to bees and other pollinating insects, so include a few borage plants in your fruit garden. It self-seeds easily, so once introduced will be there to stay.

Angelica is an architectural plant said to be an aid to fertility – so go steady! However, it also has culinary uses. The stem can be candied in sugar – it is the source of the tiny expensive pots of green sweetmeat sold by confectioners for decorating cakes and desserts.

Parsley is ubiquitous as a culinary herb, but also has great stomach soothing properties. Tea made from this plant will help to soothe cystitis. Chewing a sprig freshens spicy breath, too. Parsley is also good for livestock, and can increase milk yields.

Defining idea...

'Money was invented so we could know exactly how much we owe.'
CULLEN HIGHTOWER, US salesman and writer

Simply brilliant offer
with Bourne To Organise

BOURNE
TO
ORGANISE
THINK WHAT YOU COULD BE DOING

There couldn't be an easier way to start simplifying your life and putting some of the tips in this section into practice than with this **20% discounted offer** from **Bourne to Organise**.

Life is exciting... it's also demanding and chaotic. With only twenty-four hours a day, there is serious pressure to 'do it all'. So just stop and think – what would you rather be doing?

Bourne to Organise provide the personal touch when it comes to concierge and organising services. By letting them take care of your 'to do' lists they can guarantee to save you time, money and trouble.

Their aim is to make your life as hassle free as possible to enable you to make the most of every minute and live life to the full. If you can't think of what to do with all your spare time… then maybe they can help with that as well? With this 20% discount off their normal hourly rate (of £25), it couldn't be easier to start enjoying the things in life which *really* matter to you. For more information visit www.bourne-to-organise.co.uk

For details on how to take advantage of this fantastic offer please go to page 489, where you'll also find information on all the other great deals found throughout *Goddess*.

Terms and conditions
This offer cannot be used in conjunction with any other offer or promotion and applies to new bookings only.

Live longer, live better

**'What a wonderful life I've had!
I only wish I'd realised it sooner.'**

COLETTE

Good health doesn't require a personal trainer and good luck. Between 80 and 90 per cent of all disease is self inflicted. Fine-tuning your nutrition, sleep patterns, stress levels and activity (or lack of it) can add years to your life.

Are you a human being?

**Or are you more correctly described as a 'human doing'?
Being too busy can lead to health-wrecking stress so get a
snapshot of your stress levels with this quiz.**

1. Today, are you more likely to:
☐ a. Put aside at least 15 minutes for yourself to relax – as you do every day.
☐ b. Work through lunch, barely make a cup of tea.

2. Do you
☐ a. Hardly ever take work home?
☐ b. Frequently take work home?

3. Do you
☐ a. Work late rarely?
☐ b. Work late frequently?

4. Do you
☐ a. Cut off when you're on holiday?
☐ b. Leave a number and spend a part of most days dealing with the office?

5. Do you

☐ a. Take all of your holiday allowance?

☐ b. Take some of your holiday allowance?

6. Do you

☐ a. Usually take a lunch hour?

☐ b. Rarely take the whole lunch hour?

More 'a's. You seem to have a good grip on keeping boundaries strong between your working life and your home life. Keep it up.

More 'b's. You need to strengthen the boundaries that will help protect time for you. See idea 135, Restoration day.

Energy for life

127. Add years to your life in one day

Motivated by instant results? These simple lifestyle changes could add years to your life in one day.

There are many different ways to stay younger for longer – eating different foods, cutting others out of your diet, exercising , getting out and about, watching your stress levels, taking the right vitamins.

It can seem overwhelming, but in practice it comes down to common sense. Most of it is even fun! To give you a better idea, here's what an ideal anti-ageing day could look like.

7.30 a.m. ALWAYS START YOUR DAY WITH BREAKFAST. People who eat breakfast live longer than people who don't – as long as they choose wholegrain-based cereals. Add a cup of green tea and a piece of fruit to boost your levels of disease-fighting antioxidants.

7.45 a.m. DRINK A GLASS OF WATER AND TAKE A MULTIVITAMIN. Most people don't get the recommended daily allowance of many essential vitamins and minerals. You're more likely to remember to take a supplement every day if you take it with breakfast.

8 a.m. BRUSH AND FLOSS YOUR TEETH – it can take six years off your biological age. The bacteria that cause gum disease also cause furring of the arteries which can lead to heart disease. And bad teeth never helped anyone look younger!

8.30 a.m. WALK TO WORK. Exercising for at least thirty minutes every day is the best way to keep your heart and lungs in good shape (not to mention the rest of you).

9 a.m. DRINK A GLASS OF WATER and try to have six more throughout the day.

10 a.m. HAVE ANOTHER CUP OF TEA. Always squeeze your teabag – you'll release twice as many antioxidants that way.

10.30 a.m. CONNECT WITH YOUR FRIENDS and colleagues by email or phone. People with a strong social network of friends and family live longer and healthier lives than more solitary types.

12.30 p.m. DO SOME LUNCHTIME YOGA. It balances out all the body's systems and gets your organs working efficiently. Ever wondered why yoga teachers look so young?

1.30 p.m. HAVE A RAINBOW SALAD FOR LUNCH. Use as many differently coloured vegetables – red peppers, watercress, grated carrot and courgette, young spinach leaves, cherry tomatoes – as you can. Dress with olive oil and balsamic vinegar, and sprinkle with a handful of toasted sunflower and sesame seeds for the perfect antioxidant-packed, disease-fighting lunch.

3.30 p.m. TAKE THE STAIRS. Climb up and down a flight six times a day and you'll prevent weight gain of 2 kg a year. You take 36 days off your life for every 5 kg overweight you are.

6 p.m. MEDITATE ON THE TRAIN HOME. You'll lower your blood pressure and slow your heartbeat, both of which are good for your heart's health. Close your eyes and breathe deeply, in through your nose and out through your mouth. Try to empty your mind and simply concentrate on what the breath feels like as it enters your nostrils and leaves through your lips. Feel it filling your lungs and pushing out your abdomen. Keep this focus for around ten to fifteen minutes.

7 p.m. HAVE A SMALL GLASS OF RED WINE. Go for a deep red like a Pinot Noir for a maximum boost of disease-fighting flavonoids. Just be sure to stop at one or two.

Defining idea...

**'The best thing about the
future is that it comes only
one day at a time.'**
ABRAHAM LINCOLN

8 p.m. HAVE SALMON FOR DINNER. Oily fish like salmon – or mackerel, sardines, trout or tuna – keeps your brain healthy and can stave off Alzheimer's if eaten at least twice a week.

9 p.m. WATCH A FUNNY VIDEO. Laughter boosts your immune system and reduces the ageing effect of stress hormones on the body. So switch off the news and watch a comedy instead.

10 p.m. HAVE SEX. People who have sex more than twice a week live longer than those who don't.

11 p.m. SLEEP! It's your body's chance to release growth hormone and repair itself from the inside out. So never skimp on your shut-eye – aim for at least six to eight hours a night.

128. Upping the anti

Antioxidants could add years to your life by fighting free radical damage – if you're getting enough.

You have an army of good guys – antioxidants – which roam the body, eliminating the free radicals they find. You can boost their ranks simply by eating the right foods.

It's always important to know your enemy and in the war against ageing, it's free radicals, the unstable molecules that are a by-product of breathing and which damage the body's cells. There's nothing you can do to stop free radicals forming (except stop breathing, which would be a bit, well, radical), but antioxidants can eliminate them.

One half of the antioxidant army consists of compounds and enzymes that the body makes itself, using micronutrients found in the diet such as selenium, zinc, manganese, copper, iron, lipoic acid and glutathione. The other half are antioxidants delivered in the food we eat including vitamins A, C, E and B, and the vitamin-like compounds flavonoids, carotenoids and coenzyme Q10.

When you eat a diet high in antioxidants, a protective shield is created around each cell which fights off and destroys the attacking free radicals. But if you're depleted in any of these micronutrients, there will be cracks in the shield. Many scientists believe the rise in heart disease, Alzheimer's and some cancers can be directly linked to micronutrient depletion. Our intake of selenium, for example, has fallen by 50% in the past 50 years due to intensive farming methods that leach it from the soil.

When it comes to their antioxidant content, not all foods were created equal. Meat, fish and dairy products do contain antioxidants but they're destroyed by cooking. Fruit and vegetables, however, contain high levels of antioxidants that survive the cooking process

Here's an idea for you...

Black really is beautiful when it comes to staving off ageing. The darker the pigment – think plums, prunes, bilberries, blackberries, dates and raisins – the higher the ORAC rating. It's thought the pigment is a rich source of antioxidants. To maximise the benefits, wash rather than peel the skin of fruits and veg – the pigment is often concentrated in the skin or outer leaves. Try to eat a dark red, purple or black fruit or vegetable every day. And if you love wine, go for deep reds – they contain the most flavonoids.

(as long as you don't boil them to mush). For very basic good health, you need 'five a day' – five portions (a portion is around a handful) of fresh fruit and vegetables a day. But to fend off ageing you need to step up a level and pack in as many antioxidants as possible.

It's easier to do than you might think, thanks to the brilliant scientists at Tufts University in the States who have very helpfully rated the antioxidant value of every food. It's a system known as ORAC: oxygen radical absorption capacity. The higher the ORAC, the more powerful a food is at mopping up free radicals. In fact, eating plenty of high-ORAC foods could raise the antioxidant power of blood by 10–25%.

One Tufts study of 1300 older people showed that those who had two or more portions a day of dark-pigmented vegetables such as kale and spinach were only half as likely to suffer a heart attack – and had a third of the risk of dying of cancer – compared with people averaging less than one portion a day. Other research has shown that a diet of high-ORAC foods fed to animals prevents long-term memory loss and improves learning capabilities. It may be no coincidence that this high-ORAC diet is very similar to the one eaten by the Hunza people of the Indian Himalayas, who commonly live beyond 100.

Visit your health-food store and you'll see you can buy antioxidants as a supplement. But the researchers at Tufts think it's the whole foodstuff and the way the hundreds of micronutrients within it (some of which they're yet to identify) react together that provides its powerful antioxidant punch. If you're the cautious type, take a belt-and-braces approach – aim for a high-ORAC diet and add a good antioxidant supplement just in case.

The top ORAC-scoring foods

The following figures are the number of ORACs that 100 grams of each food provides. A high-ORAC diet will provide 3000–5000 units a day.

Prunes, 5770

Raisins, 2830

Blueberries, 2400

Blackberries, 2036

Garlic, 1939

Kale, 1770

Cranberries, 1750

Strawberries, 1540

Spinach, 1260

Raspberries, 1220

Brussels sprouts, 980

Plums, 949

Alfalfa sprouts, 930

Broccoli, 890

Beetroot, 840

Avocado, 782

Oranges, 750

Red grapes, 739

Red peppers, 710

Cherries, 670

Kiwi fruit, 602

Baked beans, 503

Pink grapefruit, 483

Kidney beans, 460

Onion, 450

White grapes, 446

129. Your anti-ageing diet

Every meal you eat is an opportunity to fend off ageing, so eat the right foods.

If feeling and looking younger than your years is important to you, you'll have already made the connection between your health and your fridge.

Here's an idea for you...

Grow your own superfood at home – you don't even need a garden! Sprouts are young green plants germinated from the seeds of vegetables, nuts, grains or beans and they've got antioxidants in super-concentrated amounts. You can buy sprouting kits or just use a large jar and some clean muslin. Simply soak the seeds overnight, place in your sprouter, then rinse with water twice a day. Keep in a dark warm place and they should be ready to eat within three days – give them a boost of sunlight before eating, then just grab a handful to add fresh crunch to salads or sandwiches.

There's a good chance there'll be broccoli, spinach and carrots in there. You won't have to rely on the lettuce in your burger for one of your five-a-day portions of fruit and veg. You probably know from experience that some foods give you energy and make you feel full of vitality, and others drag you down. You're well on the road to the perfect anti-ageing diet. Now it's time for an upgrade.

Food is our most important weapon in the war against ageing and disease. You only need to look at the differences in life expectancy around the world for proof. It's why those Japanese living in Japan, eating a diet rich in fish, vegetables and soy, and low in fat and sugar, have the longest lifespan and the lowest levels of heart disease. It's also why women in Scotland are nine times more likely to die from a heart attack than women in France.

A disease-fighting, anti-ageing diet means cooking from scratch, buying fresh ingredients and including as many foods as possible that have been identified as 'superfoods'. Here are just a few of the easiest to find and cook with. Try introducing one or two a month and experimenting with ways to eat them.

Spinach

It's all in the colour – spinach and other dark green vegetables such as kale, watercress, rocket and spring greens are packed with hundreds of disease-fighting micronutrients. Spinach is good at protecting eyesight as well as keeping the arteries clear of cholesterol, reducing blood pressure and lowering the risk of almost every type of cancer. Try using baby spinach leaves as a base for salads (it contains 90% more antioxidants than iceberg lettuce), adding them to stir-fries (right at the end – it barely needs cooking), or steaming them and serving as a side dish sprinkled with fresh lemon juice.

Broccoli

Broccoli is cancer's worst enemy. It comes from a family of cruciferous vegetables (including cabbage, kale and Brussels sprouts) that contain high levels of sulphur compounds which increase the enzymes that stop cancer cells growing. They also contain high levels of the antioxidant vitamin C and cholesterol-lowering fibre. If there are any leaves left on the stalk, don't discard them before cooking – they contain more carotenoids than the florets! Simply steam and serve, making a perfect accompaniment to meals.

Onions

Onions are high in the flavonoid quercitin, which can cut heart disease risk by 755%. Flavonoids also boost the immune system. One study showed a strong link between regular consumption of onions and a reduced risk of stomach cancer.

Sweet potatoes

While white potatoes provide low amounts of antioxidants, the orange-skinned sweet potato is packed with anti-cancer antioxidants. They can be baked in their skins, or boiled and mashed – or try cutting them into chunks and roasting them in the oven in a little olive oil to make chips.

Nuts

Nuts got a bad reputation during the 1980s fat-free diet craze – we still think of them as a naughty treat. They are high in calories, but in moderation (a handful, a few times a week) they can reduce your risk of having a heart attack by up to 50%. They're packed full of monounsaturates, which lower 'bad' LDL cholesterol and raise 'good' HDL cholesterol. Go for them raw rather than salted or roasted. They're delicious simply chopped, or toasted in a dry frying pan, and added to salads or sprinkled on soups.

Wholegrains

White, refined carbohydrates such as white bread, rice and pasta – plus refined flour products such as cakes, pastries and biscuits – have little to offer an anti-ageing diet. Refined flour is stripped of its disease-fighting fibre and nutrients. But foods that come from the wholegrain, those that still contain the antioxidant-packed wheatgerm, will help to lower your risk of heart disease, hypertension and certain cancers. So if 'whole' isn't the first word in the list of ingredients, ditch it.

Yogurt

Live bio-yogurt is a good anti-ageing food as it's full of probiotics or 'good bacteria' essential for healthy digestion and boosting the immune system. Getting your digestive system working effectively means you'll also get the most out of the other anti-ageing foods you're eating.

130. Supplementary benefits

Most nutritionists believe everyone will benefit from taking a good multivitamin and mineral supplement every day.

But what else should you take if your goal is living younger for longer?

How many times have you read that a healthy, balanced diet should provide all the vitamins and minerals a body needs, and that supplements are a waste of money? In theory, it sounds reasonable. But it doesn't explain why virtually every anti-ageing researcher and scientist takes supplements on a regular basis.

Let's face it, we never quite live up to our healthy intentions. We know we need five portions of fruit and vegetables a day, but average consumption is just about

Here's an idea for you...

When's the ideal time to take vitamin supplements? Nutritionists say it doesn't matter, as long as they're taken at roughly the same time every day. This is to ensure that levels of nutrients are consistently topped up. You're also most likely to remember to take them if it's become part of a daily routine. Many people find the easiest way to remember is to take their supplements with breakfast, as it's the meal most regularly eaten at home. Keep your bottles next to the kettle as a reminder!

half that. On top of this certain lifestyle factors, such as smoking and heavy drinking, can deplete your body of nutrients, and stress can also take its toll on the B vitamins which are required to keep the nervous system healthy. Plus, as we age, we require fewer calories on a daily basis, and so our chances of getting the right amount of nutrients from food are reduced. Add to that the fact that modern farming and food processing techniques have reduced the vitamin and mineral content of many foods, and you can see the problem.

But walk into any health-food store and you can be overwhelmed by the choice of supplements on sale. It's not simply a case of 'more is better' – your body (and your bank balance) will thank you for making an informed choice of a select few. Here's a simple four-step guide to successfully negotiating the supplement maze.

1. Start with a daily multivitamin/mineral supplement

This will make up for any deficiencies caused by trace elements missing from your diet. You don't have to spend a fortune or buy it from an obscure mail order company – you can get an affordable, good quality multi from most supermarkets and high street pharmacies. Look for one that includes selenium – a mineral needed in trace amounts that's thought to boost the immune system. One study found that 100 mcg of selenium taken daily reduced the death rate among cancer patients. Ideally, it should also include around 50 mg of magnesium, which helps to lower blood pressure.

2. Boost your vitamin C

Vitamin C's main job is to enter your cells and lie in wait to eliminate opportunist free radicals looking to damage your DNA. When it has a spare moment, it also helps heal artery walls that have become damaged, reduce cholesterol and lower blood pressure. It's also vital for boosting the immune system and plays a big role in fighting cancer. Making sure you eat some citrus food or berries every day is essential, then add a vitamin C supplement of up to 1000 mg a day – the current recommended safe upper limit. Some anti-ageing experts recommend taking up to 3000 mg a day, although it has been known to cause diarrhoea in high doses. Try starting with two daily 500 mg doses, six hours apart.

3. Boost your vitamin E

Vitamin E can lower the risk of heart attack in women by as much as 40% and in men by 35%. If vitamin E is given to people who already show signs of heart disease, it can reduce the risk of heart attack by as much as 75%. In an ideal world, vitamin E likes to work with vitamin C – they complement each other as E is fat soluble, and C is water soluble, so between them, they've got the body covered. Make sure you're eating wholegrains such as wholegrain cereals, bread, rice or pasta several times a day, and green leafy vegetables at least once a day. Then add a supplement of up to 540 mg a day.

4. Boost your Bs

Homocysteine is an amino acid which builds up in the blood as you age. Now scientists are linking high homocysteine levels with a higher risk of heart disease. But simply taking a supplement of 400 mcg of folic acid every day is usually all you need to substantially reduce your homocysteine to safe levels.

Folic acid is a B vitamin that likes to work synergistically with the other Bs, so look for a B complex supplement.

131. Save your skin

A little bit of sun exposure can help you live longer – but too much could kill you.

It may seem unfair, but there isn't a more effective way of speeding up the ageing process than lying on a sunlounger.

A glowing tan can cover a multitude of sins. Not only does the sun lead to wrinkles which make us look older, it also damages the chromosomes in our skin cells and can trigger skin cancer.

Ultraviolet light is the part of sunlight that damages skin. As UVB is 85% responsible for burning the skin – and has traditionally been thought to be the main cause of skin cancer – the first sunscreens mainly protected against these rays. However, around fifteen years ago scientists began to discover that UVA can also damage the skin in the longer term, by causing the release of harmful free radicals in the skin. These can suppress the immune system, cause allergic reactions such as prickly heat and damage the DNA of skin cells. The result is premature ageing – wrinkles, enlarged pores, bumps, pigmentation and saggy skin. There's also growing evidence that it is mainly UVA rays that cause melanoma – the most dangerous kind of skin cancer – and not UVB rays as was originally thought.

But that doesn't mean avoiding the sun altogether – the body needs to be exposed to sunlight before it can make vitamin D, essential for strengthening the immune response, healthy bones and cardiovascular health. There's also been some interesting research recently into how sunlight affects our moods, and that exposure to natural light can stave off depression. This isn't a licence to strip off and bake yourself next summer. Just ten minutes outdoors every day, without sunblock, is enough sun exposure to allow your body to make vitamin D.

Nowadays, we're clued up about the dangers of sun exposure and most of us are aware of the basic rules

Here's an idea for you...

Never know how much sunscreen is enough? A blob the size of a large coin should cover one arm and hand or your face and neck, and two blobs will do a leg and foot, your front torso or back. Sunscreen should be applied fifteen minutes before exposure, then reapplied immediately on exposure to the sun. Reapply every two hours as it gets rubbed off. And always reapply after swimming – even if it's a water-resistant sunscreen (they're designed to protect you while in the water but no sunscreen is completely waterproof, so a certain amount will come off). Try to wait five minutes after applying lotion before lying down – a protective film forms after five minutes so it's not as easily rubbed off. You'll need one 400 ml bottle of sunscreen per person for every ten days of a beach-based holiday.

to protect ourselves. But what is more worrying is that the risk of sun-related cancer is determined by how much exposure you received as a child; just one incidence of sunburn as a child more than doubles your odds of getting skin cancer and DNA damage to skin can result in cancer ten to thirty years on. It's probably not what you want to hear if you're part of the generation who grew up accepting that sunburn was a part of summer. So what (if anything) can you do to undo the damage of the past and reduce your risk of skin cancer in the future?

You could start by drinking lots of green tea (around four cups a day). Studies have also shown that compounds in green tea can fight skin cancer. Stick with it – it's an acquired taste. Eating vegetables high in beta-carotene and vitamin A such as carrots is also thought to protect against skin cancers developing.

It's important to also keep an eye on your skin (and your partner's) – 75% of melanomas are spotted by individuals, not doctors, and with early detection almost 100% of skin cancers are curable. See your doctor immediately if an existing mole or dark patch is getting larger or a new one is growing, if a mole has a ragged outline (ordinary moles are smooth and regular) or if a mole has a mixture of different shades of brown or black (ordinary moles may be dark brown but are all one shade). You should also report the following changes if they don't disappear within two weeks: an inflamed mole or one with a reddish edge, one that starts to bleed, ooze or crust, a mole that changes sensation or one that is substantially bigger than all of your other moles.

Defining idea...

'Nobody grows old merely by living a number of years. We grow old by deserting our ideals. Years may wrinkle the skin, but to give up enthusiasm wrinkles the soul.'
SAMUEL ULLMAN, poet

132. Vital energy

We need an endless supply of energy to do everything we need and want to do in our lives, yet we're often overwhelmed by a desire to have a swift forty winks.

Have you ever felt like curling up under your desk and spending the afternoon snoozing? Or been in serious need of matchsticks to prop your eyelids open? And do you ever wonder why this always seems to happen in the middle of a vital meeting, despite three cups of coffee?

The energy equation

We need sugar (glucose) to fire our system. It's the fuel that gives us our energy. However, too much is deemed by our body to be dangerous (think of diabetics).

We obtain this fuel largely from our food. A hormone called insulin specifically lowers these blood sugar levels and adjusts them according to our minute-by-minute needs. We don't have very much sugar circulating at any one time because as soon as we do, in comes insulin to normalise the level. When blood sugar levels are low, we rely on stored glucose (glycogen) found in the muscles and the liver, which helps maintain this delicate equilibrium. Once stored glucose is used, more food will be required to sustain glucose production.

Here's an idea for you...

Get a good breakfast in! A recent study revealed that people who didn't eat breakfast were likely to be overweight and less intelligent. So, if you didn't have a good reason before, you have now. A good breakfast will sustain you through to lunch, but remember that sugary cereals will pick you up and then drop you like a stone.

Not all food was created equal. Some foods 'burn' (meaning they're converted into sugar) quickly while other foods 'burn' slowly. These foods are called low and high glycaemic index foods (GI foods). The GI index is a way of measuring foods that are converted to glucose at different rates. But don't get hung up on the GI index, as confusingly you'll see it published in different places with different values. As a very simple rule of thumb, white things (e.g. potatoes, pasta, bread, parsnips, white rice) are like rocket fuel while dense, thick, fibrous, brown or green things (e.g. lentils, chickpeas, broccoli, brown rice) are going to burn more slowly and are our great energy sustainers. For example, whereas glucose (sugar) scores 100 on the GI scale, a lentil comes in at a cool 42. The important thing to remember is that it isn't necessarily foods that we traditionally think of as sweet that cause the problems. A 'sweet' potato, for instance, actually scores quite low, as it is wonderfully fibrous.

You can raise your blood sugar by another mechanism. Stick your head in the mouth of a man-eating shark, then quickly take it out again and swim like hell for the shore. This would certainly pick your blood sugar up rapidly, as powerful stress hormones would raise blood sugar to give you enough energy for your clever exit strategy. We do this all the time, but usually our boss, gas bill or deadline is the cause of our stress and not man-eating sharks. Of course there is an easier way of picking up blood sugar levels – have a fag or a cup of coffee. These are both stimulants, which stimulate the adrenal glands (where those stress hormones come from) to release sugar from storage. But what goes up, must come down, hence staying awake in the meeting becomes a challenge.

So, what's the problem with the blood sugar whizzing up and down all the time? First, the pancreas, where all that insulin is produced from, is going to get worn out. Second, you're going to get dips of energy as the blood sugar levels plummet when insulin tries to lower them. Third, insulin is also a fat storage hormone, so if it overreacts and there's continuously too much insulin in the system, eventually you'll put on weight. Commonly this appears as those cute love handles or that attractive tyre round the middle. And where do you see this phenomenon most commonly? On stressed out executives who are eating the wrong things, having too many cups of coffee and getting stressed out.

> *Defining* idea...
>
> **'Mary: I want a guy who can play 36 holes of golf, and still have enough energy to take Warren and me to a baseball game, and eat sausages, and beer, not lite beer, but beer. That's my ad, print it up. Brenda: "Fatty who likes golf, beer, and baseball." Gee, Mary, where are you gonna find a gem like that?'**
> THERE'S SOMETHING ABOUT MARY, a lesson in why you should be careful how you define 'energy'

133. Ready for a detox?

Detox is such a big buzz word these days, but what exactly does it mean?

In rebellion against the detox diet movement, someone I know did a retox diet during the football season. His method was to drink several pints of lager. The media remind us daily

Here's an idea for you...

Get a juicer and start making your own juice. You might like to try a combination of apple and blueberry or carrot and apple. Juices can be full of vitamins and minerals that help the detoxification systems important to the body. But remember to use organic fruit as there are pesticides on conventionally grown fruit.

how all the stars have detoxed, but what does this involve?

Doing a detox diet isn't quite as simple as you might think. What detox actually means to you really depends on where you are with your diet now. If you're drinking lots of alcohol, simply eliminating the booze for a few days might constitute a detox diet. To someone who already has quite a pure diet, however, eliminating wheat and dairy might be a detox. Taking stock of where you are is important because if you detox too quickly you could experience a number of unpleasant symptoms, such as headaches, lack of energy and generally feeling unwell. Don't think of doing a detox when you have an important week at work, as you might have a bit of a fuzzy head.

Don't make me

Why should we put ourselves through a detox? Isn't it really hard work? Our bodies are in a constant state of renewal at cell level, but if there's an overload of toxins either from food or environmental sources our bodies struggle to deal with them, effectively putting a strain on the kidneys and liver and taking away energy that could otherwise be used for living. A detox diet allows us to stop overloading the body with harmful substances and, if we give the body plenty of the right nutrients, it can speed up the elimination of toxins and promote cell renewal.

Warm-up

If you're afraid of becoming Mr or Mrs Fuzzy Potatohead, then the thing to do is to start slowly over a period of one month. Choose in the first week to eliminate coffee, chocolate and caffeine drinks (cola drinks), replacing them with lots of water and herbal teas. In the second week, try eliminating wheat products (cakes, biscuits, pasta) and substitute them with rye bread or other grains such as brown rice, quinoa, buckwheat or millet. In the third week, try substituting dairy products for sheep and goat products. And in the fourth week, increase your water intake up to at least 2 litres (3.5 pints) of water a day, whilst avoiding alcohol.

You might want to take into consideration environmental toxins too and try to avoid them during this period. Are you a smoker? Do you regularly use aerosol sprays? Do you take lots of over-the-counter medication (for example, for headaches)? What about your exposure to traffic fumes? If you're a cyclist, consider wearing a mask to filter fumes.

134. Are you younger than you think?

Take this quiz and find out your true biological age.

Ever told a tiny white lie and knocked off a few years when someone asks you how old you are? You may be being more honest than you think.

Here's an idea for you...

The static balance test is an instant way of assessing your biological age. Stand barefoot on a flat surface with your feet together and your eyes closed. Raise your right foot six inches off the ground (if you're left-handed, raise your left foot). See how many seconds you can maintain your balance without having to open your eyes or put your foot down. Here are the approximate values (time in seconds before falling over) for different biological ages.

- **04 seconds – 70 years**
- **05 seconds – 65 years**
- **07 seconds – 60 years**
- **08 seconds – 55 years**
- **09 seconds – 50 years**
- **12 seconds – 45 years**
- **16 seconds – 40 years**

Scientists believe that as well as a calendar age, you also have a biological or 'body' age, which is determined by your health and lifestyle. We all know people who seem younger than their years – and those who seem old before their time. Now scientists believe that it's possible to have a biological age or body age of 50 in our seventies. We're only just realising that how fast, or how slowly, we age is a process that's under our control. We now know that our diet, activity levels, and even our emotional health all have a direct effect on the ageing process. How long your body and mind stay fit, active and healthy is determined by how you live your life.

It's only a matter of time before scientists devise a definitive method of determining true body age. And who knows, in the future, perhaps we'll come to discard birth dates altogether and use personal age assessments instead for employers, insurers – maybe even dating agencies!

In the meantime, try the quiz below to find out how you're ageing so far. Don't be dismayed if it's not good news. There's plenty of information to help you knock years off your true age and keep your biological age as young as possible.

What's your body age?

Start with your calendar age. If you can answer 'yes' to any of the following questions, add or subtract years as directed to find your body age.

1. Do you get at least thirty minutes of moderate exercise (like walking) on most days?
   YES – subtract 1 year

2. Do you exercise really intensively on a regular basis?
   YES – add 3 years

3. Do you rarely, if ever, do any physical exercise?
   YES – add 2 years

4. Are you more than 10% over the recommended weight for your height?
   YES – add 3 years

5. Are you the correct weight for your height?
   YES – subtract 1 year

6. Are you under stress or pressure on a regular basis?
   YES – add 4 years

7. Do you actively practise stress-reducing techniques such as meditation or yoga?
   YES – subtract 3 years

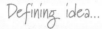

Defining idea...

'I was wise enough to never grow up while fooling most people into believing I had.'
MARGARET MEAD, anthropologist

8. Have you experienced three or more stressful life events in the past year (for example divorce, bereavement, job loss, moving house)?
YES – add 3 years

9. Do you smoke?
YES – add 6 years

10. Do you have a total cholesterol level of 6.7 or higher?
YES – add 2 years

11. Do you have blood pressure that's 135/95 or over?
YES – add 3 years

12. Do you eat five or more portions of a range of fresh fruit and vegetables every day?
YES – subtract 5 years

13. Do you regularly eat processed, packaged or fast food?
YES – add 4 years

14. Are you a vegetarian?
YES – subtract 2 years

15. Do you eat oily fish three times a week?
YES – subtract 2 years

16. Do you drink two or three small glasses of red wine, up to five days a week?
    YES – subtract 3 years

17. Do you drink more than 21 units of alcohol a week
    (if you're a man) or 14
    (if you're a woman)?
    YES – add 5 years

18. Do you have an active social life and a supportive network of friends and family?
    YES – subtract 2 years

19. Do you have an active sex life?
    YES – subtract 2 years

20. Are you happily married?
    YES – subtract 1.5 years.

135. Restoration day

When you're suffering from chronic, long-term stress. When your batteries are blown. When burnout is imminent, here is your emergency plan.

Book yourself a day out. By tomorrow, you will feel rested, stronger and more in control. (No, don't stop reading – you can make this happen.)

All you need is 24 hours. If you have children, ask someone else to look after them for as much of the day as possible. Remember that if you don't look after yourself, you will have nothing left to give to others.

The restoration day is based on three principles:

✿ Replenishing your body by giving it rest.

✿ Resting your brain by focusing on your body.

✿ Nourishing your soul with healthy simple food which will replenish the nutrients stripped away by stress.

Here's an idea for you...

Go to bed at 9.30 p.m. today and every day this week if you can manage it. Don't watch TV if you're not tired – read or listen to music. People who do this have turned around their stress levels in a week.

Before you get up

When you wake, acknowledge that this day will be different. Today you are going to shift the emphasis onto relaxation and releasing tension and replacing what stress has drained away from your body. Stretch. If you feel like it, turn over and go back to sleep. If not, read an inspirational tome – a self-help book, poetry, a favourite novel. Don't reach for your usual coffee or tea. Sip a mug of hot water with lemon: this, according to naturopaths, boosts the liver which has to work incredibly hard processing all the junk that goes into your body. Whatever, it's soothing. Every time panic hits because you're not doing anything – now and for the rest of the day – breathe in deeply for a count of eight and out for a count of eight.

When you get up

Stretch for 10 minutes. A few yoga stretches are good, but it doesn't matter as long as you try to stretch every muscle in your body. You don't have to do this 'perfectly', it's not a work out, it's a reminder – you have a body: it carries tension and pain. Feel the cricks draining out. Finish with the yoga position known as the Child's Pose. Kneel with your legs tucked under you. Bend forward so your forehead rests as near to the floor as possible in front of you. A cushion on your knees might make this more comfortable. Take your arms behind you with hands pointing back and palms upward. Rest like this and breathe deeply. This is a favourite of mine because it releases tension in the neck and shoulders, which is where I store tension. I've been known to climb under my desk at work and do this for a few moments.

Breakfast

Try a fruit smoothie: blend a cup of natural yogurt with one banana and a couple of handfuls of other fruits; peach, mango, strawberries, pineapple. Thin, if preferred, with a little fruit juice. Sip slowly, preferably outside. Imagine the vitamin C zooming around your body replacing the levels depleted by stress. My advice today is to eat lightly and avoid (except for the odd treat) foods that strain digestion too much. Drink coffee and tea if you normally do; the last thing you want is a caffeine withdrawal headache. But don't have more than, say, three caffeine drinks. Caffeine will make you jittery even if you're very used to it.

Defining idea...

'Rest as soon as there is pain.'
HIPPOCRATES

Morning

Get outside – in the most natural surroundings you can manage. Ideally, lie on your back on the grass. Stare at the sky. Let your mind drift off. Or walk in the countryside, the park, sit in your garden. If you really can't bear to be still, do some gardening.

Lunch

Have a huge salad combining every colour of vegetable you can think of – green, yellow, orange, purple, red. More vitamin C. Serve with a delicious dressing. This meal must include one absolute treat – a glass of wine, a dish of ice-cream, a piece of chocolate. Lie back. Indulge.

Afternoon

Go back to bed, or curl up on a cosy corner of your sofa. Watch a favourite movie, or a comedy show. A weepie can be great for this. A good cry is very therapeutic. Sleep if you can. Or if you'd prefer, listen to some favourite music.

Dinner

You should be hungry but feeling light. Eat another pile of vegetables – a salad or perhaps a stir-fry, following the 'eat a rainbow' advice given above. Have a fresh piece of fish grilled or fried in a little oil or butter. Think delicious but simple. Present your food beautifully; eat it by candlelight.

Go to bed early. Resist the temptation to watch TV. Read a book, listen to the radio or some music.

136. Get drunk without a hangover

The morning after. The words alone have us reaching for coffee and shades. What on earth can we do to dodge that hell? Well, just find the time it takes to read this idea.

Booze: it's not big and it's not clever. It shrivels your liver, puts pounds on your paunch and hoovers the content of your purse. Worst of all, it leads to the inevitable revelation, usually around two in the morning, that you – yes, you – are in fact the greatest dancer in the world and you don't care who knows it. Then, before you know it, the next day dawns and you've got a pounding head, bleary eyes, and that yummy baboon's armpit sort of feeling in the mouth. Frankly, if that's all you wake up with, you can consider yourself lucky. But wouldn't it be nice if it didn't have to be that way?

The obvious way of dodging hangovers would be not to get drunk, but if you wanted that kind of advice you could have asked your mum for it. There are alternatives.

Before you get drunk

The old college-boy stories about lining your stomach with milk are partly right. It's not that you can literally 'line' your stomach; it's the simple fact that your body will process the alcohol more steadily if it's absorbed along with food, so eat before your jiggle-juice bonanza.

Choose your poison

'Gin makes you sin', 'whisky makes you frisky', 'beer before wine, you'll feel fine' – lyrical verse, doubtless, but entirely fact free. What matters is clarity, purity and quality. The active ingredient in booze is ethanol, a natty little substance, part drug, part food, which your body happily gets to work on to transform so as to metabolise the sugars. So far, so good, except that en route there is a by-product called acetaldehyde: this is vile stuff and is largely responsible for the next-day nasties.

As ethanol goes stale it produces more acetaldehyde, so drinking last week's opened bottle of wine is a bad idea (tip – try finishing it off in one go first time around). The same applies to wines or mixes which are in the process of being distilled or fortified into something stronger. This means cheaper hooch made from low-quality ingredients is likely to pack a sucker punch. Avoid dodgy rum, sherry, et al. if you want to avoid the hangover from hell. And don't even think about 'shooters', in which the colour and sugar drown out any point in using good ingredients.

The other quotient is the congener count. Congeners occur naturally in fermented and distilled drinks and have been identified as another something that increases the hangover factor. Helpfully, the congener count comes with a rule of thumb that even the deeply bladdered can remember – the darker the drink, the higher the hangover risk. Thus port is one of the highest on the congener scale, vodka one of the lowest. It's not, strictly speaking, a congener factor, but drink anything green or blue and you're asking for it.

> *Defining idea...*
>
> **'He resolved, having done it once, never to move his eyeballs again.'**
> KINGSLEY AMIS

Remember this isn't the only factor – a poor-quality vodka can easily make up for its low congener count with an extra helping of acetaldehyde. That's the reason why you sometimes hear the boast that such and such booze can be drunk without risk. A product called Bismark schnapps seemed to be a likely contender but, in the end, dedicated researchers found that disproving such claims was just a matter of downing enough of the damn stuff.

During the drinking
Avoid carbonated mixers: fizzy drinks get you smashed faster, and that affects your drinking decisions (hmmm, a single malt, or one of everything in the optics?). Above all drink water – as much of it as you can before going to bed. Don't take headache pills in advance as this will put an extra strain on your liver and your liver don't love you no more as it is.

Next day
Ginger is great for settling the guts – try juicing some with apple. Water is good but an isotonic sports drink will get to your cells even better. Vitamins and minerals are also called for. NO, having a hair of the dog isn't a good idea and points the way down a slippery slope.

Special offer with mypure.co.uk

[A'kin]

Feel young and look gorgeous naturally with the award winning [A'kin] range of natural skin & hair care. **Mypure.co.uk** are offering *Goddess* readers **30% off** all [A'kin] products.

[A'kin] use gentle cleansers such as panama bark and nourishing oils including certified organic cold pressed avocado oil, macadamia oil and jojoba oil. They are rich in potent anti-oxidants such as alpha lipoic acid, vitamins A, B5, C & E, Omega 3,6,9 essential fatty acids and certified organic aromatherapy oils. They're also vegan and formulated without animal ingredients or animal testing.

[A'kin] do not use any nasty ingredients; they are formulated without sulfates, ethoxylates, parabens, propylene glycol, petrochemicals, silicones, phthalates, DEA and artificial fragrance & colours. The result is beautiful looking skin and hair with total peace of mind.

For more information visit www.mypure.co.uk

For details on how to take advantage of this fantastic offer please go to page 489, where you'll also find information on all the other great deals throughout *Goddess*.

Terms and conditions
This offer is valid until 31st December 2007. The 30% discount applies to your first online order at mypure.co.uk. It does not apply to any product already on special offer.

TRIED & TESTED
Awarded 10/10 in The Best Beauty Products Tried & Tested

Beauty Awards 06
NEWWOMAN
w w w . n e w w o m a n . c o . u k
COMMENDED

The PureBeauty Awards
Bronze 2005

natura
FINALIST
Beauty Award
2006

137. Beat jet lag

Tanned, surrounded by unpacked bags and watching telly at 4.30a.m., there is no more tragic sight than the jet-lagged traveller attempting to put their life and their sleep pattern back on track.

Here's how to minimise the effects of time-zone hopping. You get jet lag when you travel across time zones so fast that your body doesn't have time to adjust to the new day and night cues. The problem is you're messing with your internal body clock – which tells you when to sleep and when to be awake – and this takes a while to adjust to local time zones. On some long-haul flights, your jet lag can last anything from two to five days. With symptoms similar to those of a terrible hangover – tiredness during the day, inability to sleep at night, headache, diarrhoea – jet lag could easily put you off air travel altogether. Hopefully, these tips from airline crews can soften the blow. Happy holidays!

✿ Find the best time to fly. Look at the differences in time zones, the direction you're travelling in, and work out the best time to travel to minimise the effects. When you fly east you lose time and your day becomes shorter, while by flying west you gain time and your day becomes longer. So an overnight flight is best if you're travelling east, a day flight if going west.

✿ Start training for your new time zone. When going on long-haul flights, airline crews get up an hour earlier each day for a week before departure. If you're heading west, try to go to bed and get up an hour later each day. If you're going east go to bed earlier than usual.

✿ Change your watch to your destination time as soon as your plane takes off. This will help get your mind thinking in the new time and, psychologically, it will help your body to adapt itself to a different time zone.

✿ Be flight smart. Try to sleep at the new times on the plane. If you need to keep yourself awake, do crossword puzzles or listen to stimulating music. You could engage in conversation with the person next to you but there's always the risk he'll be a financial adviser who spends the entire flight trying to sell you life insurance. Don't read a novel or watch the video – they're guaranteed to send you into a slumber. And try to get a seat on the side that will get most sunlight during the flight. If you need to sleep, buy ear plugs. A sleeping pill for a night or two before the flight may make it easier to sleep on the plane.

✿ Keep on the move. During the flight, try to walk around as much as you can and, when sitting down, flex and extend your ankles to increase circulation. This will also help prevent swollen ankles and muscle stiffness. When you reach your destination, half an hour of exercise will keep you alert for up to two hours. Don't be tempted to perform star jumps in the baggage reclaim lounge, though – being escorted out of the airport by security is not a great start to any holiday. Just go for a brisk walk once you've dropped off your luggage.

❀ Adjust your daylight exposure as soon as you arrive. When you arrive in the new time zone, adjust your sleep schedule straight away to the local time. So if you arrive in the day but your body thinks it's night-time, go outside, get lots of sunshine and keep active to trick your body into staying awake (remember dark triggers sleep-inducing melatonin). Eat your meals at the local time, too. Try not to go to bed until it is bedtime in the local time zone. If you have to, take a 20-minute nap to help you get through the day.

> *Defining idea...*
>
> **'I love to travel but I hate to arrive.'**
> ALBERT EINSTEIN

138. Forty winks

If you find yourself feeling sleepy after lunch, perhaps a siesta is what you need, but does the power nap really work?

Whether you're preparing for an important meeting or tidying up at home, on some afternoons it's virtually impossible to fight the urge to sleep. Should you give in and enjoy a bit of shut-eye or will it make it even more difficult to get to sleep at night?

We're designed for two sleeps a day – the main one at night and a nap in the afternoon. A drop in temperature makes us feel sleepy between 2 and 4p.m. If you're getting enough sleep at night, you'll probably be OK – a handful of nuts may be all you need to pep you up.

433

Here's an idea for you...

To discover how naps affect your energy level and the quality of your night-time sleep, do an experiment. Take a daily nap for a week. The next week, don't nap. Every morning, rank your sleep quality on a 10-point scale. Every evening, rate your day on a similar scale. After two weeks, judge whether naps work for you.

If you're sleep deprived, though, you could be under par all afternoon. Suddenly you need to stretch, move about, yawn or sigh. You might find it harder to concentrate and your mind will start wandering. You could even start making typing errors and find it more difficult to find the right word when you're speaking.

According to fans of napping, if you just grab a coffee and push on, you're denying your body its natural restorative period. But a 15- to 20-minute nap, they say, can restore alertness and memory and relieve stress and fatigue. You're also less likely to fall asleep in front of the TV later on, then be unable to drop off at bedtime. In reality, though, it's often difficult to nap. If you're looking after children, you can't leave them unsupervised for 20 minutes and although some companies are beginning to allow napping – particularly those that rely on shift workers – most don't. But even if you don't actually fall asleep, 20 minutes of quiet time may give you the boost you need.

Nice napping

- ❀ Find somewhere quiet.
- ❀ If you're working in an office, switch your phone to voicemail and either sit at your desk or find an empty room. Ideally you'd hang a sign on your door saying 'Do not disturb' and get your secretary to wake you 20 minutes later. But we're not all company directors.

- Loosen your clothing and take off your shoes. Lie down on a sofa, stretch out on the floor or if that's not possible sit comfortably on a chair, placing your head in your folded arms on your desk.
- Close your eyes – ideally, put on an eye mask.
- Try not to think about work or all the things you have to do. Focus on what you love doing in your spare time. If you like golf, you might mentally play a round of golf on your regular course. Maybe drift back to a favourite holiday, or listen to some calming music.
- Just rest at first – if your brain needs a rest as well, you'll soon fall asleep.
- Set the alarm to go off in twenty minutes' time, in case you do fall asleep. Don't sleep for more than 30 minutes – you'll wake up groggier and foggier.
- When you wake up lie still for a minute or two – then stretch and breathe deeply and take a drink of water or a light snack to get your system going again.
- Then return to work, starting with simple chores such as opening letters or organising the work you have to do. Within just a few minutes you should feel sparky again.

> *Defining idea...*
>
> **'No day is so bad it can't be fixed with a nap.'**
> CARRIE SNOW, comedian

Napping with a baby

If you've got a young baby who wakes up constantly at night taking short naps might well help you get through the day until your baby begins to follow a more consistent sleep schedule (usually around three or four months). If you're at home with your baby, nap when she does. If you work outside your home, try flexible working or reserve blocks of time to nap during your working day if that's possible.

However, if you have problems falling asleep at bedtime, or find you are still waking in the night even though your baby is sleeping through, give up daytime naps. Don't make up for a restless night by sleeping late or going to bed earlier than usual, either. This can turn a short-term sleep problem into a long-term sleep disturbance. If you begin to feel drowsy during the day, stay active by cleaning the house, exercising or visiting a friend.

139. Sleepy foods

**What and when you eat affects how you sleep –
so read on for the dinners to make you doze.**

Late night pizzas, take-away curries, chips … If this is a list of what you've enjoyed for your evening meals over the last week, it's not surprising you've been sleeping badly.

Eating healthily and regularly is one of the best ways to keep your energy levels high, stopping you dropping off inappropriately in the day and ensuring your body releases all the hormones you need to send you off to sleep at night. The most effective sleep diet is to eat little and often rather than one or two big meals, which keeps your metabolic rate steady. This is particularly key for your evening meal – your metabolic rate and temperature will shoot up after a big meal when they should be dropping to prepare for sleep. Your digestive system has to work harder too. While you may fall asleep faster, all the intestinal work required to digest a big meal is likely to cause frequent waking and a poorer quality of sleep. Your sleep can also be affected by foods which take a long time to digest – high fat and high protein foods take twice as long as carbohydrate to metabolise. So if you were tossing and turning after last night's chicken tikka massala, you know why.

Calming foods

One of the keys to a restful night's sleep is to get your brain calmed rather than revved up. So you need to avoid foods that perk you up and opt for ones that encourage restful sleep. Steer clear of foods containing the amino acid tyrosine – found in bacon, cured meat, strong cheese (mild ones are fine) and chocolate – which stimulate the brain. Instead go for those containing tryptophan – an amino acid that your body uses to make serotonin, which it then turns into sleep-inducing melatonin. Your body doesn't make tryptophan, so the only way you can get it is by eating foods that contain it like cottage cheese, milk, chicken, turkey, rice, eggs, beans, spinach and seafood. To get the full snoozy effect, however, you need to eat these foods with carbohydrates such as pasta or potatoes. After eating carbs, your body releases insulin, which helps clear the bloodstream of other amino acids that compete with tryptophan. This means more tryptophan gets to the brain – and more of those lovely sleep hormones get made. Clever, eh?

Although you need a balance of vitamins to keep your sleep functions ticking along, there are a few key ones. Vitamin B6, for instance, triggers the pineal gland in the brain to secrete more melatonin. They're in wholegrains, bananas, dried apricots

> *Here's an idea for you...*
>
> **Write down what and when you eat and drink in your sleep diary for a week and see if there's any link between your diet and how well you sleep. You can then start by avoiding any food that's causing problems.**

and potatoes. Vitamin B3, found in red meat, chicken, oily fish and mushrooms, has been shown to improve REM sleep and decrease waking time in the night. And boosting levels of magnesium (in avocados, green leafy veg and nuts) and calcium (dairy products, broccoli, almonds) reduces the time it takes to get to sleep and the amount of times you wake up at night.

Dinners that help you drop off

Meals that are high in carbohydrates and low to medium in protein will help you relax in the evening and set you up for a good night's sleep. Good ones to try are:

- ✿ Baked potato with cottage cheese and tuna salad
- ✿ Chicken breast, potatoes and green beans
- ✿ Pasta with spinach and pinenuts
- ✿ Wholewheat spaghetti with bean, tofu or meat sauce
- ✿ Salmon fillet and green salad with yoghurt dressing
- ✿ Pasta with tomatoes and lentils
- ✿ Tuna steak with boiled potatoes and spinach
- ✿ Avocado pasta salad
- ✿ Scrambled eggs on wholemeal toast and cheese
- ✿ Tofu stir-fry
- ✿ Hummus with wholewheat pita bread
- ✿ Seafood pasta

- ✿ Chicken stir-fry with pasta and vegetables
- ✿ Tuna salad sandwich
- ✿ Tuna salad sprinkled with sesame seeds (rich in tryptophan), and wholewheat crackers

140. Wakey wakey – get up bright

Alarm clock or not? The best option for a good night's sleep.

One minute you're fast asleep, the next you're leaping out of bed, your heart thumping. What woke you may sound like a fire bell, but it's only your alarm clock. You're awake, but still feel groggy. Is this really the best way to start the day?

If you wake up naturally, the light of dawn signals your body clock to release your wake-up hormones. An alarm clock obviously interferes with this natural process and allows you to wake up when it's convenient to you. OK, it may be masking the fact that you're not getting enough sleep, but the world would be thrown into chaos if we all woke up naturally. People would be wandering into offices at all times of the day – night owls, whose body clocks run slow, would probably get in the latest as they don't wake up naturally until late morning. And in the winter, everyone would turn up late because the sun rises much later and this delays the release of your wake-up hormones. In the summer, curtains protect us from the dawn light to prevent us from waking up at 5 in the morning but it's difficult to do anything in winter when it's pitch black outside.

Train yourself to wake up at a certain time - that way, the alarm won't seem so much of a shock. It's not that difficult to do. In fact you've probably done it yourself when you've had to get up for something important. Tell yourself the night before that you need to wake up at a certain time and after a few nights, it will happen.

So what can you do?

You don't want to completely rely on an alarm clock – use one as an insurance policy in case you don't wake up in time. Ideally you should wake up just before your set time – that shows you've had enough sleep. Make sure the alarm clock you choose wakes you up how you want to. There's a lot of choice nowadays – so hunt around. Here are just a few I came across …

✿ A natural alarm clock. This simulates the sunrise and gradually becomes lighter and lighter over half an hour, so that you can wake up naturally whenever it suits you. This gradual lightening triggers your body to release all the wake-up hormones. The idea is you'll wake up more refreshed and in a better mood and have more energy all day. By putting your body clock in sync, the theory is you'll want to go to sleep earlier in the evening. There's normally a back-up-beeper for heavy sleepers and some even have a sunset go-to-sleep facility where the light slowly fades to darkness – ideal for young children or shift workers.

✿ Tailor-made alarm clock. These allow you to record your own wake-up sounds. Classical, jazz, rock … choose your favourite track of the moment. Or you can even record sounds – the sound of your children laughing perhaps or for something more surreal, your own voice telling you it's time to get up.

- Alarm clock with fade-in facility. The alarm or music gets gradually louder so you wake up more gently. Apparently, this makes it easier to remember your dreams.

- Talking alarm clock. One alarm clock I came across starts chatting to you after the alarm goes off. To turn it off you can say 'alarm off' or simply shake it. You can ask questions such as 'how do I look?' and the clock will give you a reply – either you look 'like a million dollars' or 'to tell you the truth – bleurgh!'

- Shaking alarm clock. Yes, this clock actually shakes the bed to wake you up. If that doesn't work, the flashing lights come on. Sounds like waking up to an erupting volcano to me, but it may work fo you.

Whatever type you decide on, make sure you buy an alarm clock which allows you to dim the brightness of the LED display light. This light can disrupt your sleep and wake you up – particularly if you're a light sleeper and early in the morning when you spend more time in the lighter stages of sleep. Alternatively, turn your alarm clock away from you at night or use the alarm clock in your mobile phone.

> *Defining* idea...
>
> **'If you need an alarm clock to get up, you are sleep deprived.'**
> JAMES MAAS, sleep expert

Exciting offer from Tesco Diets

www.tescodiets.com

Start on the path to a better and longer life with this exciting offer brought to you by **Tesco Diets**.

Tesco Diets, the UK's largest online dieting and healthy eating service, provides personalised diet and fitness solutions to help you lose weight, and get back into shape. The personalised plans take into account the latest nutritional guidelines, and have been developed by a team of nutritionists. The plans also take into account your personal food preferences, lifestyle, weight loss goals and health requirements.

Tesco Diets offers 3 types of plans:
General weight loss and healthy eating plans – for example, GI or low fat plans.

Health specific diets – e.g. diabetes, low cholesterol, low sodium, and gluten free.

A flexible plan, Totals – that gives you control over your diet. We give you a daily allowance, and you keep track of what you eat.

Every *Goddess* reader can get the first 3 weeks free (that's a 10 week subscription for the price of 7).

Also to help you get in shape we've got 15% off all the fitness products in our shop – including trampolines, pedometers, yoga mats and exercise bikes.

For details on how to take advantage of these fantastic offers, please go to page 490, where you'll also find information on all the other great deals throughout *Goddess*.

Terms and conditions
Both Tesco Diets offers are valid until 31 December 2007. Standard Tesco Diets terms and conditions apply.

Bounce back from disaster (because even goddesses have bad days)

'Action is the antidote to despair.'

JOAN BAEZ

'I am not a has been.
I'm a will be.'
LAUREN BACALL

Are you a bouncer?

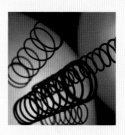

Aim to discover what psychologists call your 'bounce factor' – your resilience. People who are resilient in the face of problems are happier – and richer, incidentally – than those who aren't.

1. Imagine that you and everyone you work with are suddenly called into your boss's office and told you're being made redundant. What would be your almost instant reaction.

☐ a. You'd be numb and it would take about 15 minutes before you could compute what was going on.

☐ b. You'd panic. On the outside you'd behave like everyone else, but inside it would be meltdown.

☐ c. You'd be shell-shocked but still it could have been worse and for some of your colleagues it's a great deal worse.

2. You believe that successful people:

☐ a. Are born successful.

☐ b. Have to work really hard at it no matter how they appear.

☐ c. Aren't always successful; every life has its down sides.

3. You volunteer your services to other people:
- ☐ a. When you have the reserves of energy to do it properly.
- ☐ b. When you think you can truly help them.
- ☐ c. Routinely – giving back is one way you stay sane.

4. Your glass tends to be:
- ☐ a. Half empty.
- ☐ b. You're too busy to see the bloody glass.
- ☐ c. Half full.

5. If someone does you a bad turn you are more likely to:
- ☐ a. Resent them no matter how hard you try to get over it.
- ☐ b. Ignore them, scratch them from your 'list'.
- ☐ c. Think about it a lot, and try really hard to see it from their point of view with the aim of trying to forgive them.

6. What frightens you more?
- ☐ a. Poverty.
- ☐ b. Dying alone.
- ☐ c. Being unable to control your destiny.

Score 0 for an a, 1 for a b, 2 for a c

How did you do?

Score **9** or less and improving your resilience will help you deal with life's vicissitudes more easily. Try idea 45 Make like tigger – learn to bounce.

141. Should I stay or should I go?

Love life hit an iceberg? How do you know when to hang in there and salvage a wrecked relationship and when to swim for new shores?

Call us die-hard romantics, but we believe most relationships are salvageable. Even after betrayal, arguments, debt or months of sexual drought, it's possible to recapture the spark and ignite something rich and purposeful.

Even the best relationships feel like sinking ships sometimes, and the urge to escape with the nearest lifeboat man can be strong. But the decision about whether to stay in a lacklustre love affair or find a new port in the storm should be a rational one.

Resist making decisions on a whim. Even if you've caught your new groom in bed with your bridesmaid, stay put. Sometimes you'll find yourself changing your mind from day to day, or even hour to hour. In truth, many people who leave relationships impulsively later regret it, only to find it's too late to return. You've probably invested many months or years in your alliance. Parents, in-laws and friends will all give you their views, but it's not really any of their business. They've all got their own agenda, so we suggest you avoid discussing your dilemma until you've reached your decision.

Write stuff

Writing your thoughts down brings clarity and helps you decide. Try keeping a diary of thoughts and feelings. What do you want from your relationship? Why do you feel like leaving? Is it your relationship that is making you unhappy or could there be other reasons, like a career crisis or mounting debts? If there has been a catastrophe, like infidelity, be honest with yourself about what your relationship was like before. Do you have something worth saving or were you thinking about leaving anyway? If your relationship was good before, you may well decide to give it another go. See if you can discover what your partner wants. Even if your problems seem insurmountable, good intentions on both sides go a long way. Can you see the difficulties as a catalyst for change?

> **Here's an idea for you...**
>
> When it's hard to decide whether to stay or go, it's usually because both options have a lot going for them. Whatever you decide, an informed choice is better than an impulsive one. When you have a moment, make a list of what first attracted you to your partner. What are his good qualities? What would you miss? In what ways does he bring out the best in you?

What can you do if you are incompatible? Charlie wants six children, but Denise doesn't want any. Russell wants a pet tarantula and Sally's arachnophobic. Stephanie wants to live in a city, but Jo's a committed country dweller. George wants sex twice a day, Jenny would be happy with twice a year. As we said, we're die-hard romantics and think we can reconcile most so-called irreconcilable differences with goodwill, compromise and imagination. But romance alone won't do. It takes both of you to look at problems and come up with creative solutions. Charlie retrained as a childminder. Sally had her phobia treated and has grown rather fond of Gideon the tarantula. Stephanie and Jo live in a country-style cottage in a small commuter town. And Jenny and George? Don't be so nosy – that's their business!

Having said that, we've identified four relationship scenarios that are bad news. There's no point staying together if:

His pants are on fire

Persistent liars cause big trouble. Relationships are about trust. Can't believe a word he says? Get packing.

He's mad, bad and dangerous to know

Rachel's partner Damien was convinced she was having an affair. She wasn't. He hired a private detective to follow her and then accused her of bribing the detective to lie on her behalf. He went through her laundry, checking her knickers for semen stains. Every day when she came home he interrogated her about where she'd been. This sort of jealousy is rare and is a sign of illness, often related to hitting the bottle. In the trade it's called Othello Syndrome. Rachel was advised to get out of the relationship, as there was a risk that Damien might kill her. If this sort of behaviour sounds at all familiar, get out and get expert help for your partner. You may be able to re-energise your relationship, but they need treatment first.

He subjects you to degrading treatment

If he persistently puts you down in public or
humiliates you in front of your friends, don't stand for
it. Nobody deserves to have her self worth eroded by
an insecure gronk who helps themselves to feel better
by making their lovers look stupid, useless or inept.

He's hitting home

You can't salvage your relationship if your partner is threatening, hitting or sexually
assaulting you. Domestic violence happens in every sort of relationship, and is
hardly ever a one-off. Sometimes it's there from the start; sometimes it won't
surface for years. Lots of people stay because they are frightened, or hope things
will improve. But it usually gets worse over time. Get out and get help from the
police, doctor or local helpline.

142. Breaking up is hard to do

Sometimes it just isn't there. You have pushed, prodded and tried to shoehorn this person into a relationship, but it just isn't going to work.

So you need to grab the bull by the horns (or rather let go of it) and move on. And there is a right and a wrong way to do it.

Getting it right lets both of you move on with dignity and calm, but getting it wrong can leave you both licking your wounds and making voodoo dolls for months, if not years, to come.

How to split up with a good one

Oh, if only it was possible to flip the X factor like a light switch. Sometimes it just doesn't work and you've got to cut a nice guy loose. The best way to deal with men like this is face to face and showing them the respect they deserve, even if it makes things a little harder for you. That way they, and you, can rest assured that you did the dignified thing. But once you are sitting opposite, what do you say?

✿ Don't lie. Making up a dead aunt or work stress is unfair. If they have done right by you don't slope off under the cover of a fib; they will probably be able to tell and worry about what else you have lied to them about.

Here's an idea for you...

If you think a break-up may turn ugly, do it in a public place and have a friend come and meet you at a prearranged time. That way, you are making a clear statement that the meeting is over.

❁ Be as honest as you can be. If the spark is just missing, tell them that. It's not uncommon for lots of things to be right but one thing to be wrong and you can even commiserate with them; chances are if you aren't feeling it, they won't be either.

❁ Don't suggest it might happen further down the line. If they really like you they will keep hanging in there waiting for you to change your mind, which is stopping them from finding someone else. No matter how reassuring for you it would be to have a nice guy waiting in the wings in case you don't find Mr Right, it's wrong, wrong, wrong...

❁ Answer any questions with the best framing possible. When people are upset they may level a lot of hurt questions at you; try not to respond in kind. If they ask if it was because you didn't like their knobbly chicken legs, don't start clucking. You can simply say you didn't feel a sexual chemistry; after all, one woman's chicken legs are another woman's lean, athletic pins. There is no point in dashing his confidence. At the same time, if his fifteen phone calls a day did irritate you, you could let him know. It might stop him from making the same mistake again.

❁ Balance criticism with positivity. If you are going to mention the fifteen calls a day, then make sure that you let him know that while being attentive was great, it could be moderated (not stopped). You don't want to release him onto an unsuspecting female population imagining that the best way to take things forward is never to pick up the phone.

- ❀ Don't use them for ex sex. What for you is just a convenient lay, might keep their hurt alive and erode their confidence, whilst fostering false hope.

- ❀ Don't tell them how they feel. You have had time to get used to the idea; it's news to them and they may feel disappointed or that you had more potential.

- ❀ Stick to your guns. Just because they think you still have something between you if you really haven't, keep reminding them that you don't think that it's the case. You will only have to go through this again further down the line. And do you really want people lying in bed at night trying to interpret what you said? Heartless!

- ❀ Try not to get defensive. If they start blaming you, keep calm and don't blame them back. They will start brooding on what you have said when the dust has settled and may find it hard to let it go.

How to split up with a bad one

Well, I'm showing my dark side here, but who cares? If someone has been mean or destructive towards you, they are not entitled to any respect in return. The problem is that sometimes our judgement gets a little bit clouded. I suggest that if you aren't sure, just keep it short and sweet. If they are real meanies, and have left you hanging on for phone calls/stood you up/left you dying of thirst in a desert, try

Defining idea...

'Saying goodbye doesn't mean anything. It's the time we spent together that matters, not how we left it.'
TREY PARKER and MATT STONE, creators of South Park, the US cartoon show

some of the silent treatment back. A few days in dating no-man's-land waiting for the phone to ring might teach these men a few lessons about empathy. And if they hate you for it, who cares? Save your good stuff for those who deserve it.

143. Getting over rejection

Along with the highs and the fun of dating, comes some of the rough stuff.

That's to be expected, but it doesn't make it any easier when someone says, 'thanks, but no thanks'.

The key to enjoying dating is to accept that just as everyone you meet can't light your fire, you're not everyone's idea of petrol either. But that's all very well in theory. You need some practical tools to make sure that you can stay afloat when buffeted by romance's vagaries.

Smile, smile, smile!

When someone wants to make a break, let them go. Even if you think someone is making a mistake and there is potential in your relationship, no one normally wants to be anyone else's jailer. By all means, ask some questions if you think it will help, but don't plead, beg or whine. You'll be glad you kept your dignity when the initial discomfort has paled. Help is at hand...

> ## Here's an idea for you...
>
> **If you are finding it hard to get over the knock to your confidence, try going somewhere where taking risks is all part of some good harmless fun. Speed-dating is a good way to see that this is all just a numbers game, to some degree; your right number just hasn't come up yet.**

✿ Where is it coming from? You've only had three dates and you feel like you will never get over the rejection? This guy probably isn't the reason; hell, you don't even know this guy. You may just have some old feelings that are coming up to do with your own confidence; a man shouldn't have this much effect so early on; you may need to look more closely at your own demons. You may also worry that he was your last shot at children, a home, someone to strut down the aisle with. This is just fear talking. Relax, you will get another shot at fulfilling your dreams.

✿ Letting go of control. You might think that if you had tried a different technique, worn different clothes or could just have one more chat with him you could turn things around. You can't. The great thing about being in a relationship is that two willing people choose it; once you can accept that you can't control everything, you can enjoy the fact that you aren't responsible for everything either.

❀ Get back in the swing. If someone wanted to end a brief fling, catching a glimpse of you sloping round the supermarket in your pyjamas will just reaffirm their conviction. It also means that the fantastically handsome guy fumbling through the meals for one is only going to speak to you to ask you where the air fresheners are. Even if you don't feel perky, act it: before you know it, the balance will be less act and more reality.

❀ What were you expecting? Something to do every Saturday night? Someone to rely on? Maybe you need to get a life that doesn't revolve around someone else and theirs. You will be much more likely to take rejection and break-ups more easily if your whole social structure isn't hinged around the other person.

Defining idea...

'**Finish each day and be done with it. You have done what you could. Some blunders and absurdities no doubt crept in; forget them as soon as you can. Tomorrow is a new day; begin it well and serenely and with too high a spirit to be cumbered with your old nonsense.**'
RALPH WALDO EMERSON, US essayist and poet

❀ Don't put words in his mouth. Don't imagine that you know what he is thinking. You don't know whether he wants to get back with his ex or try naked wrestling with his best friend Stuart. The point is, he doesn't want you and the worst kind of guy you can try and get involved with is one that doesn't really want you. You could get arrested for it, but worse, you could spend pointless months, years even, staring at the ceiling in the small hours of the morning trying to work out what went wrong when he doesn't even remember your name.

❀ Get the chocolate out. Get the duvet on the sofa, have a good sob, drink a glass of wine and eat some chocolate all the while berating this fool that can't see what a prize you are to your most supportive mate. A knock to the confidence deserves a little ego stroke. Then get up tomorrow and move on.

And finally, remind yourself what this is about. Dating in itself is not a solution to all your problems, but then neither should a man be. Remind yourself that you are meant to be having fun and taking a few risks. Then put on your best outfit and hit the dance floor again.

144. How to love the job you've got

Sometimes you can't have the one you want. So you have to love the one you've got.

One in four of us wants to leave our jobs. We can't all do it at once, so here's how to cope until your personal Great Escape.

The bottom line

Hate your job? It's probably for three reasons – you hate the work (it's monotonous or stressful), you hate the environment, including your colleagues, or something else has happened in your life that makes work seem meaningless and you're ready

Here's an idea for you...

Boost work morale in a stressful workplace by starting group traditions beyond getting drunk on Friday night and moaning. Go out for a Chinese on pay day or book an awayday at a spa or have a whip-round every birthday and celebrate with champagne and cake.

for a lifestyle change. Or it could be that you're in denial. I'm going to come over a bit mystical here, because I firmly believe that sometimes we hate our job because we can't be bothered to address what's really stressing us out in our lives. Our energy is focused elsewhere and until we sort out whatever drama or sadness is soaking up our concentration, we're not likely to find the dream job anytime soon. So the advice here is not about refocusing your CV – there are plenty of other places where you can read up on that. But it will help you relieve stress in the short term and make you feel better about yourself in the long term. And that hopefully will help you raise your energy enough to eventually find another job.

Love your surroundings...

...Just as much as you can. If your workplace is grim and drear, you are not going to feel good. Clear your desk. Sort out clutter. Personalise your work space with objects of beauty and grace. Pin up photos of beautiful vistas you've visited or would like to visit. (It's a bit less personal than family pix.) But whatever you choose to put on your desk, change the visuals every couple of weeks, otherwise your brain stops registering them.

Love your lunchbreaks

A lunch break shouldn't be a scramble for bad food and a desultory walk round a shopping mall. Spend time planning. Every lunch hour should involve movement, fresh air, delicious healthy food and at least one work of art. Works of art are easily available for your perusal (art galleries, department stores) and easily transportable (books, CDs). Always, always take an hour to relax at lunch.

Love your colleagues

Tough one. These could well be the reason you hate your job in the first place. If there are people who specifically annoy you, then find a way to deal with them. Your local bookshop is full of manuals that will teach you how. Allow yourself no more than five minutes a day unloading your woes about work colleagues to a trusted friend or partner – not anyone you work with. This is not goody-goody – it's self-preservation. The more you unload your negativity all over the place, the more you are talking yourself into a hole of unhappiness and stress.

Love yourself

Turn up. Work hard. Do better. Lots of people who are unhappy with their work kid themselves that they are working really hard, when in fact their work is shoddy and second-rate. If you're not up to speed, improve your knowledge base and skills. If your work is lazy, look at everything you produce or every service you

> Defining idea...
>
> **'People get disturbed not so much by events but by the view which they take of them.'**
> EPICTETUS

offer and ask yourself how you can make it special, imbue it with your uniqueness, breathe creativity and a little bit of love into it. Doing every task diligently and with positivity will vastly increase your self-esteem.

Love your dreams

Most of us couldn't have got through school without the ability to drift away on a pleasant reverie of future plans. For five minutes in every hour allow yourself to dream. Read through job pages that aren't related to your present job. You may see a position or course that fires your imagination in a completely new direction.

145. Make like Tigger – learn to bounce

Everyone gets stressed. Everyone gets disappointed. But how come some people are better at dealing with it than others?

The answer is that they're natural 'bouncers'. But you don't have to be born that way.

Disappointment does one of two things: it makes you 'bouncy' (resilient) or it makes you 'bitter' – and which one you end up is a more telling predictor of future happiness than 'rich ' or 'poor', 'nice' or 'nasty'.

Bounceability is easy in your twenties. Underneath the veneer of sophistication most twenty-somethings are teenagers at heart convinced that their life is going to be fabulous. But during our thirties, the decisions we make pretty well determine what sort of person we're going to be, and how we decide to deal with setbacks is one of the greatest determinants.

According to psychologist Dr Al Siebert, bouncers exhibit flexibility. 'If you look at someone who doesn't handle life well,' he writes, 'it's often because they think, feel or act in only one way and can't see any alternative.' That means they get stuck in an idea of the sort of person they have to be, the sort of job they were meant to do, the sort of partner that's right for them, the sort of life that they 'deserve'.

> Here's an idea for you...
>
> **Next time you're in the middle of a crisis, try to laugh every chance you can. And if you can't laugh, cry. One way or another vent your emotions. Your mind will work better when strong feelings aren't interfering with your ability to think straight.**

I saw a documentary recently about the after-effects of Black Monday, the catastrophic plummet of the stock market in October 1987. Brokers who had lost everything were interviewed. Nearly all of them had gone off and made another fortune in a business that suited them better. Clearly, these entrepreneurs didn't give up on the dream of being successful but they didn't assume there was only one route, that they had to drive a certain car, live a certain lifestyle. The most successful of all had been on the dole for a year while he licked his wounds. He'd been wiped out but he used it as a learning experience and then went off to become a multi-millionaire in another field.

Each of us is born, apparently, with a happiness set-point which is genetically influenced, but crucially, not fixed. We can come from a long line of grumpy bastards but at the end of the day our genes only seem to account for about half of our propensity for happiness – or unhappiness, depending on how you look at it. However, what we learn from grumpy parents is likely to be a lot more influential than what we inherit. We learn that life is fixed, that we can't change, that we're not in control. But that's wrong. The thing to remember is this: your brain chemistry is not fixed. You can change it.

How? When bad stuff happens, ask yourself what's known as 'coping' questions which challenge inflexible thinking. What would be useful for me to do right now? What is the reality, and what is merely my fantasy about this situation? Can I salvage anything from this?

Then ask yourself some 'serendipity' questions. Why is it good that this has happened? What am I learning from this? What could I do to turn this situation around?

Ultimately, what it comes down to is remembering that everything changes and change itself is the source of stress. Bad stuff happens to good people. But there are plenty of people who have had every disappointment in the book and still lived useful, happy lives. And before you mutter 'bully for them', science will tell you that there's no reason why you can't be one of the bouncers too.

> Defining idea...
>
> **'Hope begins in the dark. The stubborn hope that if you just show up and try to do the right thing the dawn will come. You wait and watch and work. You don't give up.'**
> ANNE LAMOTT, writer

146. Clawing your way back from a fatal faux pas

There are many books about etiquette and how to avoid social gaffes written by people who are skilled in the subject. These books are not for you.

The problem with etiquette books is that they don't take account of the environmental factors involved. The people that write them have long ago achieved power over their own destiny and manners, while you have not. This is a fancy way to say that you're often drunk, trying to get drunk, or thinking that the only way to get through the following three-hour social situation is to get even more drunk.

This is a disadvantage. Your short- and long-term memory is impaired by the effects of alcohol, as is your judgement of situations. In combination, the two factors can have awkward consequences – such as simultaneously having sex with someone and forgetting his or her name. In case you were wondering, this example is a serious gaffe, especially if the person is a relative, a relative of your spouse, or the guy who came to install satellite TV.

All of the techniques below can be performed drunk. In fact, that's the only time most people could get away with any of them. The key is total commitment. Don't worry about practice: trust us, you'll get plenty of that.

The maiden aunt: This is strictly for when you have more social status than the person you are talking to. It has the advantage of honesty and can be used for any

Here's an idea for you...

To avoid forgotten name embarrassment, use the 'buy one, get one free' tactic. You're standing with a good friend or partner (let's call him Derek) and someone whose name you have forgotten approaches. Make a one-sided introduction. 'Hi! Great to see you again!' you say to the stranger, who is either your boss or the guy who collects the pint glasses – you can't quite remember – 'This is Derek!' Hopefully, the boss/glass collector will give his or her name without a prompt. If not, you're stuffed.

gaffe. It has the disadvantage that you will regularly cause offence. You stop talking, stare at the person as if they have just arrived on the planet at that moment and then say, loudly and firmly, 'You know, I've completely forgotten who you are' or 'I think that was your girlfriend I just goosed'. There is a limit on the number of times you use this on the same person.

The designated driver: Travel everywhere with a friend who is more charming and responsible than you. When you insult or offend someone, your chaperone is on hand to clear up the mess. This is an approach favoured by upper class British males, among whom it is known as 'marriage'.

The bon vivant: This one has the advantage that it can be used repeatedly throughout an evening. Whenever two people approach whose names and personal details you can't for the life of you remember, grab them warmly and shout 'My guys! Now I'm sure you two must have met before!' Do this confidently enough, and they will bask in your approval. You can thereafter say or do more or less what you like, because you are The Man. Take care that they aren't already good friends, or they may turn round and say, 'Yes, but who are you?' In which case, use the Cleese (see below).

The Cleese: A panic measure, to be used only in extreme situations. Elaborately feign a distraction. This may involve attending to an untied shoelace (if possible, your own) or pretending to choke on a cocktail sausage. Fainting is usually too extreme and potentially hazardous.

The woolly: This is often employed in a family situation. For example, when you have children, you are so tired you can barely remember their names, never mind the names of all the babies that belong to the people who used to be your friends. Your friends, however, consider their children's names to be somewhat important, and would be offended if they knew you had forgotten. So on emails, cards and letters, use general forms of greeting if in doubt. 'The Smith family' is slightly formal. 'Ian and Deb and family' is better, but remember, if they only have one child, you've just given the game away. Using 'How are the little ones?' normally gets a response that 'Jemima is extraordinary, she's reading already, and Jason still has that twitch.' Forget the dull anecdotes (you'll hear them again), just write down the names. If you think this isn't true, just wait until Christmas and see how many of your cards are addressed to 'All at number 42'. They're all doing it.

> *Defining idea...*
>
> **'Murder is always a mistake. One should never do anything that one cannot talk about after dinner.'**
> OSCAR WILDE

147. Jumping job when you've been rumbled

Here's how to get another job with a fat-cat salary when in your current job you've done nothing, nada, nix, not a sausage, and until now you've got away with it.

You've got away with it for two years. You're a legend at work; people talk about your continuous inactivity with awe. You've bumped up your 'working at home' days to two and a half a week and you've got a team that covers for you. But, you've been sussed. Your boss has discovered, or more likely been briefed, that you are what you actually are – a complete waste of space. It's time to move on.

We need to make another assumption here: it's much easier to move on in the same organisation than a new one. Where you are, you already know the levers to pull and the buttons to press to avoid work and, more importantly, avoid trouble. It's just not the time to relearn all of that in another place. No, you've got to move on in the same organisation. But you've got to get a new job against a background that the boss you've got right now thinks you're a skiver. And as sure as eggs are eggs, any potential new manager will ask your current boss for his or her opinion of you. However, this is much less of a problem than it seems.

It may surprise you, but your biggest allies in this enforced change of job are the people in the human resources department. 'But', we hear you gasp, 'they're the people who measure productivity, who check progress against objectives and generally are trained to spot skill gaps and non-jobs.' Correct, but they're also the people who make absolutely sure that managers adhere rigidly to dismissal and other personnel processes. That's why they're your best friends right now. Firing someone is very hard work and no managers want to go through the whole bureaucratic rigmarole if they don't have to, and that includes your boss. Think about it from your boss's point of view. The personnel department will dig for evidence. They'll find and brandish your last appraisal where the person who's trying to fire you said such nice things about you and your dedication to the organisation and hard work. They'll make your boss fill in forms, make statements and struggle through a long series of verbal warnings, written warnings, having witnesses at the meetings, offering you the chance to have a witness at the meetings and so forth. No one wants to do this; it's like swimming in treacle or kicking a sponge. Most people will do anything not to have to do it.

Here's an idea for you...

Never treat an appraisal as an ego-trip. An appraisal is an important document to be used in evidence as you pursue your route to the top without actually doing anything. Think about the wording with the HR department in mind. All you need is to make sure it says that you've done what you were expected to do and that you're a loyal servant of the organisation. Those are the two things an employment tribunal are looking for.

You need a reference

OK, you've searched the house magazine and found a new job that's suitable. It's a bit more money (nobody believes that anyone voluntarily moves sideways) but it's not so much that it would make your old boss jealous or even hopping mad. You've gone to the interviews and knocked their socks off. There's only one small cloud on the horizon – the new people are bound to talk to your boss. Answer: get your retaliation in first.

Talk to your boss. You have two objectives. First, help him or her to understand that you're not likely to give up easily if they try to sink you. Make it quite clear that you're not going to go quietly. This one is going to end in court and they're going to have to explain to a lot of people why they didn't realise that you've done absolutely bugger all for two whole years. Now find some positives. Why is the new job more suitable for your talents? Give them ammunition to fire that makes them enthusiastic about your ability and willingness to do the new job without saying anything at all about how you've done the old one. Remember: they're only looking for reasons to advance your case; they've already decided to avoid the pain of sacking you.

Think about this reference business before you choose your new manager. Anyone your boss hates is a good candidate. 'Not only have I got rid of Julie, but she's gone to Deborah. That should slow her down a bit.' Anyone your boss doesn't know can also be the right person: 'Well, it's no skin off my nose'.

148. Dear diary

Fancy trying some therapy that's free, versatile and there whenever you need it? Writing a diary's not just for lovelorn teenagers or third-rate politicians. Here's how to write wrongs.

Pausing to record things brings peace and serenity into troubled hearts and lives. Discover what really matters: what grieves you and what brings you joy.

Keeping a daily diary of important events, thoughts, observations, fears, disappointments, hopes, memories and distress can reduce anxiety, assuage sorrows and help you defeat depression.

Write the good fight

Aimless ranting? Far from it. As well as putting problems on paper, keeping a diary can help you find answers for stuck or recurring problems. A diary is much more than a friend to confide in. Used effectively, diaries are supporters and collaborators in the struggle against depression. After a few weeks you'll start to notice patterns. Some times of the week or parts of your life make you happy and they'll stick out. Once you've realised what they are, doing more of them is a failsafe remedy. Of course, problems and worries can also seem more real once they're on paper, but this doesn't have to be a bad thing. At least you'll know who the enemy is and what you need to work on. Over months, your diary will be a great mood barometer, and

Here's an idea for you...

Put this book down, grab a pen and paper, or sit at your computer and spend twenty minutes writing about how you feel.

you'll be able to use it to track your recovery and predict what you need to do to get through future tough times.

Melancholic memoirs

Writing creates a bit of distance that helps you be much more objective about experiences and how they make you think and feel. A nurse I used to work with called diary writing a 'psychic enema'. Using your diary as a dumping ground for resentment or depression saves you from feeling guilty about unloading on friends. The great thing about putting your thoughts on paper is that you can really be yourself. We all censor ourselves when talking to friends or other helpers, but when it's just you and your journal, you can really let rip. Notebooks don't hold it against you if you bleat like a selfish, attention-demanding diva. And where else do you get to turn over a new leaf and make a fresh start every day?

Defining idea...

'The truth is that writing is the profound pleasure and being read the superficial.'
VIRGINIA WOOLF, depression sufferer and author of A Writer's Diary

Spell it out

Writing daily gives you a routine and structure, essentials for beating depression. Try to write at the same time of day, as this gets momentum going and wards off inertia in other areas of your life too. You know how your moods vary during the day, so you're well placed to decide when to write. Mornings work for me, but if you regularly wake up at lunchtime feeling awful, mornings are clearly out. Some people like to create a soothing writing corner, with scented candles. Others prefer perching on the end of their bed with a chewed biro and spiral notebook. I think the key is to find somewhere you can sit comfortably and be relatively uninterrupted.

Write away

Getting started is easy. All you need is something to write in (and a pen of course!). That said, those page-per-view appointment diaries just don't cut it. A page per day is the absolute minimum, but why not opt for a loose-leaf binder? You can add pages or cuttings and turn it into a valuable coping resource. Alternatively going for the luxe factor and splashing out makes writing a more sensual experience. Invest in a monogrammed leather journal or embroidered velvet notebook and enjoy filling those thick vellum pages with gorgeous coloured inks. Whatever style of diary you go for, reflecting on your day and capturing your feelings is a great way to get started.

> *Defining idea...*
> '**I can shake off everything if I write; my sorrows disappear, my courage is reborn.**'
> ANNE FRANK

149. Nothing short of a miracle

Sometimes we all hope for miracles to get us through tough times. Ever considered conjuring your own? Discover a question that'll turn colossal problems into solutions of miraculous proportions.

Ask a question, end up with a miracle.
I know, it sounds dodgy, but it's about finding what works and doing it often. Far easier than changing what you – or your friends and family – do wrong.

'Suppose one night there is a miracle while you are asleep and your problem is solved. What do you suppose you will notice different the next morning that will tell you there has been a miracle?' Insoo Kim Berg and Steve de Shazer are pros who reckon it's easier to create solutions than solve problems. They ask their clients this question and it's part of what they call brief solution-focused therapy; it doesn't take long and gets results. It's great for those of us wary of becoming therapy junkies. Don't get me wrong, some of my best friends are psychoanalysts, but if forty years of Freudian analysis hasn't flicked your switch, it's time to try this quirky quickie.

It's easy to dismiss techniques that sound a bit too good to be true and that applies, ooh, at least double when you're being offered a quick fix. So if you've been thinking of doing a runner, stay right where you are. It might make you cringe but it can cure.

I suggest you grab a pen and paper, re-read the miracle question, and jot down imagined changes in as much detail as you can muster. Try and include small, tell-tale signs that would let you know there is something different. Who would be the first person to notice something different about you after the miracle? What would your partner/children/parents/friends/Pilates instructor notice was different about you if there had been a miracle? What would they all do differently? What would be different in your relationship with them?

Ronnie is a young widower who was depressed and lonely. Mornings were a nightmare of squabbling children, who missed breakfast and were always late for school. He felt a failure before the day had properly started. On a scale of 1 to 10, where 10 was the best Robbie had ever felt and 1 was suicidal despair, he gave himself a 3. Say Robbie woke up to find a miracle had happened. He'd bounce out of bed when the alarm rang, instead of hitting the snooze button several times. The kids would get up without fighting him or each other, and while they got ready, he'd make breakfast which they'd enjoy together before collecting packed lunches and heading off to school with plenty of time. People in his street, who had been avoiding him since his wife died five years ago, responded to his smiles and new-found contentment. They even noticed how good looking he was. Robbie's life is pretty much like that now. He started doing some of the miracle solutions and now rates his mood as 8 out of 10. Fancy trying some of what he's got?

> *Here's an idea for you...*
>
> **Be a time traveller for five minutes. Cast your mind back to the last thing you did really well. Perhaps it's bringing up four children on your own, rescuing your elderly neighbour from that ferocious toy poodle or leaving your cheating boyfriend on the other side of the world before sneaking off and flying home with his return ticket and passport. Remind yourself how you did it. Where did you find your inspiration, muscle or audacity?**

Suspend reality and pretend your miracle has happened. And ask yourself these toughies: What will you need to do differently at work? What will you need to do differently at home? What will be the first thing your grumpy boss/bitchy colleagues/whining children will notice? What will they do differently?

If you've been jotting answers down, you might have had a Eureka moment. If you haven't, don't worry, it took me a while to get this, but to have the sort of changes in your life that it seems only a miracle could bring, you need to alter a few things. The catch? You're the one who does the altering. But you're already well on your way. Answering these questions helps you find ways out. So next time you think 'only a miracle could get me out of this mess', remember: there can be a miracle, because you can produce one.

Bounce back from disaster with this luscious offer

The Chocolate Fondue Fountain is an unforgettable conversation piece which creates an atmosphere of luxury. **The Chocolate Fondue Company** uses the very best Belgian chocolate, available in Dark, Milk, Creamy White and an abundance of other specialist Chocolate flavours which cascade off each tier of the chocolate fondue. *Goddess* readers, with their **20% discount** off any first time purchase, can easily turn their next party into the event of a lifetime.

THE
CHOCOLATE FONDUE
COMPANY

The Chocolate Fondue Company is an established company specialising in providing chocolate fountain fondues. Accessories such as Bamboo Skewers, delicious Jumbo Marshmallows and Stainless Steel Forks are provided. Whether it's with strawberries, marshmallows, or a sneaky finger tip – it's time to get dipping with this great offer. To view all available products please visit www.chocolatefonduecompany.co.uk

For details on how to take advantage of this fantastic offer please go to page 490, where you'll also find information on all the other great deals found throughout *Goddess*.

Terms and Conditions
Offer available until 30 June 2007, excluding December 2006, only to mainland UK new customers, does not apply to rental hire.

Where it's at...

brilliant ideas

Goddess: Be the woman you want to be is published by Infinite Ideas, publishers of the acclaimed **52 Brilliant Ideas** series. If you found the tips and techniques in this book helpful, you can't go wrong with this special offer exclusive to all *Goddess* readers. Buy any **52 Brilliant Ideas** book from the selection below and you'll get a second book of your choice for free*.

Stress proof your life
52 brilliant ideas for taking control
By Elisabeth Wilson

Inspired creative writing
Secrets of the master wordsmiths
By Alexander Gordon Smith

Look gorgeous always
Find it, fake it, flaunt it
By Linda Bird

Healthy cooking for kids
52 brilliant ideas to dump the junk
By Mandy Francis

Cellulite solutions
52 brilliant ideas for super smooth skin
By Cherry Maslen and Linda Bird

Re-energise your sex life
Put the zing back into your lovemaking
By Elisabeth Wilson

Unleash your creativity
Secrets of creative genius
By Rob Bevan and Tim Wright

Incredible orgasms
Yes, yes, yes, yes, yesss!
By Marcelle Perks

Lose weight and stay slim
Secrets of fad-free dieting
By Eve Cameron

Detox your finances
Secrets of personal finance success
By John Middleton

Whole health
Inspirational ideas for mind and body well-being
By Kate Cook

For more detailed information on these books and others in the **52 Brilliant Ideas** series please visit www.infideas.com

See overleaf for prices and details on how to place your order.

* If books vary in price we'll give the lowest priced one for free. Postage at £2.75 per delivery address is additional.

Choose any two titles from below and receive the cheapest one free.

Qty	Title	RRP
	Stress proof your life	£12.99
	Inspired creative writing	£12.99
	Look gorgeous always	£12.99
	Healthy cooking for kids	£12.99
	Cellulite solutions	£12.99
	Re-energise your sex life	£12.99
	Unleash your creativity	£12.99
	Incredible orgasms	£9.99
	Lose weight and stay slim	£12.99
	Detox your finances	£12.99
	Whole health	£12.99
	Subtract lowest priced book if ordering two titles	
	Add £2.75 postage per delivery address	
	Total	

Name: ....

Delivery address: ....

....

....

E-mail:...Tel (in case of problems): ....

By post Fill in all relevant details, cut out or photocopy this page and send along with a cheque made payable to Infinite Ideas. Send to: Goddess 52, Infinite Ideas, 36 St Giles, Oxford OX1 3LD, UK.

Credit card orders over the telephone Call +44 (0) 1865 514 888. Lines are open 9am to 5pm Monday to Friday. Just mention the promotion code 'Goddess 52'.

Please note that no payment will be processed until your order has been dispatched. Goods are dispatched through Royal Mail within 14 working days, when in stock. We never forward personal details on to third parties or bombard you with junk mail. This offer is valid for UK and RoI residents only. Any questions or comments please contact us on 01865 514 888 or email info@infideas.com.

Exclusive special offers

You and a guest will receive a **free upgrade** on any booking you make with **Elite Hotels**. The first ten bookings (across the group) will also receive a complimentary afternoon champagne cocktail for two. Details on page xxii.

To take advantage of this offer please call the reservations desk of the hotel of your choice quoting 'Goddess reader offer' when making your booking. Ashdown Park Hotel - 01342 824988. Tylney Hall - 01256 764881. The Grand Hotel - 01323 412345. For more information on each hotel visit www.elitehotels.co.uk

Treat yourself or a friend to a subscription for one of Natmag's fantastic magazines for **ONLY £23.99!**, as featured on page 102.

Call **0870 124 1050*** and quote the promotional code **'AD01'**.
Lines are open weekdays 8am-9.30pm, Saturdays 8am-4pm.
Alternatively order online, safely and securely, at
www.qualitymagazines.co.uk/AD01

*BT Landline calls to 0870 numbers will cost no more than 10p per minute; calls from mobiles usually cost more.

Pamper yourself at **Champneys** and enjoy a **15% discount** on any standard booking (see page 176 for details). For more information visit www.champneys.com.

To take advantage of this exciting offer please call Champneys directly on 08703 300 300 and quote 'Goddess' when making your booking.

All offers are valid for UK and RoI residents only

Get in touch with your inner sex goddess with help from **LoveHoney.co.uk.** When you spend £40 or more you'll get **£10 off.** (As featured on page 214.)

> To take advantage of this offer simply visit www.lovehoney.co.uk/goddess and follow the straightforward instructions on how you can get your £10 off any LoveHoney product when you spend £40 or more.

Goddess readers are eligible for a **£10 discount** on any **Grape Vine Social** event when booking online. (As featured on page 260.)

> To take advantage of this great offer visit www.grapevinesocial.com. When you make an online booking for an event at one of the many participating venues across the UK simply enter promotional code 'Goddess' when prompted at checkout. Your discount will automatically be applied.

This offer is valid until 31 December 2007.

Treat yourself or a friend to a special offer of **£5 off The Pink Toolbox**. (As featured on page 294.)

> To take advantage of this fantastic deal simply call 01983 248 678 (Mon-Fri, 9am-5pm excl. Bank holidays) and quote the promotional code 'goddess'.

See page 294 for terms and conditions.

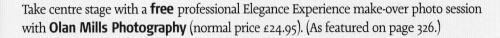

Take centre stage with a **free** professional Elegance Experience make-over photo session with **Olan Mills Photography** (normal price £24.95). (As featured on page 326.)

To take advantage of this special offer simply e-mail info@infideas.com quoting the promotion code 'Olan Mills Offer'. Make sure you give your full name and address and we'll send you a special voucher, detailing the offer, which you will need to take with you when you go to your **Elegance Make-over session**.

Bourne to Organise is offering all *Goddess* readers **20% off their normal hourly rate** (which is usually £25). You can also sign up for a newsletter which provides top tips to keep your life stress free and a monthly offer. (As featured on page 394.)

To take advantage of this special offer simply ring Bourne to Organise directly on 01962 779225 and quote the promotional code 'Goddess' when making a booking. You'll receive a 20% discount on any of their numerous services.

See page 394 for terms and conditions.

Mypure.co.uk are offering *Goddess* readers **30% discount** off all [A'kin] products. (As featured on page 430.)

To take advantage of this exciting offer visit www.mypure.co.uk/goddess. Please quote the offer password 'goddess' when prompted and you'll receive 30% off any products from the [A'kin] range.

See page 430 for terms and conditions.

Every *Goddess* reader can get a **30% discount** off the **Tesco Diets** service (that's a ten week subscription for the price of seven) on www.tescodiets.com/goddess, along with 15% off any product from the Tesco Diets fitness shop – www.tescodietsshop.co.uk. (As featured on page 442.)

Tesco Diets - to claim your first 3 weeks free (10 weeks for the price of 7) - please visit www.tescodiets.com/goddess.
To buy anything from the Tesco Diets shop, and receive a 15% discount, please visit www.tescodietsshop.co.uk, and enter the promotional code "GDSS ONE" when prompted.

See page 442 for terms and conditions.

Goddess readers, with their **20% discount** off any first time purchase, can easily turn their next party into the event of a lifetime **with the Chocolate Fondue Company**. (As featured on page 475.)

To take advantage of this special offer simply ring The Chocolate Fondue Company directly on 01376 584 669 and quote the promotional code 'Goddess'. You'll automatically receive a 20% discount off your first purchase. To view all available products please visit www.chocolatefonduecompany.co.uk

See page 475 for terms and conditions.